S0-BAF-950

The MICHELIN Guide

Chicago

RESTAURANTS

2012

Manufacture française des pneumatiques Michelin

Société en commandite par actions au capital de 504 000 004 EUR
Place des Carmes-Déchaux — 63000 Clermont-Ferrand (France)
R.C.S. Clermont-Fd B 855 200 507
No part of this publication may be reproduced in any form without the prior
permission of the publisher.

© **Michelin, Propriétaires-éditeurs**
Dépot légal Octobre 2011
Made in Canada
Published in 2011

The MICHELIN Guide
One Parkway South
Greenville, SC 29615 USA
www.michelinguide.com
michelin.guides@us.michelin.com

Dear Reader

*W*e are thrilled to present the second edition of our MICHELIN Guide to Chicago.

Our dynamic team has spent this year updating our selection to wholly reflect the rich diversity of Chicago's restaurants and hotels. As part of our meticulous and highly confidential evaluation process, our inspectors have anonymously and methodically eaten through all of the city's neighborhoods and suburbs to compile the finest in each category for your enjoyment. While these inspectors are expertly trained food industry professionals, we remain consumer driven: our goal is to provide comprehensive choices to accommodate your comfort, tastes, and budget. Our inspectors dine, drink, and lodge as 'regular' customers in order to experience and evaluate the same level of service and cuisine you would as a guest.

We have expanded our criteria to reflect some of the more current and unique elements of the city's dining scene. Don't miss the scrumptious "Small Plates" category, highlighting those establishments with a distinct style of service, setting, and menu; and the comprehensive "Under $25" listings which also include a diverse and impressive choice at a very good value.

Additionally, you may follow our Michelin Inspectors on Twitter @MichelinGuideCH as they chow their way around town. Our anonymous inspectors tweet daily about their unique and entertaining food experiences.

Our company's two founders, Édouard and André Michelin, published the first MICHELIN Guide in 1900, to provide motorists with practical information about where they could service and repair their cars, find quality accommodations, and a good meal. Later in 1926, the star-rating system for outstanding restaurants was introduced, and over the decades we have developed many new improvements to our guides. The local team here in Chicago enthusiastically carries on these traditions.

We sincerely hope that the MICHELIN Guide will remain your preferred reference to the city's restaurants and hotels.

Dear Reader

Contents

© MICHELIN

© City of Chicago / GRC

Contents

5

The Michelin Guide

"This volume was created at the turn of the century and will last at least as long".

This foreword to the very first edition of the MICHELIN Guide, written in 1900, has become famous over the years and the Guide has lived up to the prediction. It is read across the world and the key to its popularity is the consistency in its commitment to its readers, which is based on the following promises.

→ Anonymous Inspections

Our inspectors make anonymous visits to hotels and restaurants to gauge the quality offered to the ordinary customer. They pay their own bill and make no indication of their presence. These visits are supplemented by comprehensive monitoring of information—our readers' comments are one valuable source, and are always taken into consideration.

→ Independence

Our choice of establishments is a completely independent one, made for the benefit of our readers alone. Decisions are discussed by the inspectors and the editor, with the most important decided at the global level. Inclusion in the guide is always free of charge.

→ The Selection

The Guide offers a selection of the best hotels and restaurants in each category of comfort and price. Inclusion in the guides is a commendable award in itself, and defines the establishment among the "best of the best."

How the MICHELIN Guide Works

→ Annual Updates

All practical information, the classifications, and awards, are revised and updated every year to ensure the most reliable information possible.

→ Consistency & Classifications

The criteria for the classifications are the same in all countries covered by the Michelin Guides. Our system is used worldwide and is easy to apply when choosing a restaurant or hotel.

→ The Classifications

We classify our establishments using ％％％％-％ and 🏠🏠🏠-🏠 to indicate the level of comfort. The ✿✿✿-✿ specifically designates an award for cuisine, unique from the classification. For hotels and restaurants, a symbol in red suggests a particularly charming spot with unique décor or ambiance.

→ Our Aim

As part of Michelin's ongoing commitment to improving travel and mobility, we do everything possible to make vacations and eating out a pleasure.

The Michelin Guide

How to Use This Guide

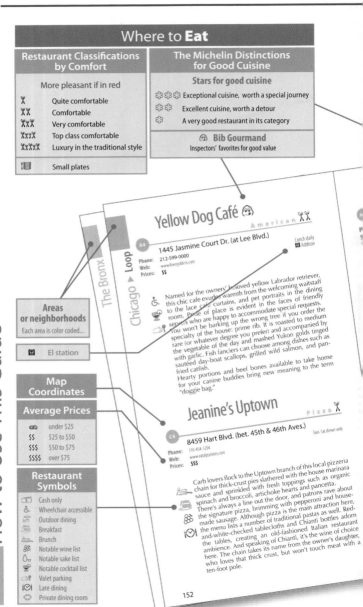

Where to **Eat**

Restaurant Classifications by Comfort

More pleasant if in red

X	Quite comfortable
XX	Comfortable
XxX	Very comfortable
XxxX	Top class comfortable
XxXxX	Luxury in the traditional style
🔢	Small plates

The Michelin Distinctions for Good Cuisine

Stars for good cuisine

🏵🏵🏵	Exceptional cuisine, worth a special journey
🏵🏵	Excellent cuisine, worth a detour
🏵	A very good restaurant in its category

🅑 Bib Gourmand
Inspectors' favorites for good value

Areas or neighborhoods
Each area is color coded...

🚇 El station

Map Coordinates

Average Prices

⊜	under $25
$$	$25 to $50
$$$	$50 to $75
$$$$	over $75

Restaurant Symbols

💳	Cash only
♿	Wheelchair accessible
🌳	Outdoor dining
🍴	Breakfast
🥂	Brunch
🍷	Notable wine list
🍶	Notable sake list
🍸	Notable cocktail list
🚗	Valet parking
🌙	Late dining
⊘	Private dining room

The Bronx   Chicago ▶ Loop

Yellow Dog Café 🅑
American XX

A4   1445 Jasmine Court Dr. (at Lee Blvd.)

Lunch daily
🚇 Addison

Phone: 212-599-0000
Web: www.ilovegaldens.com
Prices: $$

Named for the owners' beloved yellow Labrador retriever, this chic cafe exudes warmth from the welcoming waitstaff to the lace cafe curtains, and pet portraits in the dining room. Pride of place is evident in the faces of friendly servers who are happy to accommodate special requests. You won't be barking up the wrong tree if you order the specialty of the house: prime rib. It is roasted to medium rare (or whatever degree you prefer) and accompanied by the vegetable of the day and mashed Yukon golds tinged with garlic. Fish fanciers can choose among dishes such as sautéed day-boat scallops, grilled wild salmon, and pan-fried catfish.

Hearty portions and beef bones available to take home for your canine buddies bring new meaning to the term "doggie bag."

Jeanine's Uptown
pizza X

C4   8459 Hart Blvd. (bet. 45th & 46th Aves.)

Tues-Sat dinner only

Phone: 310-454-5294
Web: www.eatofpannies.com
Prices: $$$

Carb lovers flock to the Uptown branch of this local pizzeria chain for thick-crust pies slathered with the house marinara sauce and sprinkled with fresh toppings such as organic spinach and broccoli, artichoke hearts and pancetta. There's always a line out the door, and patrons rave about the signature pizza, brimming with pepperoni and house-made sausage. Although pizza is the main attraction here, the menu lists a number of traditional pastas as well. Red-and-white-checked tablecloths and Chianti bottles adorn the tables, creating an old-fashioned Italian restaurant ambience. And speaking of Chianti, it's the wine of choice here. The chain takes its name from the owner's daughter, who loves that thick crust, but won't touch meat with a ten-foot pole.

152

How to Use This Guide

8

Where to **Stay**

Average Prices	Hotel Symbols	Hotel Classifications by Comfort
Prices do not include applicable taxes	149 rooms — Number of rooms & suites	**More pleasant if in red**
$ under $200	Wheelchair accessible	🏠 Quite comfortable
$$ $200 to $300	Exercise room	🏠 Comfortable
$$$ $300 to $400	Spa	🏠 Very comfortable
$$$$ over $400	Swimming pool	🏠 Top class comfortable
Map Coordinates	Conference room	🏠 Luxury in the traditional style
	Pet friendly	
	Wireless	

...s Palace ✿ ✿

Italian ✗✗✗✗

...ner Pl. (at 30th Street) Dinner daily

...fabulouspalace.com

...ome cooked Italian never tasted so good than at this ...npretentious little place. The simple décor claims no big-...ame designers, and while the Murano glass light fixtures ...are chic and the velveteen-covered chairs are comfortable, ...his isn't a restaurant where millions of dollars were spent on the interior.

Instead, food is the focus here. The restaurant's name may not be Italian, but it nonetheless serves some of the best pasta in the city, made fresh in-house. Dishes follow the seasons, thus ravioli may be stuffed with fresh ricotta and herbs in summer, and pumpkin in fall. Most everything is liberally dusted with Parmigiano Reggiano, a favorite ingredient of the chef.

For dessert, you'll have to deliberate between the likes of creamy tiramisu, ricotta cheesecake, and homemade gelato. One thing's for sure: you'll never miss your nonna's cooking when you eat at Sonya's.

Manhattan ▶ Chelsea

David Burlington/Getty Images

153

The Fan Inn

D1

135 Shanghai Street, Oakland 🏠

Phone: 650-345-1440 or 888-222-2424
Web: www.superfaninnoakland.com
Prices: $$

45 Rooms 5 Suites

...oused in an Art Deco-era building, the venerable Fan Inn ...ently underwent a complete facelift. The hotel now fits ...with the new generation of sleekly understated hotels ...ring a Zen-inspired aesthetic, despite its 1930s origins.

...othing neutral palette runs throughout the property, ...uated with exotic woods, bamboo, and fine fabrics. ...e lobby, the sultry lounge makes a relaxing place for ...mixed cocktail or a glass of wine.

...ens and down pillows cater to your comfort, while ...en TVs, DVD players with iPod docking stations, ...less Internet access satisfy the need for modern ... For business travelers, nightstands convert to ...les and credenzas morph into flip-out desks. ...ter, fax or scanner? It's just a phone call away. ...st, the hotel will even provide office supplies.

...alf of the accommodations here are suites, ...xury factor ratchets up with marble baths, ...ng areas, and fully equipped kitchens. ...nn doesn't have a restaurant, the nearby ...rly everything you could want in terms of ...dumplings to haute cuisine.

San Francisco ▶ Civic Center

John A. Rizzo/Getty Images

315

Where to Eat

Chicago

Andersonville, Edgewater & Uptown
Lincoln Square · Ravenswood

This rare and diverse collection of spirited neighborhoods in Chicago's north side is like a real-world Epcot theme park, with visitors easily flitting from one immigrant ethnic tradition to the next, and all the while sampling international cuisines, but without a passport. Lauded as one of the most charming neighborhoods in the Windy City, Andersonville also struts a plethora of quaint "Places to Stay" including popular bed-and-breakfasts and beloved hotels. A food mecca of sorts, the **Andersonville Farmer's Market** (held every Wednesday) houses an array of bakeries, farm produce, and Oriental fruit orchards.

Swedish Spreads

From the art on the lamppost banners to the Swedish American Museum Center, you can see the influence of Andersonville's historical roots upon arrival on Clark Street. Happily, much of that can be explored with your taste buds, starting the day at **Restaurant Svea**. This well-known spot is also home of the hearty Viking breakfast that may reveal Swedish-style pancakes, sausages, roasted potatoes, and toasted *limpa* bread (to name a few of the offerings).

Meanwhile, **Wikström's Gourmet Foods** is one of the last standing Swedish emporiums of packaged and prepared favorites, still stocked with everything needed for a traditional smörgåsbord, from Swedish meatballs and herring, to lingonberry preserves. Locals yearning for authentic baked goods eagerly take a number and wait in line at the **Swedish Bakery**. Many of its traditional baked treats are available in individual sizes, as well as larger portions perfect for those looking to entertain. For more instant gratification, scout a seat at the counter by the window and enjoy that miniature coconut-custard coffeecake right away, perhaps with a complimentary cup of coffee.

Andersonville also caters to its worldly community with **Middle East Bakery & Grocery**. Make a massive meze feast from spreads, breads, olives, and an impressive range of hummus among other goodies available in the deli. Or, stock up on dried fruits, spices, rice, rosewater, nuts, and teas from the grocery section. Either way, you will have ample options for a magnificent Middle Eastern menu.

All Italia

On the pizza front, **Great Lake** has won many raves for its pizza, despite the infamously long lines and a lack of interest in expansion that, according to some hungry pizza-lovers, is downright un-American. Nonetheless, these delicious

Chicago-style pies are made with the country's premium ingredients—its menu is a virtual Who's Who of local, organic vegetable farmers and heirloom breeders. Whether you choose to dine-in or take-out, their fabulous pies usually feature organic tomato sauce, farmer's cheese, and a flurry of herbs paired with deliciously fresh green garlic, spring onions, mortadella, or chorizo. After this indulgence, stop by **The Coffee Studio** for a cup of joe prepared by what critics have named one of the country's best boutique coffee shops. Superlatives aside, take home a pretty little green box of chocolate-dipped glacée fruits to devour all by yourself.

An Asian Affair

Uptown's Argyle Street is renowned for being a pocket of intermixed East Asian culture—even the Argyle Red Line El stop is thematically decorative. A terrific concentration of Chinese, Thai, and Vietnamese delis, as well as bakeries, herbalists, noodle shops, and restaurants line these streets; and there is endless tasting to be done along these blocks. Speaking of which, **Sun Wah BBQ** is a forever beloved spot for Cantonese cuisine. Walk in and be greeted by their glistening selection of bronzed meats. These are offered on their own or over rice for a complete meal.

The real draw in Edgewater is its art deco architecture, especially evident along Bryn Mawr Avenue and Lake Michigan's beaches. This neighborhood also boasts a vibrant community who convene at **The Metropolis Café**, an offshoot of Chicago's lauded Metropolis Coffee Company. Watch a crowd of students, professionals, and locals gulp down oodles of their creative coffee quenchers.

Hot Dog Haven

This is Chicago, so there's always a good hot dog nearby, and one of the best red-hots uptown is as delicious as it is easy to spot. Just look for the iconic pitchfork piercing a sausage over the name **Wolfy's**, and know that you have arrived. Try the classic dog, but know that by the time the limitless listing of toppings are piled on, the meat will be invisibly buried beneath piccalilli, pickles, peppers, and other impossibly colored yet divine condiments.

LINCOLN SQUARE AND RAVENSWOOD

Evidence of the German immigrants who helped develop Lincoln Square still lingers in this quaint area. Highlights include a century-old apothecary as well as the new, yet Old World-inspired butchers and specialty items that abound at **Gene's Sausage Shop**. For an impressive array of fresh chops, steaks, free-range poultry, smoked European sausages, as well as bacon in its many glorious forms, plan to sample the many wears of **Lincoln Quality Meat Market**. The **Lincoln Square Farmer's Market** has long been loved and frequented (on Tuesdays); they now showcase a new Thursday evening market, pumping with live music alongside a medley of fruits, vegetables, and flowers, which remains a draw for locals with day jobs.

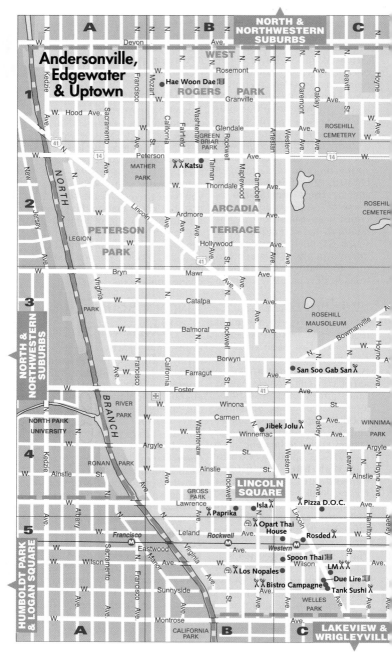

Andersonville, Edgewater & Uptown

A · **B** · **C**

NORTH & NORTHWESTERN SUBURBS

Devon Ave.

WEST

Rosemont

● Hae Woon Dae 🏠

ROGERS PARK

Granville Ave.

Glendale

GREEN BRIAR PARK

Peterson Ave.

MATHER PARK

🙏 🙏 Katsu

Thorndale Ave.

ARCADIA

Ardmore Ave.

TERRACE

ROSEHILL CEMETERY

ROSEHILL CEMETERY

PETERSON PARK

Hollywood Ave.

LEGION

Bryn Mawr Ave.

ROSEHILL MAUSOLEUM

Catalpa Ave.

PARK

Balmoral Ave.

NORTH BRANCH

Berwyn

Farragut

● San Soo Gab San 🙏

Foster Ave.

NORTH & NORTHWESTERN SUBURBS

RIVER PARK

Winona

Carmen

WINNEMAC PARK

NORTH PARK UNIVERSITY

● Jibek Jolu 🙏

Winnemac

RONAN PARK

Argyle

Ainslie St.

Ainslie St.

GROSS PARK

LINCOLN SQUARE

Lawrence

🙏 Paprika   ● Isla 🙏   🙏 Pizza D.O.C.

🙏 Opart Thai House

Leland *Rockwell* Ave.   ● Rosded 🙏

Francisco Ⓜ

Eastwood

Western Ⓜ

Wilson   ● Spoon Thai 🏠   LM 🙏🙏

Ⓜ 🙏 Los Nopales ●   Due Lire 🏠

🙏 Bistro Campagne   Tank Sushi 🙏

Sunnyside

WELLES PARK

HUMBOLDT PARK & LOGAN SQUARE

Montrose Ave.

A · **B** · **C**

CALIFORNIA PARK

LAKEVIEW & WRIGLEYVILLE

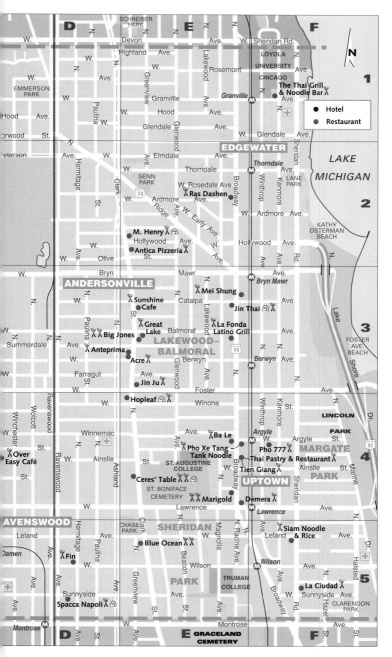

Legend:
- ● Hotel
- ● Restaurant

Map labels:

SCHREIBER PARK
W. Devon Ave.
W. Highland Ave. W. Sheridan Rd.
W. N. LOYOLA UNIVERSITY CHICAGO
EMMERSON PARK
W. Rosemont Ave.
Hood Ave. W. Granville Ave. Granville The Thai Grill & Noodle Bar
orwood St. W. Hood Ave.
eterson Ave. W. Glendale Ave. W. Glendale Ave.
EDGEWATER
Elmdale Ave.
SENN PARK Thorndale Ave. Thorndale LANE PARK
W. Rosedale Ave. Ras Dashen
Ardmore Ave. W. Ardmore Ave.
Ridge KATHY OSTERMAN BEACH
M. Henry
Hollywood Ave. Hollywood Ave.
Antica Pizzeria W. Olive St.
W. Bryn Mawr Bryn Mawr Ave.
ANDERSONVILLE Mei Shung
Sunshine Cafe Catalpa Ave. Jin Thai
Great Lake Balmoral La Fonda Latino Grill
Summerdale Ave. Big Jones FOSTER AVE. BEACH
Anteprima LAKEWOOD-BALMORAL
Acre Berwyn Berwyn Ave.
Farragut Ave.
Jin Ju Foster Ave.
Hopleaf Winona
LINCOLN PARK
Winnemac Ave. Ba Le Argyle Argyle St. MARGATE
Over Easy Café Pho Xe Tang - Tank Noodle Pho 777
Ainslie St. Thai Pastry & Restaurant
ST. AUGUSTINE COLLEGE Broadway Tien Giang Ainslie St.
Ceres' Table UPTOWN
ST. BONIFACE CEMETERY Marigold Demera
Lawrence Lawrence Ave.
RAVENSWOOD CHASE PARK SHERIDAN
Leland Siam Noodle & Rice
Blue Ocean Leland
Fin Wilson Wilson Ave.
PARK TRUMAN COLLEGE
Sunnyside La Ciudad
Spacca Napoli Sunnyside Ave. CLARENDON PARK
Montrose Montrose Ave.
GRACELAND CEMETERY

LAKE MICHIGAN

17

Acre

5308 N. Clark St. (bet. Berwyn & Summerdale Aves.)

Phone: 773-334-7600   Lunch & dinner daily
Web: www.acrerestaurant.com
Prices: **$$**   🚇 Berwyn

Putting its own slightly global spin on the ever-expanding field of seasonal American cuisine, Andersonville's Acre also brings beer to the table with more than 25 craft selections on draft at any given moment. Those in the mood for suds with their meal will likely eschew the muted banquettes of the dining room for a seat at the long, undulating wooden bar in the Tap Room, where blackboards highlight beers from the extensive list.

The kitchen aspires to elevate regional comfort food with ambitious fare like baked Delaware oysters with preserved lemon stuffing, and Amish chicken liver pâté crostini with pickled ramps. Casual lunch options may include a fresh and tangy smoked trout sandwich on caraway rye with sauce *gribiche* and pickled carrot.

Anteprima

5316 N. Clark St. (bet. Berwyn & Summerdale Aves.)

Phone: 773-506-9990   Dinner nightly
Web: www.anteprimachicago.net
Prices: **$$**   🚇 Berwyn

Located along a stretch of Clark populated with attractive storefronts, the 50-seat Anteprima is steeped in all things Italian. From the painted landscapes and bustling atmosphere to the regionally inspired menu, this place exudes a rustic vibe.

Don't wave away the bread basket—tender focaccia, rosemary *grissini*, and sliced country bread are irresistible. Choose from a long list of appetizers (grilled polenta steeped with greens), then move on to traditional dishes like spaghetti *cacio e pepe* and tender Chianti-braised pork osso buco. Pay attention to the specials, where you may find the likes of veal sweetbreads with squash purée, wild mushrooms, and balsamic. Top it all off with some homemade limoncello.

Antica Pizzeria

 Italian

5663 N. Clark St. (bet. Hollywood & Olive Aves.)

Phone: 773-944-1492   Dinner Wed – Mon
Web: www.anticapizzeriachicago.com
Prices:

Antica Pizzeria's chef hails from Catania and serves up a roster of pizza and pasta that brings a decidedly Sicilian attitude to the regional Italian menu. The pizzas here–chewy, crusty, and tender–are a bit thinner than their Neapolitan-style cousins and are offered with myriad toppings that include the *fattoressa* (inspired by the chef's own mother) that piles on cooked ham, hard-boiled eggs, green peas, and mushrooms. Pastas are numerous and entrées offer the likes of grilled swordfish with *salmoriglio* sauce and eggplant *caponata*.
The comfortable and friendly room brings on a rustic mien showcasing bright yellow walls hung with black-and-white photography, wood furnishings, and a visible workstation installed with a wood-fired brick oven.

Ba Le

 Vietnamese

5014 N. Broadway (at Argyle St.)

Phone: 773-561-4424   Lunch & dinner daily
Web: www.balesandwich.com
Prices: Argyle

Moving just a few doors down did exactly what the owners hoped it would. This storefront is still the north side's hot spot for authentic French-Vietnamese sandwiches; but now within a more sleek sphere, starring an L-shaped counter overlooking Broadway (also a first-rate perch for people-watching).
The menu is heavy on *banh mi* variations, that tasty ensemble made with crusty French bread and swelled with fixings like grilled pork, cilantro, and house-pickled daikon. The affordable price tags plus large portions make for a sweet pair with leftovers for later. Natives in the know gulp down the quirky Vietnamese FOCO pennywort drink; while salads, pastries, desserts, sodas, and teas round out the menu and sate the more prudent palate.

 Chicago ▶ Andersonville, Edgewater & Uptown

19

Big Jones

Southern XX

5347 N. Clark St. (bet. Balmoral & Summerdale Aves.)

Phone: 773-275-5725   Lunch & dinner daily
Web: www.bigjoneschicago.com
Prices: $$ Berwyn

Y'all will definitely want to come back here. Big Jones brims with big Southern charm and hospitality. Green brocade wallpaper, glass-and-iron chandeliers, and cute bistro tables give the place a welcoming look and feel. And it's no surprise it reminds you of your long-lost Aunt Weezie's place, since this spot shines a little Southern warmth in oft chilly Chicago. There wouldn't have been a war between the states if they had food this good. It all starts with fluffy cornbread beside a glass of sweet tea, and continues with Southern specialties like shrimp and grits; Cajun boudin fritters; gumbo; and Carolina barbecue pork. Honey, with fried green tomatoes, red velvet cake, and bourbon bread pudding, it's definitely worth putting off the diet for a day.

Bistro Campagne

French XX

4518 N. Lincoln Ave. (bet. Sunnyside & Wilson Aves.)

Phone: 773-271-6100   Lunch Sun
Web: www.bistrocampagne.com   Dinner nightly
Prices: $$ Western (Brown)

This cozy bungalow in the middle of Lincoln Square's busiest drag is unassuming. But behind the gates find a stunning oasis-in-the-city outdoor garden. Whether you eat indoors or out, the spaces offer a warm and inviting experience complemented by an unfussy French staff.

The rustic French menu (with floods of French wines, of course) covers all of the classics (think escargot in a classic garlic-Pernod butter; or a plump buckwheat crêpe stuffed with wild mushrooms, sorrel, spinach, and topped with a béchamel gratineé). Traditional desserts like a chocolate *pot de crème*, profiteroles, or tart citron are delightful cap-offs. A cozy spot for romantic dinners, Bistro Campagne also pleases the larger lot by hosting live music on different evenings.

Chicago ▶ Andersonville, Edgewater & Uptown

Blue Ocean

E5

Japanese ✗✗

4650 N. Clark St. (at Leland Ave.)

Phone: 773-334-6288
Web: www.blueoceansushi.net
Prices: 💰💰

Lunch Mon – Fri
Dinner nightly
🚇 Wilson

One of the neighborhood's newcomers, Blue Ocean is a large, contemporary, and colorful addition to Uptown. Its menu, described as "contemporary sushi," brings a modern sensibility to the Asian favorite. The sleek sushi counter does not offer seating; instead enjoy your meal at one of the dark blue-stained wood tables.

In addition to sushi, the menu includes an offering of small plates such as braised short ribs (soy, sake, and ginseng served with short rib maki,) plus appetizers such as a bacon-wrapped scallop cake and yuzu hamachi. Sushi is souped-up. For example, the Blurashi features an oversized rice bowl served on a deep square platter topped with sea urchin, salmon roe, salmon, tuna, snapper, raw shrimp, and cooked octopus.

Ceres' Table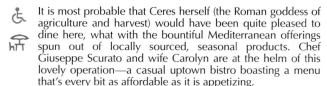

E4

Mediterranean ✗✗

4882 N. Clark St. (bet. Ainslie St. & Lawrence Ave.)

Phone: 773-878-4882
Web: www.cerestable.com
Prices: $$

Dinner nightly

🚇 Lawrence

It is most probable that Ceres herself (the Roman goddess of agriculture and harvest) would have been quite pleased to dine here, what with the bountiful Mediterranean offerings spun out of locally sourced, seasonal products. Chef Giuseppe Scurato and wife Carolyn are at the helm of this lovely operation—a casual uptown bistro boasting a menu that's every bit as affordable as it is appetizing.

A mosaic-tiled entry leads you into a room designed with tranquil blues, black leather booths, and a full bar. Try fried squash blossoms stuffed with mozzarella and anchovies; grilled quail over a panzanella salad; or rich calf's liver with white corn polenta. The Wednesday night prix-fixe is a steal—an appetizer, entrée, dessert, and glass of wine for under $40.

Chicago ▶ Andersonville, Edgewater & Uptown

Demera

Ethiopian ✗

E4

4801 N. Broadway (at Lawrence St.)

Phone: 773-334-8787   Lunch & dinner daily
Web: www.demeraethiopianrestaurant.com
Prices: $$ 🚇 Lawrence

♿ A short skip off the red line at Lawrence, this bright corner location is as welcoming for a quick bite or drink and good people watching as it is for an authentic Ethiopian feast. On the weekends Demera also welcomes musicians for live performances, promising that this spot goes beyond other ethnic eateries.

As is tradition, Demera serves *injera*, the spongy, pancake-like bread used as a utensil on a communal plate. Its tangy flavors pair wonderfully with the *ye beg alicha* dish of tender lamb in a rich and creamy aromatic green sauce; as well as the *ye-kwanta firfir*, featuring beef tips stewed in a spicy *berbere* sauce. Don't skip the Ethiopian tea, which is an oregano tea infused with anise, clover, and cinnamon. Sweeten with honey and savor.

Due Lire

Italian

C5

4520 N. Lincoln Ave. (bet. Sunnyside & Wilson Aves.)

Phone: 773-275-7878   Dinner Tue – Sun
Web: www.due-lire.com
Prices: $$ 🚇 Western (Brown)

Contemporary Italian cuisine comes to this Lincoln Square address courtesy of Naples native Massimo Di Vuolo and Chef Kevin Abshire. Di Vuolo's warm welcome is a gracious entrée to this trattoria bearing a perfectly neighborhoody ambience with its casual décor of parchment-colored walls and polished dark wood furnishings.

The kitchen presents a tastefully edited canon of preparations beginning with *antipasti* such as local Italian sausage with rapini; *arancino* Milano dotted with asparagus and fontina; or drunken mussels in Belgian-style ale with pretzel-roll crostini. The selection of *primi* may offer a spot-on risotto whirled with charred ramps and nuggets of langoustine; while main dishes may include grilled ahi tuna with Sicilian caponata.

Fin

1742 W. Wilson Ave. (at Hermitage Ave.)

Phone: 773-961-7452   Lunch & dinner Tue – Sun
Web: www.finsushibar.com
Prices: 💰💰

🚇 Montrose (Brown)

While this may not be an authentic Japanese restaurant, it is in fact a flavorful, fresh, and budget-friendly hybrid of sushi-meets-Thai cuisine. Inside this pleasant Ravenswood newcomer, find a white-dominated room complemented by chocolate brown accents, plenty of windows, a cheerful staff, and bright disposition.

Enjoyably prepared nigiri and sashimi of fine quality contribute to an extensive menu bolstered by a plethora of maki. Standard rolls like spicy tuna coated with tempura crunch seem humble against the likes of a crunchy plantain, cream cheese, and avocado maki as featured among the listing of special rolls. Entrées bring a Thai accent in the likes of shrimp pad Thai; duck with red curry sauce and organic soba; or tom yum fried rice.

Great Lake

Pizza 🍴

E3

1477 W. Balmoral Ave. (bet. Clark St. & Glenwood Ave.)

Phone: 773-334-9270   Dinner Wed – Sat
Web: N/A
Prices: $$

🚇 Berwyn

The outside seats at Lydia Esparza and Nick Lessins' pizza parlor, Great Lake, aren't so much for alfresco diners, as they are for the throngs of waiting (BYOB to bide the time) patrons. When the door unlocks, peek in a space simply dressed with wood floors and exposed brick walls, welcoming guests to a tiny, communal room.

Service can be slow (the pizza oven can hold only two at a time), but fresh, beaming salads (heirloom tomatoes joined with basil, *Mona* cheese, Tellicherry black pepper, and walnut oil); and a blackboard touting pristine purveyors make Great Lake a culinary cult-hit. Your patience may be rewarded with a perfectly charred thin-crust laden with cheese and tomatoes; or the more familiar tomatillo salsa, farmer's cheese, and arugula.

Hae Woon Dae

Korean

 B1

6240 N. California Ave. (bet. Granville & Rosemont Aves.)

Phone: 773-764-8018	Lunch Sat – Sun
Web: www.letseat.at/haewoondaebbq	Dinner nightly
Prices: ᏣᏱ	

Located in a low-slung strip mall and labeled by a plain black awning, Hae Woon Dae looks simple and unimpressive. While appearances may be lacking, the tasty Korean specialties served inside more than satisfy.

Mandoo, pan-fried or boiled dumplings; three varieties of savory Korean-style pancakes; and *yookhwae* (spiced beef tartare) start off the list of hearty specialties that include soul warming stews and casseroles. Of special note is the barbecue selection. Each table features a recessed pit into which a cauldron of glowing wood charcoal is lowered for tabletop grilling. Serving scissor-cut strips of sizzling marinated *kalbi* brushed with fermented chili paste and wrapped in cool crisp daikon and romaine, Hae Woon Dae offers pizzazz indeed.

Hopleaf

Gastropub

E4

5148 N. Clark St. (bet. Foster Ave. & Winona St.)

Phone: 773-334-9851	Dinner nightly
Web: www.hopleaf.com	
Prices: $$	🖳 Berwyn

Don't be confused when you arrive with a hankering for mussels and see a standing room-only bar. First and foremost, Hopleaf is a tavern and no one under 21 is admitted. But it is an excellent tavern with more than 200 beers on offer, many of them on draught, craft, and from Belgium.

Slide back through the bar to find a charming full-service hideaway waiting to exceed your culinary expectations of a bar. Starters always include mussels and sometimes crawfish-corn fritters with pappadew salad and sweet pea aïoli. Creative entrées may feature twists on classics, like the CB&J sandwich, made creamy with homemade cashew butter, fig jam, and *Morbier* cheese.

Epansion plans will double the space and allow their chefs more room to cook.

Chicago ▶ Andersonville, Edgewater & Uptown

24

Isla

B4

Filipino

2501 W. Lawrence Ave. (bet. Campbell & Maplewood Aves.)

Phone: 773-271-2988
Web: www.islapilipina.com
Prices:

Lunch & dinner Tue – Sun

Western (Brown)

A favored spot for Filipino cuisine in Lincoln Square, Isla now sports a freshened look to accompany its friendly vibe and heaping plates. The former steam-table setting offers pale mint green walls hung with artwork for sale, sleek seating, and cheerful signs scrolled in Tagalog that welcome and thank diners for their patronage.

The menu is well endowed in distinct pork specialties: crispy *pata*, deep-fried pork knuckle; *paksiw na lechon*, tangy pork stew with peppercorns and soy sauce; and *inihaw na baboy*, marinated and grilled pork strips served with tart vinegar dipping sauce. Saving room for dessert may prove challenging, but the *halo-halo* could tempt—an otherworldly colorful layering of ice cream, crushed ice, candied fruit, beans, and flan.

Jibek Jolu

B4

Asian

5047 N. Lincoln Ave. (bet. Carmen & Winnemac Aves.)

Phone: 773-878-8494
Web: N/A
Prices:

Lunch & dinner daily

Jibek Jolu (translates as Silk Road) is a tasty spot serving the cuisine of Kyrgyzstan. The culinary makeup of this landlocked Central Asian republic melds the influences of Turkish, Russian, Persian, and Chinese cuisines to produce a unique representation of the region.

To start, the menu utilizes halal products to offer meat-stuffed pastries, as in the *cheburek* (fried lamb turnover), along with soups that include *borsh*, and an incredibly crunchy Korean carrot salad with julienned carrots, onion, garlic, parsley, and dried chilies. *Lagman*, hand-pulled wheat noodles tossed with a stew of tender seared beef, sweet peppers, and daikon, is featured among the entrées that may also reveal *pelmeni* and charcoal-grilled cubes of marinated chicken.

Jin Ju

Korean ✗

5203 N. Clark St. (at Foster Ave.)

Phone: 773-334-6377   Dinner nightly
Web: N/A
Prices: **$$**

A sexy spot on a stretch of bustling Clark Street, Jin Ju spins out luscious Korean classics with aplomb. Inside, dim lighting, dark wood furnishings, and lush red walls create a sophisticated coziness, while servers are gracious and attentive.

The menu showcases a range of specialties to start, like plump *mandoo*, batter-fried spicy chicken wings, or *paj un*, a savory Korean-style pancake filled with the likes of kimchi, served sliced in wedges with a tangy soy and rice vinegar dipping sauce. The *dak tori tang* could warm the coldest day in the Windy City—its fiery red pepper broth is brought to the table bubbling and brimming with braised chicken, potato, carrots, and leafy herbs served with sticky rice, along with a tasty assortment of *banchan*.

Jin Thai

Thai ✗

5458 N. Broadway (at Catalpa Ave.)

Phone: 773-681-0555   Lunch & dinner daily
Web: www.jinthaicuisine.com
Prices: 🍜   🚇 Bryn Mawr

It's an auspicious beginning for a restaurant to have its space blessed by Buddhist monks—and though it sounds like urban legend, neighbors attest that this really happened at Jin Thai. Benevolent Buddha figures continue to keep watch over the dining room, their serene vibe amplified by the hospitality of husband-and-wife team Chai and Jintana Roongseang.

This might be the place to convince your pad-Thai-loving friends to try a new menu offering. The standards are available, but lively creations like Vietnamese crêpes plump with tofu, coconut flakes, shrimp, and cucumber make a case for sampling other items on the menu. *Nam tok* doesn't fall prey to sogginess here; grilled steak gets a kick from fresh mint, cilantro, lime, chilies, and onion.

Katsu

B2

Japanese ✗✗

2651 W. Peterson Ave. (bet. Talman & Washtenaw Aves.)

Phone:	773-784-3383
Web:	N/A
Prices:	**$$**

Dinner Wed – Sun

Lovingly run by Chef Katsu Imamura and his wife, this charming Japanese spot offers sushi fans countless reasons to head over to Katsu's counter. Mrs. Imamura is a gracious presence in the dining room and, despite its age, the setting is attractively maintained. Its minimal décor bears personality, as in a sepia-toned print of Johnny Cash in the bathroom and robotic action figures stationed at the sushi bar.

Raw fish is the focus, prepared as sushi, sashimi, or *chirashi*. The deluxe platter brings pleasing mouthfuls of embellished nigiri—yellowtail with slivers of green onion, super-white tuna topped by caviar, and *amaebi* with tobiko—along with sashimi and *tamagoyaki*. The tasty cooked fare includes veal liver sautéed with garlic chives.

La Ciudad

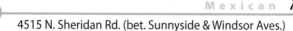

F5

Mexican ✗

4515 N. Sheridan Rd. (bet. Sunnyside & Windsor Aves.)

Phone:	773-728-2887
Web:	www.laciudadgrill.com
Prices:	

Lunch & dinner daily

🚇 Wilson

From first sight, within a strip mall of pawn shops and iron bar-covered windows, this newcomer is not the most inviting. But walk through the doors, and things sure change. This little BYOC (*cervezas*) is not your typical, grubby taqueria. Fire engine red walls are modestly dotted with black and white prints of D.F.

The food is as pleasant a surprise as the interior; appetizers like plump shrimp with corn salsa and chipotle cream demonstrate the kitchen's ability to think outside the quesadilla box. Go all out with the *parilla*—a plate brimming with chicken, steak, chorizo, and cactus salad. One upside of this dicey 'hood is liquor stores are plentiful and reasonable. You bring the tequila, they'll provide the lime.

La Fonda Latino Grill

Latin American ✗

E3

5350 N. Broadway (bet. Balmoral & Berwyn Aves.)

Phone: 773-271-3935
Web: www.lafondalatinogrill.com
Prices: **$$**

Lunch Tue – Fri
Dinner Tue – Sun

🖼 Berwyn

Quality ingredients and an extensive pan-Latin menu are the hallmarks of this small Edgewater gem. The grill is the centerpiece of the kitchen, with an emphasis on meats–pork, beef, and chicken–that are grilled as ordered.

The menu here may not be ambitious, but what La Fonda does, it does extremely well. Meals may begin with silky tamales stuffed with luscious chicken and green olives, topped with an avocado "hot" sauce. Favorite entrées may include the beef *lengua*, served tender with a tomato sauce and crunchy green peas. Diners are sure to leave feeling full, particularly if they have been wise enough to save room for dessert. Their flan is a wonderfully silky and caramel-lacquered custard, served with strawberries and just the right hint of rum.

LM

French ✗✗

C5

4539 N. Lincoln Ave. (bet. Sunnyside & Wilson Aves.)

Phone: 773-942-7585
Web: www.lmrestaurant.com
Prices: **$$**

Dinner Mon – Sat

🖼 Western (Brown)

A persimmon-colored awning marks the entry to this boxy and brownish townhouse. From an opening in the romantic little dining room, peer into LM's kitchen where Chef Justin Perdue holds court. Dripping with casual elegance, this French *bijou* now draws a trendier crew—the white tablecloths are gone, but the sophistication still remains.

Close-knit tables set with orange-tinged accents match the décor, and a lengthy mirror stands to create the illusion of space. While luxe leather chairs draw you in, stay focused on such belly-warming, French-inspired dishes as creamy polenta set beneath a soft-boiled egg and a scattering of mushrooms, or grilled hanger steak sliced and fanned over potato purée with crispy lardons. The $38 prix fixe is delicious steal.

Los Nopales

Mexican ⚒

C5

4544 N. Western Ave. (bet. Sunnyside & Wilson Aves.)

Phone: 773-334-3149
Web: www.losnopalesrestaurant.com
Prices: 💰💰

Lunch & dinner Tue – Sun

🚇 Western (Brown)

As much a feast for the eyes as the belly, "nopales," which literally translates to "cactus," is an efficacious ingredient on the menu and in the design of this bright and enticing Mexican storefront. One of the owners used to helm the stoves at the Palmer House Hilton and Heaven on Seven, and due to that corporate experience, Los Nopales rises above and beyond the typical taqueria.

Embark on this feast with chips and salsa, made new and exciting with a duo of homemade salsas: one is smoky and spicy with chipotles, the other silky with avocado and tomatillo. Don't miss the tortilla soup, teeming with shredded chicken, avocado chunks, and fried tortilla strips; or an outstanding *tres leches* cake, frosted with hints of maple, caramel, and chocolate.

Marigold

Indian ⚒⚒

E4

4832 N. Broadway (bet. Ainslie St. & Lawrence Ave.)

Phone: 773-293-4653
Web: www.marigoldrestaurant.com
Prices: 💰💰

Dinner Tue – Sun

🚇 Lawrence

♿
🏠

As popular as it is ambitious, this Indian eatery knows how to please local crowds—right down to sitar music in the background, playing classic rock. Visually, the long dining room is attractive and kitsch-free with vivid colors and polished woods lending a slightly industrial look. Friendly, upbeat service enhances the relaxed, neighborhood vibe.

The menu offers a tasty departure from the expected Indian classics. Here, find a concise listing of dishes that highlight contemporary twists, such as mussels steamed in turmeric-infused coconut broth or duck confit cured in Indian spices. "Naanwiches" and curries in tasting and entrée portions are a hit, as are the signature dishes, like Kalonji chicken, which are as artfully plated as they are delicious.

Mei Shung

Chinese

E3

5511 N. Broadway (bet. Bryn Mawr & Catalpa Aves.)

Phone:	773-728-5778
Web:	www.meishungtogo.com
Prices:	

Lunch & dinner Tue – Sun

🚇 Bryn Mawr

No one goes to Mei Shung for the décor. This storefront looks like 1,001 other Chinese joints, and once you open the door and step inside and see the paper tablecloths, your mind will not be changed.

What will make you think differently is the extensive menu, chock-full of authentic Taiwanese and Mandarin dishes (particularly from the Shandong region). The hot and sour soup is just the right degree of spicy, thanks to white pepper and vinegar. Other must-tastes include the flavorful, chewy steamed bean curd roll, Taiwanese sausage, and noodle soups. The Mandarin dishes might include Peking duck, that aforementioned hot and sour soup, and fish with spicy salt. And if you have room, order the Taiwanese-style steak—it is also über popular.

M. Henry

American

E2

5707 N. Clark St. (bet. Edgewater & Hollywood Aves.)

Phone:	773-561-1600
Web:	www.mhenry.net
Prices:	

Lunch Tue – Sun

🚇 Bryn Mawr

The line out the door is the first sign that this hot spot is beloved by locals, but grab a mug of coffee and wait it out. Breakfast and brunch are M. Henry's strong suits, and diners flock here for the stacks of pancakes ranging from simple hotcakes with maple syrup and berries to the more over-the-top dulce banana rumba hotcakes layered with rum and raisins and a drizzle of crème caramel.

Salads and sandwiches are equally creative and filling. Both breakfast and lunch menus are vegetarian-friendly and made from seasonal, organic ingredients when possible. Can't wait? Hit the bakery showcase with everything from quiche and flatbreads to sweet treats. For an equally pleasing bite with a slight twist, visit sister spot M. Henrietta.

Opart Thai House

Thai ✕

C5

4658 N. Western Ave. (bet. Eastwood & Leland Aves.)

Phone: 773-989-8517
Web: www.opartthai.com
Prices: ⊜⊜

Lunch & dinner daily

🖳 Western (Brown)

Steps from the El, Opart Thai is a simple spot serving an extensive selection of Thai dishes that range from enjoyable to excellent. Inside the pleasant dining room warmed with carved woodwork and exposed brick, find ample seating for groups large or small as well as a window for orders to-go.
The large menu features well-prepared curries, soups, and entrées, like the crispy, deep-fried catfish served with a rich red curry that makes the flavorful coconut and spices stand out more than the heat. Another highlight is the classic *tom yum koong*, which arrives piping hot and deliciously tart with meaty straw mushrooms, fresh shrimp, and Kaffir lime leaves. Coffee with condensed milk sweetens the meal's end.

Over Easy Café

American ✕

D4

4943 N. Damen Ave. (bet. Ainslie & Argyle Sts.)

Phone: 773-506-2605
Web: www.overeasycafechicago.com
Prices: ⊜⊜

Lunch Tue – Sun

🖳 Damen (Brown)

Folks line up for yolks at the Over Easy Café. Come breakfast, brunch, or lunch and there's always a line. Once your table is clear, you'll find yourself digging in and rubbing elbows, since this place really packs them in, but after a few bites of these sweet or savory offerings, and you won't notice anything but the food. Many of the dishes have a south-of-the-border flavor (eggs with chorizo and guacamole); while others are pure down-home American comfort food.
Go savory with El Gordito's corn cakes, which include two eggs, grilled ham, and spicy red pepper sauce; or go sweet with Emily's dream pancakes layered with blackberries and topped with orange butter, raspberry coulis, whipped cream, and a dusting of powdered sugar. Yum!

Paprika

Indian

 2547 W. Lawrence Ave. (bet. Maplewood Ave. & Rockwell St.)

Phone: 773-338-4906 Dinner nightly
Web: www.paprikachicago.com
Prices: $$ 🚇 Rockwell

Chef Shah Kabir and his family know hospitality. Prepare to be swept up in their warmth and care the minute you enter; and even be greeted at the door by the chef himself and likely be welcomed to sit and sip a cool, refreshing *lassi*. After a 13-year run at his former spot, Indian Gourmet in Rogers Park, Kabir went out in search of smaller digs, re-routing to this delectable destination in Lincoln Park.

From aromatic, homemade curries to tasty twists on *dahls* (*turka dahl ki shabzi* is a revelation), the menu bursts with expert deliciousness. Even your everyday veggie samosa gets a yummy revival—a soft, light shell replaces the standard crunchy exterior, stuffed with spices, potatoes, peas, and cauliflower, served up with a trio of tangy chutneys.

Pho 777

Vietnamese

 1063-65 W. Argyle St. (bet. Kenmore & Winthrop Aves.)

Phone: 773-561-9909 Lunch & dinner daily
Web: www.pho777chicago.com
Prices: 🍜 🚇 Argyle

This strip of Argyle Street is destination No. 1 when it comes to Vietnamese food. The décor may not distinguish Pho 777 from the pack, but good quality makes it an easy choice.

Of course, the namesake dish is a must. The broth of the *tai bo vien pho* (beef noodle soup with round steak and meatballs) is scented with cardamom, ginger, and clove. It might be a bit mild but tables are topped with an assortment of chili pastes and oils to spice things up. Start off with some spring rolls, filled with rice noodles, shrimp, mint, carrots, bean sprouts, and basil, served with a punchy peanut sauce. Charbroiled pork rice plates, catfish simmered in a clay pot, and an assortment of flavored bubble teas (think: papaya, taro, plum, and mango) complete the menu.

Pho Xe Tang - Tank Noodle

Vietnamese ✗

4953 N. Broadway (at Argyle St.)

Phone: 773-878-2253
Web: www.tank-noodle.com
Prices:

Lunch & dinner Thu – Tue

🚇 Argyle

♿ Also known as "Tank Noodles," Pho Xe Tang is one of the highlights of Little Saigon. Tables are dotted with caddies containing chopsticks, plastic and steel flatware, *sriracha*, soy sauce, and pickled jalapeños. Unlike other nearby eateries, Pho Xe Tang has a louder vibe, with lots of pulsating bass in its music.

No visit to a Vietnamese restaurant would be complete without slurping up *pho*, traditionally served with a plate of lime wedges and fresh greens (bean sprouts, fresh mint, basil, and sliced jalapeños). The *pho tai nam ve don* is as good a choice as any; its tender skirt steak spiced with star anise and cinnamon. Starters like the papaya salad and steamed rice flour roll provide additional (and authentic) tastes.

Pizza D.O.C.

Italian ✗

2251 W. Lawrence Ave. (at Oakley Ave.)

Phone: 773-784-8777
Web: www.mypizzadoc.com
Prices: $$

Lunch Fri – Sun
Dinner nightly
🚇 Western (Brown)

♿ In Italy, where purity of products is a matter of national pride, D.O.C. (*denominazione di origine controllata*) is a government-controlled seal of quality. Here in Chicago, self-ordained Pizza D.O.C. assures each diner that it takes its ingredients just as seriously, from the Sicilian olive oil drizzled on the lightly charred crusts to the thinly sliced salami that tops it.

These uncut 12-inch pies are as good for taking out as eating in, whether at the large, popular bar or group-friendly dining room with exposed brick and festive wreaths. Just keep in mind that pizza here isn't your typical Chi-town pie, so the thin crusted, lightly sauced delicacies that emerge after only minutes in the brick oven won't hold up to heftier toppings.

Chicago ▶ Andersonville, Edgewater & Uptown

Chicago ▶ Andersonville, Edgewater & Uptown

Ras Dashen

Ethiopian ✗

5846 N. Broadway (bet. Ardmore & Thorndale Aves.)

Phone: 773-506-9601
Web: www.rasdashenchicago.com
Prices: $$

Lunch & dinner daily

🚇 Thorndale

Welcoming and all-embracing, Ras Dashen is a good pick for both the neophyte to Ethiopian cuisine as well as the loyal enthusiast who wants authentic eats. The friendly staff is happy to explain the drinks, the *mossab* (that covered dish on each table used as the communal serving plate), and even the restrooms (men's and women's facilities are in different parts of the restaurant).

As is traditional, dishes are served with *injera*, the fermented pancake-like bread used to ladle food, such as the *yebeg wat*, a dish of tender lamb cubes stewed in a spicy *berbere* sauce. Ras Dashen even offers a warm and creamy bread pudding made with *injera,* spices, and flax seeds. An ample offering of signature drinks and hard-to-find beers are poured at the full bar.

Rosded

Thai ✗

2308 W. Leland Ave. (bet. Lincoln & Western Aves.)

Phone: 773-334-9055
Web: N/A
Prices: ✑

Lunch & dinner Tue – Sun

🚇 Western (Brown)

This BYOB Thai fave has seen quite a bit of traffic in its day, as evidenced by the lived-in feel of the tiny, eleven-table dining space. But we get it. Belly-pleasing dishes keep the place packed for lunch and dinner, while maintaining a hearty take-out business to boot.

Soups, noodles, rice dishes, curries, and salads are offered in vast varieties on the menu; as are yummy mains like flaky catfish fritters, battered and deep-fried, smothered with a glaze of sweet chili sauce and fragrant Thai basil; or Rama Chicken with curry-peanut sauce. Try the *pad prik khing*—curried green beans with a choice of meat; or smoky, tender pork satay, marinated in flavorful yellow curry, grilled, and served with a dipping sauce and zesty cucumber salad.

San Soo Gab San

Korean ✗

5247 N. Western Ave. (bet. Berwyn & Farragut Aves.)

Phone: 773-334-1589
Web: N/A
Prices: ☺☺

Lunch & dinner daily

Beloved by families by day and large groups on the late night, this neigborhood standby appeals to locals and visitors thanks to the grill-top tables offering do-it-yourself feasts and lived-in décor.

A meal commences with the typically mammoth parade of *banchan* including several types of kimchi, sesame oil-flavored vegetables, cold noodle salads, and even a steaming bowl of savory soup. The sheer number served forgives a few misses in quality. The massive menu shows all the classics like *dol sot bi bim bap* and *bulgogi*. Try the giant *mandoo* accompanied by a pungent, spicy dipping sauce, as well as char-broiled chicken in a smoky-sweet glaze. San Soo Gab San is open almost all night, perfect for a boozey Korean barbecue feast with friends.

Siam Noodle & Rice

Thai ✗

4654 N. Sheridan Rd. (at Leland Ave.)

Phone: 773-769-6694
Web: www.siamnoodleandrice.com
Prices: ☺☺

Lunch & dinner Tue — Sun

 Wilson

This cozy mainstay opened its doors over twenty years ago and has been going strong ever since. Family-run and charming to boot, this Thai favorite churns out scrumptious specialties with a unique home-style twist; collard greens get sprinkled into a number of dishes, like *pad see ew*, and sliced ham hocks are stewed Thai-style over rice in the *kao kha moo*.

To start, settle into a glass-topped table and try the papaya salad, neatly piled high with julienned green papaya, basil, and chilies topped with pungent dried shrimp, all perfectly drenched in a bright lime dressing. Meat lovers should explore the list of chef's specials, like basil meatballs—sliced and stir-fried with strips of green chili and bamboo shoots, tossed in a salty-sweet sauce.

Spacca Napoli

Pizza

D5

1769 W. Sunnyside Ave. (bet. Hermitage & Ravenswood Aves.)

Phone: 773-878-2420
Web: www.spaccanapolipizzeria.com
Prices:

Lunch Wed – Sun
Dinner nightly
Montrose (Brown)

Lines out the door aren't unusual at this Neapolitan-style bistro, which takes its pizza very seriously. In fact, the bistro's pizza ovens were built by third- and fourth-generation artisans from the old country, and owner Jon Goldsmith is a certified *pizzaiolo*. Important soccer games often play on the TV here, thereby furthering the authentic aspect.

The menu, of course, is built around twelve varieties of pizza along with a selection of antipasti (marinated anchovies) and desserts (*spumoni*), which are good, but not the centerpiece. Try the classic *Margherita*, made with *fior di latte* mozzarella, fresh basil, and olive oil, and charred just right, so it is crispy, but not too smoky. A decent wine list and authentic espresso round out the offerings.

Spoon Thai

Thai

C5

4608 N. Western Ave. (bet. Eastwood & Wilson Aves.)

Phone: 773-769-1173
Web: www.spoonthai.com
Prices:

Lunch & dinner daily

Set along a strip of Western Avenue that is rich in Asian offerings, Spoon Thai is certainly worthy of consideration. The room is simple but clean and warmed by the affable service.

Look past the spring rolls and satay for a more enriching experience. Homemade Thai sausages and the *yum pla muk* salad of squid tossed with spicy lime dressing and fragrant herbs are two fine preludes. The array of vibrant cooking goes on to feature the likes of *ka nom jeen nam ya*, ground catfish in curry sauce over wide noodles; and intriguing house specialties such as banana blossom salad, a meaty combination of chicken and shrimp with slivers of tender banana blossom in a warm coconut milk sauce bright with lime and red chili and showered with crispy shallots.

Sunshine Cafe

J a p a n e s e

5449 N. Clark St. (bet. Catalpa & Rascher Aves.)

Phone:	773-334-6214	Dinner Tue – Sun
Web:	N/A	
Prices:	👓	🚇 Bryn Mawr

While many dining establishments succeed at being hospitable, it's an absolute pleasure when one encounters an ambience that is truly welcoming and laid-back, case in point Sunshine Cafe. The setting is modest but does bear one note of embellishment: a bright yellow sign that reads "You are my sunshine."

This sprightly spot showcases home-style Japanese cooking that is hearty and heartwarming. Starters include *shu mai*, potato croquettes, and *inari zushi* (fried tofu skin pouches filled with seasoned sushi rice). Entrées, accompanied by miso soup and green tea, focus on broiled fish, tempura and donburi. The *katsu don* is a bowl of top quality rice decked with slices of tender, panko-crusted pork tenderloin, sautéed onions, egg, and light brown sauce.

Tank Sushi

J a p a n e s e

4514 N. Lincoln Ave. (at Sunnyside Ave.)

Phone:	773-769-2600	Lunch & dinner daily
Web:	www.tanksushi.com	
Prices:	**$$**	🚇 Western (Brown)

Step aside, sushi purists. This diverse gang of chefs whips up a frenzy of artful and innovative creations, throwing fried bananas into a maki alongside lobster and spiced honey mayo; and drizzling butter-soy sauce, red *tobiko*, and chives over tender chunks of steamed king crab. Traditional maki, classic sashimi, and various nigiri also line the multi-page menu, as do hot and cold small plates like the decadent crisp chopstick roll stuffed with mushrooms and cream cheese.

Happy hour specials offer selections at half price, though there's usually a crowd to contend with. Grab a spot in the sleek, modern space and refresh with a flight of fragrant sake—there's an ample selection to choose from. End the feast with tasty mango *mochi*.

The Thai Grill & Noodle Bar

Thai

F1

1040 W. Granville Ave. (bet. Kenmore & Winthrop Aves.)

Phone: 773-274-7510
Web: www.thaigrillchicago.com
Prices:

Lunch & dinner Tue – Sun

Granville

In the ground floor of the Sovereign apartment building, Thai Grill & Noodle Bar sports a more contemporary (and less clichéd) take on the typical Thai eatery. Amid the grey walls, striped zebrawood tables, and dark banquettes, diners will find locals and families enjoying good renditions of Thai standards and sipping bubble teas (with those tapioca "bubbles").

Diners who are new to Thai cuisine, or just shy about the heat of their food, should not fear as these dishes are friendly to western palates. Even the spicy fish–a fillet of sole with a blend of Asian eggplant, beans, basil, Kaffir lime leaves, and chilies–highlights flavors rather than overwhelms with heat. Traditional dishes run the gamut from five different curries to pan-fried noodles.

Thai Pastry & Restaurant

Thai

E4

4925 N. Broadway (bet. Ainslie & Argyle Sts.)

Phone: 773-784-5399
Web: www.thaipastry.com
Prices: $$

Lunch & dinner daily

Argyle

Just south of Argyle Street in the heart of the city's Little Saigon district is this Thai marvel, standing out among many Vietnamese restaurants. This storefront is brighter and less cluttered than most of its neighbors—the lime colored walls surround cases of, as its name suggests, Thai pastries.

There are pre-packed *klong-klang, a-kare*, taro custard, curry puffs, and many others. But pastry is not the only dessert here: quarts of local favorite, Village Creamery ice cream are available for take-out, which many customers do with the pastries, too. But this neighborhood mainstay is worth coming to for pre-dessert savory dishes. Don't miss the traditional *Panang* curry, sweetened with coconut milk and seasoned with Kaffir lime and good quality chicken.

Tien Giang

Vietnamese

4925B N. Broadway (bet. Ainslie & Argyle Sts.)

Phone: 773-275-4928
Web: www.tiengiangrestaurant.com
Prices: ⊜⊜

Lunch & dinner daily

🚇 Argyle

Here, the vast Vietnamese offerings revolve around a single grain: rice noodle soups, *congee* (rice porridge), *bún* (rice vermicelli), and fried rice—with a robust list of tasty appetizers, fish, and meat specialties rounding out the menu. Named for a province in South Vietnam vital to the region's rice production, Tien Giang styles its simple space in dark woods, white walls, and a cheery ceiling inset painted sky blue with puffy clouds; tables are topped with a range of sauces, from chili pastes and *sriracha* to hoisin. The house-made noodle soup (*phở đặc biệt Tiền Giang*) is a sure thing—beef broth brimming with rice noodles, strips of brisket and tongue, accompanied by a plate of mung bean sprouts, mint, basil, lime, and sliced jalapeños.

Feast for under $25 at all restaurants with ⊜⊜.

Chicago ▶ Andersonville, Edgewater & Uptown

Bucktown & Wicker Park

Ukranian Village · West Town

Finesse and Flair

Like many of the Windy City's neighborhoods, Bucktown and Wicker Park have seen its fair share of transition. Ranging from Polish immigrants to wealthy businessmen (who have built stately mansions on Hoyne and Pierce avenues), it has been home to people from all walks of life. But, don't let the hushed residential streets and bewitching brownstones fool you—this neighborhood still knows how to mix it up. While you're more likely to run into bankers than Basquiats these days, Bucktown and Wicker Park remains an international hotbed of creative energy and trendsetting style.

Shopping Sanctum

Shake out the remains of your piggy bank before arriving. After all, this neighborhood has some of the most stylish shopping in the Midwest. It is worlds away from the international chains of the Magnificent Mile. Instead, think über-cool indie shops. Don't have time to travel the world for funky home accessories, or love the flea market look but don't want to get out of bed on the weekends? Fake the well-traveled look and visit Fenway Gallery, where you can pick up an exotic home accessory or two. To experience a taste of Wicker Park's vast and vivid

music scene, be sure you make the time to stop by Reckless Records and get schooled on the latest underground band. You can even get creative and design your own t-shirt at the appropriately named T-Shirt Deli—and rest assured as this is only the beginning of a wonderful journey.

Gathering of the Arts

The neighborhood shows off its artistic roots by hosting two of the city's largest festivals. Wicker Park Fest is an annual two-day music festival held each July that features no less than 28 bands. The Around the Coyote festival held each fall shines a spotlight on local artists practicing creative and visual arts. Wicker Park is also home to a number of art galleries, including the unique 4Art Inc., where artists create their works during the opening night show.

Even starving artists can find something to eat in foodie-friendly Bucktown and Wicker Park. Hot dog fanatics simply must take a tour of the famed **Vienna Beef Factory**—visitors are bound to be blown away by the production lines of products made here. After a view of the manufacturing line, return to your appetite and dine in the employee cafeteria. Parched after all the meat-eating? Quench your thirst by heading straight for **Black Dog Gelato**, where you can savor outstanding whisky gelato bars dipped in milk chocolate and candied bacon; or taste unusual flavors like goat cheese-cashew-caramel.

Fascinating Foods

The name sounds a little sketchy, but vegetarians love the **Earwax Café** for its over-the-top, funky décor, which is kind of Grateful Dead-meets-India. This inexpensive and idyllic eatery presents tasty, multinational all-veggie meals, including a breakfast menu that is served all day. So if you're craving eggs Benedict for dinner, you know where to head. Other food faves include the seitan ruben overflowing with sauerkraut, Swiss cheese, and creamy dressing; as well as the sweet potato and black bean quesadilla spread with cilantro pesto.

Go whole hog and bone up on your cooking skills at **Cooking Fools**, and you won't ever be teased about your tiramisu again. If you're planning to entertain friends with a delicious meal at home, be sure to swing by the **Wicker Park & Bucktown Farmer's Market** for fresh produce, glorious cheeses, and other specialty items. And while basking in cheese paradise, don't forget to grab a pie at **Piece**— hugely frequented by locals and considered Chicago's most favored pizza place. However, Piece has garnered a following that come by not only for their crunchy pizzas, but also for their hand-crafted beers and delicious spectrum of appetizers, sandwiches, and desserts.

Sweet tooths worth their salt certainly know all about **Red Hen Bread**. Atkins would turn over in his grave if he ever got a taste of the bread and pastries from this terrific bake shop. Lauded as a "premium purveyor of high quality artesian breads and pastries," Red Hen sates scores with the likes of croissants, muffins, scones, cookies, tarts, quiche, and Red Hen Signature treats. Think your mama makes good pie? Grab a fork and taste a lip-smacking piece from **Hoosier Mama Pie Company**. Run by Paula Haney, the former pastry chef at Trio, it's a little slice of paradise. No bake shop is complete without cake, and **Alliance Bakery**'s window display of cakes is quite stupendous.

Crowning Cocktails

Speaking of stupendous, lull on the late night at **Violet Hour**, the speakeasy that serves some of the most heavenly cocktails in town. Slurp up these concoctions while chowing on toasty treats like spiced nuts, deviled eggs with smoked paprika and goat cheese, and smoky chili cheese mini-dogs topped with mustard and onion.

Marie's Rip-Tide Lounge is a bit of retro fun. With soulful beats emanating from a jukebox and an incredibly energetic vibe, the hopping lounge draws a regular group of late night revelers. Marie, now in her 70s, lives upstairs and decorates this frozen-in-time space for all of the holidays. The perennially-packed **Moonshine Brewing Company** shows a solid and serious beer collection, with

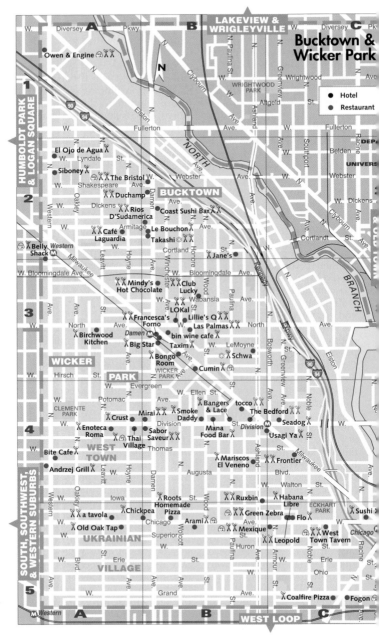

W. Diversey A Pkwy. B W. Diversey C Pk

Wrightwood Ave.

WRIGHTWOOD PARK

Altgeld St.

● Hotel
● Restaurant

Owen & Engine XX

HUMBOLDT PARK & LOGAN SQUARE

I-90 I-94

Elston

N. Paulina St.
N. Clybourn
Ashland
Greenview

N. NORTH Ave.

Fullerton Ave.

Belden
UNIVERS

Racine
Southport
DEP

El Ojo de Agua X
W. Lyndale St.
Siboney X
W. Shakespeare Ave.
XXX The Bristol W. Webster Ave.
Duchamp X
BUCKTOWN Ave.
W. Dickens
Dickens
Rios X X Coast Sushi Bar X X
D'Sudamerica
XX Café Le Bouchon X Ave.
Laguardia Takashi ●
Cortland Cortlandt St.
X Jane's ●

Western
Oakley
Damen
Leavitt
Hoyne
Milwaukee
Winchester
Honore
Wood
Paulina

Belly X
Shack M
W. Bloomingdale Ave. W. Bloomingdale Ave.

Mindy's XX XX Club
Hot Chocolate Lucky
W. Wabansia Ave.
LOKal X X

3

X X Francesca's Lillie's Q XX
Forno Las Palmas XX
W. North North Ave.
X Birchwood Damen M bin wine cafe X
Kitchen X Big Star Taxim X LeMoyne
St.
X Bongo ✿X Schwa
W. Hirsch St. Room
WICKER Cumin ✿ X
PARK
WICKER PARK Ave.
W. Evergreen

Bosworth
Greenview
N. Elston
Noble

W. Ellen St.
Potomac X Bangers tocco XX
Ave. & Lace The Bedford XX
CLEMENTE Mirai XX Smoke
PARK X Crust Daddy St. Division M Seadog X
W. Division Mana
Enoteca Sabor Food Bar X Usagi Ya X
Roma ✿ Thai Saveur XX
Village
Bite Cafe X WEST Thomas
TOWN X Mariscos XX Frontier
Andrzej Grill X El Veneno
Augusta
Blvd.
W. Walton St.

Leavitt
Hoyne
Damen
Oakley
Western

W. Iowa X Roots St. XX Ruxbin X Habana
Homemade Libre ECKHART
X X a tavola X Chickpea Pizza Ave. PARK X Sushi
Arami X ✿ XX Green Zebra X Flo ●
X Old Oak Tap ● Chicago XX Mexique Chicago
UKRAINIAN W. Superior XX Leopold ✿XX West
VILLAGE St. Town Tavern
Huron Armour Noble Erie St.
W. Erie St. Ohio St.

SOUTH, SOUTHWEST, & WESTERN SUBURBS

5

W. Grand Ave.

M Western A B WEST LOOP C Ave.

42

packs brewed on-site; while **Silver Cloud** is foolproof for sidewalk boozing, chicken pot pie, or a grilled cheese sandwich. This comfort food haven makes one feel at home—it exudes a casual vibe and is flooded with warmth. Whether you're here for "small bites," "big bowls," or a crowning cocktail, Silver Cloud is sure to be a crowd-pleaser and wreaks of Bucktown.

Late Night Fun

Definitely defining the 'tude of the 'hood is the **Cellar Rat Wine Shop**. If you thought exceptional wines at excellent value was never a possibility, think again, as this place will prove you wrong. Displaying a splendid array, this neighborhood delight never fails to satisfy, no matter the day or time. Carry on your Saturday

night fever at **Salud Tequila Lounge**. Alongside a sinfully delightful range of tequilas, Salud also salutes foodies with south-of-the-border spreads from gooey guacamole, nachos, and quesadillas, to tortas, tacos, and other deliciousness. Straight from the horse's mouth, eat well but drink better at **Angels and Mariachis**. This bar may be rustic-looking, but it reverberates nightly with a raucous set. Watch them groove to the beats of rock and country, whilst sipping and savoring a menu of eats 'n treats. From martinis, margaritas, tequila, and cerveza, to a range of Mexican faithfuls, this cantina struts it all.

Wholesome Ways

Local Folks Food is a family-run enterprise whose chief charge is to develop delicious, natural, and gourmet condiments (mustard and hot sauce anyone?) perfect for slathering upon burgers. Find these tangy, tantalizing treats at the **Green Grocer** and elevate your burger to ethereal.

And finally, much to every foodie's delight, Bucktown and Lincoln Park now share a fabulous and fantastically unique **Whole Foods**. Lauded as *the* third largest store nationwide, this particular paragon is complete (and replete) with food stations (like mini restaurants), an International Cookie Club, and a delightful wine (**Da'Vine**) and beer bar.

Pick your favorite food, then your best beverage (wine and beer either by the bottle or glass), and while away an evening at this wholesome haven. Don't really have time to linger? Push a cart around, sipping as you shop!

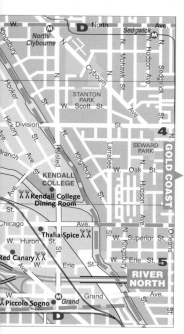

Andrzej Grill

A4

1022 N. Western Ave. (bet. Augusta Blvd. & Cortez St.)

Phone: 773-489-3566
Web: www.andrzejgrillrestaurant.com
Prices: ⊜⊜

Lunch & dinner Mon – Sat

No trip to Chicago would be complete without a super filling, inexpensive, and authentic Polish feast. If you're not invited into someone's home for such a satisfying meal, the homey Andrzej Grill is as good a choice. The diminutive, no-frills stop is as popular for take-out as dining in.

Service is efficient and straightforward, which can be said of the food, too. For less than $10, diners can fill up on the Polish platter, which includes a crisp potato pancake; stuffed cabbage roll (tender leaves of cabbage surrounding a steamed filling of herb-scented rice); a smoky, well-seasoned, grilled kielbasa; and that star of the Polish culinary world: plump *pierogi*. And on top of all this comes a side of tasty sauerkraut, made with cabbage and carrot.

Arami

B5

1829 W. Chicago Ave. (bet. Wolcott Ave & Wood St.)

Phone: 312-243-1535
Web: www.aramichicago.com
Prices: $$

Lunch & dinner Tue – Sun

🚇 Division

You won't find fat, gimmicky sushi rolls anywhere at Arami; in a skylit, bamboo-framed atmosphere, unembellished fresh fish and light but artful Japanese cuisine have the chance to shine. Sit in the back for a view of the sushi bar and absorb the wide sake selection or a Japanese spirit-infused cocktail while the chefs work with a deft touch.

The word *fresh* bears repeating with each plate's presentation— listen to the chef when he politely recommends leaving soy sauce off the rolled coins of maki *mono* stuffed with hamachi and *maguro*, then crowned with cooked shrimp, spicy mayo, and Japanese salsa. Need warmth? Sweet and spicy pickled Fresno chilies and kumquat rings complement duck confit's richness in one of the stellar donburi.

a tavola

A5

Italian

2148 W. Chicago Ave. (bet. Hoyne Ave. & Leavitt St.)

Phone: 773-276-7567

Dinner Mon – Sat

Web: www.atavolachicago.com

Prices: $$

This long-time mainstay is housed in a small brick townhouse, and inside both the dining room and menu continue this petite trend. The dining area is simply decorated with striking black-and-white photographs (a combo of nudes and landscapes) and white linen tablecloths. But that old saw, "good things come in small packages," applies here.

The regular menu is selective, with a few specials, which the server will read to you. For years, the don't-miss dish has been the brown butter gnocchi, topped with fried sage leaves. Order it as a starter, leaving room for a seasonal entrée special, such as the pork shank braised with white wine, cloves, and juniper berries, served aside cannellini beans. The waiter will also pair wines with the meal on request.

Bangers & Lace

B4

Gastropub

1670 W. Division St. (at Paulina St.)

Phone: 773-252-6499

Lunch & dinner daily

Web: www.bangersandlacechicago.com

Prices: $$

🔲 Damen (Blue)

Brat and brew lovers take note: this hopping gastropub is taking things far beyond your average ballgame fare. "Bangers" get serious sprucing up here. Smoked venison sausage is served in a toasted challah roll and topped with rhubarb jam, candied bacon bits, black currants, and house-made beer mustard; a French garlic sausage is wrapped in soft brioche cornbread with orange marmalade, foie gras mousse, and maple butter; and a veal brat is paired with melted Gouda and sauerkraut.

Exposed brick walls lined with beer taps, blackboards with daily specials, and lace curtains all give warmth to the hipster-packed space. The thirty-plus beer list includes locally crafted brews as well as a slew of international and regional offerings.

The Bedford

American 🍴🍴

B4

1612 W. Division St. (at Ashland Ave.)

Phone: 773-235-8800
Web: www.bedfordchicago.com
Prices: $$

Lunch Sun
Dinner nightly
Damen (Blue)

This old bank continues to service its community, but now as a restaurant honoring the foods of America's Midwest. Look for the doorman to find the portal that "deposits" you down the slate stairwell and into the glamorous Bedford. The bar and dining room turns back the clock with vaults, safe deposits, and Americana pictures. If scenes from family road trips come to mind, you're on track. Either way, it is idyllic for a romantic tryst.

Peruse the nibbles as you nestle: buttermilk crackers spread with pimento cheese are a perfect teaser for chili-glazed chicken wings with chunky blue cheese. Pan-seared hanger steak paired with creamy chard and homemade tater tots, and a chocolate-strawberry pie filled with fresh berries will hook any cool Chicagoan.

Belly Shack 😊

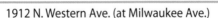

Fusion 🍴

A2

1912 N. Western Ave. (at Milwaukee Ave.)

Phone: 773-252-1414
Web: www.bellyshack.com
Prices: 🪙🪙

Lunch & dinner daily

Western (Blue)

Chef/owner Bill Kim is worlds away from his ex-luxury lair, Le Lan, at this Asian-Latin snack shop. A hip crowd fills this minimalist-urban spot, burrowed beneath the El. Order at the counter and wait for the flava' to arrive.

Sandwiches like the tasty pocket with savory meatballs, dressed noodles, and an ample squirt of *sriracha*; or the hot and sour soup with hominy and cilantro, show the chef's terrific melody of Mexican and Asian tones. A sometime special of *bulgogi*, thinly shaved cheesesteak-style beef doused with spicy mayo and cilantro, wedged between crisp, salty plantains is a work of Korean-Latino fusion genius.

Belly Shack's soft serve swirls in playful scoops of mint brownie, with a guest chef appearance by Mindy Segal, on the brownie topping.

Big Star

B3

M e x i c a n

1531 N. Damen Ave. (bet. Milwaukee & Wicker Park Aves.)

Phone: 773-235-4039
Web: www.bigstarchicago.com
Prices:

Lunch & dinner daily

Damen (Blue)

The team behind Blackbird, Avec, and Publican have built one heck of a rollicking hot spot here for Wicker Park scenesters. Loud music, a grungy but hip vibe, and abundant drink specials keep the lofty garage-like space filled to the rafters. Arrive seriously early to claim a spot at the bar, or just go with the standing room flow and raise a glass with 200 of your closest friends and neighbors.

Order up an outstandingly refreshing michelada or prepare to succumb to the addictive La Paloma. Highlights of the tasty menu include a satisfying *queso fundido*, smoky tacos *al pastor*, a killer Sonoran hot dog plus some solid guacamole. With three dollar shots and pitchers of Schlitz you'll want to keep the food coming to survive the booze consumption.

bin wine cafe

B3

A m e r i c a n

1559 N. Milwaukee Ave. (bet. Damen Ave. & Honore Sts.)

Phone: 773-486-2233
Web: www.binwinecafe.com
Prices: $$

Lunch Sun
Dinner nightly
Damen (Blue)

Just south of the Bucktown/Wicker Park epicenter intersection, this American café attracts young families, older gaggles, eclectic locals, and others, for its spot-on eats.

A particularly satisfying treat is the frittata, moistened with sweet crab and crunchy artichokes. This perfect opener is served hot, with just the right amount of tang. The kitchen's take on the BLT is made with smoked bacon and whole grain bread that is kissed with the right amount of basil pesto; the crispy French fries are a pefect match for this sandwich. As ought to be the case at a place known for its brunches, Bin's mugs of coffee are served hot and strong. The wine list is interesting, and all of the wines served here are available to take home, too.

Birchwood Kitchen

American

A3

2211 W. North Ave. (bet. Bell Ave. & Leavitt St.)

Phone: 773-276-2100
Web: www.birchwoodkitchen.com
Prices:

Lunch Sat – Sun
Dinner Tue – Sun
Damen (Blue)

Birchwood Kitchen's periwinkle façade sparkles like a gem from a stretch of brick storefronts lining North Avenue. Daily specials written on a cookie sheet and old church pews lining the exposed brick walls hint of quirky country charm and mirror the ethos of the utterly fresh and ever-changing menu, which might include a quiche with country pork sausage and slivered apple, or house-cured gravlax. The café takes pride in supporting local edibles like Burton's maple syrup and the Metropolis Coffee Company.

Prepared foods in a glass case make the idea of a picnic completely sensible and inspiring, and homemade sweets beg to be wrapped up for dessert. It's hard to pin down a choice from the jars of soft cookies, banana nut bread, and gooey brownies.

Bite Cafe

American

A4

1039 N. Western Ave. (bet. Cortez & Thomas Sts.)

Phone: 773-395-2483
Web: www.bitecafechicago.com
Prices: $$

Lunch & dinner daily

Though Bite's black-framed windows barely stand out on its block of industrial brick storefronts, gals with a roller derby edge serve up unforgettably bold dishes inside. Grab a seat at the small back counter or take up residence at distressed oak tables armed with powder blue metal chairs, and settle in for an eccentric but filling ride.

Eat all day, if you can: breakfast *poutine* gilds the lily with poached eggs atop house-cut fries, cheese curds, and smoked bacon gravy. Lunch? How about a fried chicken leg sandwich with pickled cabbage slaw and Tabasco aïoli? Dinner could be bison Salisbury steak or a Porterhouse pork chop paired with watermelon and tomato salad. And don't stop before dessert; there's pie, pound cake, or ice cream to be had.

Bongo Room

American

B3

1470 N. Milwaukee Ave. (bet. Evergreen Ave. & Honore St.)

Phone: 773-489-0690

Lunch daily

Web: www.thebongoroom.com

Prices:

 Damen (Blue)

This cheerful spot with a jaunty name offers Wicker Park residents a hearty start to the day. Fuel up on eggs any style, a heaping breakfast burrito, and sides such as Canadian bacon; but when gifted a puckish collection of pancakes, grab 'em! Be warned though that the banana Oreo hotcakes, a decadent stack with bananas, crushed cookies, warm vanilla bean crème, and chocolate crème anglaise, may send you back home for a nap. For lunch, an array of sandwiches and salads will perfectly pacify you until sundown.

The sunny room, offset by an upbeat staff, is outfitted with yellow painted furnishings and a dining counter that doubles as an excellent roost for those kooks who are best left alone until after that all-important first cuppa'.

The Bristol

American

B2

2152 N. Damen Ave. (bet. Shakespeare & Webster Aves.)

Phone: 773-862-5555

Lunch Sun

Web: www.thebristolchicago.com

Dinner nightly

Prices: $$

Whether you seek familiar dishes or feel like gnawing on less appreciated and boldly cariverous cuts, Chef/owner Chris Pandel is sure to meet your needs. At The Bristol, he aims to reward cravings head-on, sending out strongly satisfying plates with a comfortable and convivial spirit.

Fresh tagliatelle garnished with anise essence, earthy anchovy, and bright lemon pleases even the most straightforward taste buds. On the other hand, a crispy pig's tail reminiscent of traditional *pernil* sports crackling, fatty pork skin balanced by a spicy, minty tomatillo sauce, while slices of beef heart confit pack a punch of flavor and texture. Timid and adventurous palates meet for dessert to share a monumental chocolate pecan pie swirled with bacon caramel.

Café Laguardia

Cuban ✕✕

A2

2111 W. Armitage Ave. (bet. Hoyne Ave. & Leavitt St.)

Phone: 773-862-5996
Web: www.cafelaguardia.com
Prices: ☙☙

Lunch & dinner daily

🔲 Western (Blue)

A portrait of one of history's most fervent Cuba-lovers, Ernest Hemingway, hangs on the wall in this second-generation Cuban haunt. Red-topped tables are paired with chairs upholstered in a riot of animal prints, lending the place a marked south-of-the-border expat feel.

The menu renders an armchair trip to Cuba, with an affordable sampling of filling sides and entrées. A particular bargain is the Taste of Cuba platter, which shows off the kitchen's specialties: *picadillo criollo*, a ground beef dish with raisins and olives, is hot and flavorful; the fried pork medallions are crunchy, caramelized, and tender; and the ham croquette sports an appealing (and golden) exterior. Black beans, white rice, and grease-free fried plantains complement the meaty menu.

Chickpea

Middle Eastern ✕

B5

2018 W. Chicago Ave. (bet. Damen & Hoyne Aves.)

Phone: 773-384-9930
Web: www.chickpeaonthego.com
Prices: ☙☙

Lunch & dinner daily

Jerry Suqi has brought some of the most scene-y spots to Chicago nightlife over the last decade. There was Sugar: A Dessert Bar, La Pomme Rouge, Narcisse, and then Jam. His newest spot looks like an unassuming campus sandwich shop, but it is no less ambitious than his other previous efforts. With his mom (Amni Suqi) as executive chef, Suqi is trying to bring the vibe and the food of his native Palestine to the city. Posters and signage in Arabic set the scene, but the scene-stealer is the affordable, get-it-and-go food. The star is the *kufta* pita, made with lamb, grilled green peppers, and a remarkable tahini sauce. Mama's lentil soup should not be missed either as it's unbelievably creamy and delicious touched with favas and a swirl of olive oil.

Club Lucky

Italian ✗✗

B3

1824 W. Wabansia Ave. (at Honore St.)

Phone: 773-227-2300
Web: www.clubluckychicago.com
Prices: $$

Lunch Mon — Fri
Dinner nightly
🚇 Damen (Blue)

Quiet by day but boisterous by night, this family-friendly favorite brings to life a bygone era of classic Italian-American dining from its commanding location on the corner of Wabansia and Honore. The nostalgic ambience also includes cordial service and a generous sidewalk for alfresco dining in fair weather.

Inside, the dusky room highlights red vinyl booths, painted brick walls, and crowds indulging in this idyllic Italian-American experience. The black Formica tables display a quintessential spread of antipasti starring portobellos, carrots, beets, and beans in balsamic; as well as pastas like rigatoni with veal meatballs, creamy mozzarella, and tomato sauce, all served family style. Desserts showcase crispy cannoli and a sweetened martini slate.

Coalfire Pizza

Pizza ✗

C5

1321 W. Grand Ave. (bet. Ada & Elizabeth Sts.)

Phone: 312-226-2625
Web: www.coalfirechicago.com
Prices: 💰💰

Lunch & dinner Tue — Sun
🚇 Chicago (Blue)

Few restaurants are as aptly named as Coalfire. The pizzas from this local favorite are cooked in an oven fueled by a coal fire. That 800-degree fire sets the stage for the kitchen and the menu.

The menu does include a few other Italian favorites like salads and calzones, but really there's no reason to consider them, because you (and everyone else in town) are here for the pizza, and that in itself says a great deal. These are not Chicago-style pies. Rather, thin-crusted, 14-inch, Neapolitan-style pies. Pick from one of nine combos or create your own. Options include fresh or regular mozzarella cheese, thin sliced hot salami, and pesto. A decent beer and wine list round out the offerings, but bring patience, since they don't take reservations.

Chicago ▶ Bucktown & Wicker Park

Coast Sushi Bar

Japanese ✕✕

B2

2045 N. Damen Ave. (bet. Dickens & McLean Aves.)

Phone: 773-235-5775
Web: www.coastsushibar.com
Prices: $$

Dinner nightly

Animated chatter and softly thumping music give Coast Sushi Bar a definitive vibe and immediate sense of vitality. Choose to sit at the counter staffed by personable sushi chefs for a first-row seat as the broad, crowd-pleasing menu of sushi, maki, and a range of cooked dishes and daily specials are prepared and artfully arranged.

The fish here is fresh and appealing, as in the starter of warm shrimp salad with sweet-tasting garlic-wasabi dressing and corn tempura. Sushi selections are highlighted on a blackboard of fresh specials, all thinly sliced and beautifully draped over small balls of rice; they may include ivory white hamachi, fatty salmon, or pristine cuts of ruby red tuna. Upgrade to the freshly grated wasabi for a nominal charge.

Crust

Pizza ✕

A4

2056 W. Division St. (at Hoyne Ave.)

Phone: 773-235-5511
Web: www.crustchicago.com
Prices: $$

Lunch & dinner daily

🚇 Division

If you're thinking Crust is just another Chicago pizza joint, you couldn't be more mistaken. This beloved place feels more like a fresh California breeze in the heart of Wicker Park, with nary an oozing deep-dish in sight. Think thin, since it's all about California-style pizza with organic and unusual toppings in combinations like shrimp, cheese, and lime; or the carbonara with bacon, peas, and egg. Wash it down with a local micro-brewed beer. Nightly specials include entertainment (trivia night and DJs).

Billed as the first certified organic pizzeria in the Midwest, this haunt is undeniably cool. Bright and cheery with framed photographs against whitewashed brick walls, it lures everyone from hipsters and intellectuals to young moms with strollers.

Cumin

B3

Indian ✗

1414 N. Milwaukee Ave. (bet. Evergreen & Wolcott Aves.)

Phone: 773-342-1414
Web: www.cumin-chicago.com
Prices:

Lunch Tue – Sun
Dinner nightly
Damen (Blue)

Polished wood, steel, and leather accents, and white linen tables draped with butcher paper make it clear this isn't your run-of-the-mill, divey Indian joint. Whether for the well-priced lunch buffet or for the à la carte dinner menu, diners come out en masse for Cumin's flavorful food and creative, original cocktails.

Contemporary versions of Nepalese and Indian dishes split the menu. *Mirchi masala naan*, stuffed with green chilies and spices and baked to order, comes out flaky and moist from the kitchen. Tender white and dark meat bathed in a golden-hued almond and cashew curry makes for an exemplary chicken *sahi korma*; thick mango lassi served over ice does the trick of balancing the palate after pummeling it with the pleasures of heat and spice.

Duchamp

B2

American ✗✗

2118 N. Damen Ave. (at Charleston St.)

Phone: 773-235-6434
Web: www.duchamp-chicago.com
Prices: $$

Lunch Sun
Dinner Tue – Sun

Folks from the West Loop nightclub Lumen gave birth to Duchamp—a global baby whose comfort food beats what's being served at most taverns across town. The interior feels a trifle dark and swanky and emanates a modern, sleek sense. The inspired menu demonstrates east-meets-west twists. Watch these unfold in small plates like hot wings, braised duck rillette, and Maine lobster tempura; or large portions including sage roasted pork chop, mushroom risotto-stuffed acorn squash, chicken paillard, and beef cheek stew. Locals rave about the signature burger, made from flavor-rich, juicy, ground beef, served on a toasted brioche spread with tangy tomato remoulade, and topped with a flood of creamy Havarti cheese.

53

El Ojo de Agua

 Mexican

A2

2235 N. Western Ave. (at Lyndale St.)

Phone: 773-235-8807
Web: N/A
Prices:

Lunch Sun – Fri
Dinner Sun – Thu
 Western (Blue)

 Hankering for a taco? Get over to this no-frills Bucktown taqueria, where they come fresh and piled high on delicious homemade corn tortillas, for just a handful of change. Though burritos, quesadillas, and other standard goodies are offered, the tacos are a critical fave. Munch on the *al pastor* taco— smoky spit-roasted pork marinated with dried chiles, onion, and pineapple; or the mouthwatering *carne asada*, splashed with spicy red salsa.

All are adorned with sliced radishes and charred jalapeños, and topping choices come in "regular" (cilantro and chopped white onions); or "super" (sour cream, cheese, and guacamole), which are generously heaped onto whichever tasty taco you fancy. Wash it all down with a creamy cinnamon *horchata* or a cool *agua fresca*.

Enoteca Roma

 Italian

A4

2146 W. Division St. (bet. Hoyne Ave. & Leavitt St.)

Phone: 773-342-1011
Web: www.enotecaroma.com
Prices: $$

Lunch & dinner daily

 Division

 Roman goddess Letizia Sorano presides over the candlelit cavern housing Enoteca Roma, a rustically welcoming spot with a big heart and an appetite for sharing. Adventurous and studious oenophiles can test themselves with multiple wine flights, and casual noshers can pick through *antipasti*, *salumi*, and nearly a dozen kinds of bruschetta.

Come early for the square Roman-style pizza, because when the dough runs out, it's gone for the night. Late arrivals can still get a bowl of Letizia's lasagna, arriving screaming hot in a round crock and bubbling over with venison Bolognese, béchamel, gooey mozzarella, and salty Parmesan. If the irresistible brownie of the day isn't enough, sleep on it and grab more treats next door at Letizia's Natural Bakery.

 Chicago ▶ Bucktown & Wicker Park

Flo

Mexican ✗

1434 W. Chicago Ave. (bet. Bishop St. & Greenview Ave.)

Phone:	312-243-0477	Lunch & dinner daily
Web:	www.eatatflo.com	
Prices:		Chicago (Blue)

A cornerstone of this rapidly gentrifying neighborhood, Flo's packs 'em in. The joint is open for three squares a day, but it is the breakfast and brunch menus that draw lines out the door. The pretty exterior sets the tone, with a plant-filled window and an array of mirrors down one inside wall.

Quality ingredients and a playful menu mimic the décor with a funky yet wholesome vibe. The vibrant spice of the Southwest is evident in the vast offerings starting with signature breakfast dishes such as *huevos rancheros*, breakfast tacos, and *chilaquiles*, all made with fresh salsa, warm tortillas, and savory black beans. Lunch and dinner playfully continue with a vamped-up Frito pie, hearty pork tamale bowl, or the spicy and saucy sloppy Flo.

Fogon

Mexican ✗✗

1235 W. Grand Ave. (at Ogden Ave.)

Phone:	312-421-2000	Lunch & dinner daily
Web:	www.fogonchicago.com	
Prices:	$$	Chicago (Blue)

In a departure from the typical primary paint jobs of most Mexican joints, much of the color at Fogon comes from the sophisticated food on the plates. Ceiling fans help aromas waft from the sparkling-clean kitchen into the dining room, a space that's further brightened by walls of windows and a steady stream of margaritas and mojitos coming from the glossy granite bar.

Italian, French, and Chinese influences weave their way into the upscale Mexican menu to great effect, upping the culinary ante far beyond rice and beans. Familiar dishes like quesadillas get a double dose of earthy fungus with the pairing of truffles and *huitlacoche*, while charred *chiles de arbol* meet applewood-smoked bacon and roasted red peppers in fiery *camarones a la diabla*.

Francesca's Forno

✗✗

B3

1576 N. Milwaukee Ave. (at Damen Ave.)

Phone: 773-770-0184
Web: www.miafrancesca.com
Prices: $$

Lunch Sat – Sun
Dinner nightly
🚇 Damen (Blue)

Francesca's Forno underwent a slight yet propitious face-lift, so say good-bye to those huge portions of pastas and *primi* in favor of lighter, ingredient-driven Italian thrills. Old-timers shouldn't sweat as the reduced portions have brought about reduced prices—now groups can indulge in many more Lilliputian dishes instead of attacking one Gulliver.

Enveloped in walls of windows, wooden floors, glass light fixtures, and a pressed-tin ceiling, fans hanker for their sumptuous *cicchetti*. Expect the likes of *granturco arrostito*, sweet corn with truffle oil and Grana Padano; Padrón peppers in spicy *pomodoro*; and *orecchiette con salsiccia* tossing crumbled sausage, tender rapini, and Calabrian chilies that may have a soft mien, but explode with flavor.

Frontier

✗✗

C4

1072 N. Milwaukee Ave. (bet. Division & Noble Sts.)

Phone: 773-772-4322
Web: www.thefrontierchicago.com
Prices: $$

Lunch Sat – Sun
Dinner nightly
🚇 Chicago (Blue)

Corral a crew of carnivores and mosey on in to this sexy saloon-style eatery for a good ole fashion meat-feast. Dining in numbers comes in handy at Frontier, where banquet options like "Whole Animal Service" get you and a dozen cohorts an entire house-smoked pig, goat, lamb, or wild boar, plus a starter and lip-smacking sides. (Equally handy is remembering to order this five days in advance.)

Bend an elbow at the handsome bar with one of several craft beers or specialty drinks, which pair perfectly with snacks such as dilled habeñero pickles, deviled eggs, or pristine fresh oysters. Grub on tasty apps like duck confit tacos (corn tortillas plump with onion, yucca, salsa verde, and *queso fresco*); lollipop chicken wings; or lamb spare ribs.

Green Zebra

C5   V e g e t a r i a n   ✗✗

1460 W. Chicago Ave. (at Greenview Ave.)

Phone: 312-243-7100   Lunch Sun
Web: www.greenzebrachicago.com   Dinner nightly
Prices: $$ 🚇 Chicago (Blue)

Named for the Green Zebra heirloom tomato, this is a sleek, serene arena with a Zen-like attitude and accommodating vegetarian menu that even carnivores can abide.
Come with a friendly bunch, since Green Zebra is all about small plates and shared entrées designed for grazing. Vegan options are plentiful, but you'll even find a meat dish or two toward the bottom of the list. The minimalist décor complements the subtle flavors and seasonings of dishes such as smoked sweet potato croquettes with brown butter and cauliflower; and Riesling-poached pear salad with feta, mint, and almonds. Playful desserts, like the white chocolate banana Bavarian with homemade nutella, are not to be missed.
The wine list features organic and bio-dynamic selections.

Habana Libre

C5   C u b a n   ✗

1440 W. Chicago Ave. (bet. Bishop & Noble Sts.)

Phone: 312-243-3303   Lunch & dinner daily
Web: www.habanalibrerestaurant.com
Prices: $$ 🚇 Chicago (Blue)

The spirit of Cuba is more than alive and well—it's a celebration amid the festive faux banana tree, swaying paper lanterns, and Latin tunes at Habana Libre. Let time ease by as the kitchen pulls together a pleasant parade of plantains in versatile forms: mashed and fried into cups that hold tender, beefy strings of *ropa vieja*; or cut wide and smashed, thin as a slice of bread, then fried into *tostones*, layered with mayo, braised chicken, and grilled onions for a fantastically messy *jibarito* sandwich.
Instead of settling for the pedestrian bottled red sauce on hand, ask for the fresh jalapeño-laced salsa verde, and dollop it all over dishes like succulent *lechon asado*, which dodges the "dry pork" bullet that befalls so many versions of the entrée.

Jane's

Contemporary ✗

B2

1655 W. Cortland St. (bet. Marshfield Ave. & Paulina St.)

Phone: 773-862-5263
Web: www.janesrestaurant.com
Prices: 🅰🅰

Lunch Fri – Sun
Dinner Tue – Sun

A neighborhood charmer in an 1890's house typical of the area, Jane's can hardly be called hip, yet it is regularly packed with hipsters (and their offspring) who live in the neighborhood.

The menu has not evolved much since Jane's opened in 1994, and some of the dishes such as the Asian chicken salad and the goat cheese-stuffed chicken, may seem dated, but Jane's does what it does well. Portions, such as the fettucine with roasted poblano, are ample and well-prepared. The potato leek soup–available during winter months–is creamy, but not so rich that it fills you up before your entrée arrives. The menu is exceedingly vegetarian-friendly, and breakfast is available until 3:00 P.M. on weekdays. Expect a wait for a table during the popular weekend brunch.

Kendall College Dining Room

International ✗✗

D4

900 North Branch St. (at Halsted St.)

Phone: 312-752-2328
Web: www.kendall.edu/diningroom.com
Prices: $$

Lunch Mon – Fri
Dinner Tue – Sat
🖳 Grand (Blue)

Imagine that dining out could be a sneak peek at a future Michelin-starred chef. That's a real possibility in this dining room and kitchen, which doubles as a test space for culinary arts students. Forgive the jitters as servers-in-training deliver your meal, which you can watch being prepared through floor-to-ceiling windows onto the kitchen.

The lunch prix-fixe menu includes three courses for under $20, with dishes such as a green gazpacho and a buttermilk panna cotta that rivals what may be served in nearby fine restaurants. Additionally, enjoy many other fine dining indulgences, such as an amuse-bouche, intermezzos, and very good bread.

It is not just the chefs who come from the school: many of the herbs and vegetables are grown in campus gardens.

Las Palmas

 Mexican

1835 W. North Ave. (at Honore St.)

Phone: 773-289-4991
Web: www.laspalmaschicago.com
Prices: $$

Lunch Wed – Sun
Dinner nightly
 Damen (Blue)

What looks like a small but bright and cozy neighborhood Mexican hangout is a deceptively creative spot. Inside, find a warm and lively space with vibrant artwork that can seem psychedelic after too much mezcal, glowing and intimate glassed-in atrium, and a garden that's a warm-weather oasis for inventive margaritas and mojitos muddled to order with mint and fresh fruit.

Likewise, the menu tweaks Mexican standards with 21st century details. A crisp, light chili relleno bursts with Manchego, goat, and Chihuahua cheeses plus a hint of *epazote*. Pineapple- and tequila-marinated skirt steak is perfectly tender atop rum-soaked roasted plantains and mango salsa. Who would pair sangria gelée and cocoa nib brittle with simple bread pudding? Las Palmas, that's who.

Le Bouchon

French

1958 N. Damen Ave. (at Armitage Ave.)

Phone: 773-862-6600
Web: www.lebouchonofchicago.com
Prices: $$

Lunch & dinner Mon – Sat

 Damen (Blue)

In lieu of intercontinental travel, head straight for Le Bouchon. One step inside this endearing restaurant and you'll think you've died and gone to bistro heaven. Pressed-tin ceilings, red walls, tile floors, framed pictures of Paris, and cramped tables only enhance its authenticity.

Still, Le Bouchon embodies more than the classic bistro look. Wholesome and fuss-free preparations of French comfort food headline the menu, as Chef/owner Jean-Claude Poilevey flits about from table to table. This kitchen knows how to soothe the soul with its cooking, as in salad Lyonnaise with a perfectly poached egg and crisp bacon lardons; steaming bowls of Bouillabaise brimming with clams, mussels, and shrimp; or the smooth, lovely chocolate marquis.

Leopold

C5

1450 W. Chicago Ave. (bet. Bishop & Noble Sts.)

Phone: 312-348-1028
Web: www.leopoldchicago.com
Prices: **$$**

Dinner Tue – Sun

🚇 Chicago (Blue)

Having cradled a potpourri of cultures and cuisines, it is only fitting that Chicago's own Leopold adds to the influx of beer-friendly Belgian options in West Town. Let the wafting aromas lure you inside—the serene front lounge is a nice place to linger and will divert thoughts of moules and frites.

Inside, fans fill chic nailhead chairs set atop dark wood floors. The dining room hugs a glass-lined bar and rightly so, they have all the booze and brews to match. This is upscale bar food which flaunts French and German influences, yet standouts like a tart filled with garlicky escargots and melted Grayson; *potatis korv*, pork and veal sausages with currant mustard; and crispy waffles licked with maple gelato and bourbon butter are nothing if not divine.

Lillie's Q

B3

1856 W. North Ave. (at Wolcott Ave.)

Phone: 773-772-5500
Web: www.lilliesq.com
Prices: **$$**

Lunch & dinner daily

🚇 Damen (Blue)

A note to traditionalists: the goods here are referred to as urban barbecue, so expect a few tasty tweaks on some cherished favorites. Meats are massaged with "Carolina Dirt"–the house dry rub–and then may be given a glaze; or finished with one of five flavorful sauces, all of which can be found neatly lined on the tables. Feast on tangy apple-glazed baby back ribs, tender tri-tip, smoky baked beans, hush puppies, and fried pickles.

The popular spot rocks a rustic chic style, with exposed ducts and brick walls; metal chairs beneath wooden tables; and filament bulbs in iron fixtures. Service pieces follow the theme—steamy sides roll out in cast iron dishes, meats on paper-lined metal trays, and cold bevs in old-fashioned Mason Ball jars.

LOKal

B3

American ✕✕

1904 W. North Ave. (bet. Winchester & Wolcott Aves.)

Phone: 773-904-8113
Web: www.lokalchicago.com
Prices: $$

Lunch Sat – Sun
Dinner nightly
🚇 Damen (Blue)

This European-flecked American café gets the urban vibe going with its stylish interior dressed in square tables, white molded chairs, and large canvases of modern art. The lounge area hosts guest DJs who pump up the volume when the lights go down, augmenting the retro feel.

At LOKaL, lunch and dinner offer wholly different experiences, but each is worthy on its own. Lunches are a simpler affair (see: a flurry of sandwiches and salads); while the dinner menu is more complex (showcasing the likes of bison steak with pepper cress mashed potatoes, lobster *pierogi*, and braised rabbit salad). LOKaL is lauded for its fresh, first-rate ingredients that may present themselves, for example, in an artisan greens salad with rhubarb vinaigrette.

Mana Food Bar

B4

Vegetarian ✕

1742 W. Division St. (bet. Paulina & Wood Sts.)

Phone: 773-342-1742
Web: www.manafoodbar.com
Prices: 🍃🍃

Lunch Sat
Dinner nightly
🚇 Division

Located in a neighborhood that is partly grungy, partly chic, and completely trendy, this compact vegetarian spot satisfies every appetite with big, fresh flavors. The space is suitably industrial-chic: one wall is exposed whitewashed brick and the other is smooth and gray, set off by a wood bar, hand-hewn chairs, tables, and booths.

The menu is small but very tasty, with just a few soups, salads, and plates that can be ordered as appetizer or entrée portions. Inspiration may range from the refreshingly tangy avocado, arugula, and tomato salad with roasted garlic-chili dressing, to the eggplant-filled ravioli, to Mana Sliders—mini brown rice burgers made meaty with mushrooms.

Mana is mainly a nighttime spot, though it is open for lunch on Saturdays.

Mariscos El Veneno

Chicago ▶ Bucktown & Wicker Park

Seafood

B4

1024 N. Ashland Ave. (at Cortez St.)

Phone: 773-252-7200   Lunch & dinner daily
Web: N/A
Prices: $$ Division

Searingly hot sauces steal the show at Mariscos El Veneno, focused on the seafood-centric cuisine of the Mexican state Nayarit. Look past the fish tank in the rear to appreciate the bustling activity and tantalizing aromas escaping from the kitchen. Service is friendly and fast, though speaking Spanish can be useful here.

The kitchen turns out serious heat and wonderful complexity in each gartantuan dish. *Pulpo especial*, a house signature, smothers tender octopus with creamy and spicy stewed onions. Bright red *camarones* arrive sizzling in a diabolical hot sauce, and piquant sour tomatillo salsa dresses *tacos de pescado*, made with their own soft corn masa tortillas. Cool down with a piña colada mousse pie, layered over a thick chocolate cake base.

Mexique

Mexican

C5

1529 W. Chicago Ave. (bet. Armour St. & Ashland Ave.)

Phone: 312-850-0288   Lunch & dinner daily
Web: www.mexiquechicago.com
Prices: $$ Chicago (Blue)

As its name infers, Mexique melds Mexican cuisine with classical French techniques—a tip of the historical hat to France's occupation of Mexico in the 1860s. A subdued and minimal dining room punctuated with crimson and brick makes it clear that though it's a playful fusion, the kitchen aspires to serious cooking that avoids kitsch.

Cochinita rillettes showcase silky pork braised in an achiote-tequila marinade. Duck confit, that rustic French standard, may be paired with seared breast glazed in spicy-sweet chipotle-tamarind sauce. A "pescamal" substitutes delicate seafood mousse for the tamale's traditional *masa harina*, and to finish, dessert enchiladas ooze rich, dark chocolate ganache from rolled crêpes drizzled with ancho chile-chocolate sauce.

Mindy's Hot Chocolate

B3

Contemporary ✕✕

1747 N. Damen Ave. (bet. St. Paul Ave. & Willow St.)

Phone: 773-489-1747
Web: www.hotchocolatechicago.com
Prices: $$

Lunch Wed – Sun
Dinner Tue – Sun
 Damen (Blue)

The name, the cocoa-colored interior, and Chef/owner Mindy Segal's reputation may tempt you into this oft-crowded, industrial-chic restaurant and straight to dessert.

Dessert can't–and shouldn't–be skipped here, but neither should the savory contemporary items. Daily soups may change, but the macaroni and cheese made with Wisconsin Gruyère and cheddar is a year-round sensation. Recommending just a handful of desserts is like being asked to select your favorite child. When pressed, though, the warm brioche doughnuts with hot fudge sauce have been a best seller since the restaurant opened. There are also six variations of hot chocolate on the menu. The wine list is impressive and, unsurprisingly, offers a nice selection of dessert wines.

Mirai

B4

Japanese ✕✕

2020 W. Division St. (bet. Damen & Hoyne Aves.)

Phone: 773-862-8500
Web: www.miraisushi.com
Prices: $$

Dinner nightly

 Damen (Blue)

Mirai is a bit like Disney World. You know it's not real, but who cares? The Japanese food is westernized and by no means traditional, but unless you're dining out with Mr. Miyagi, rest assured that nobody will cry foul.

Bold and appetizing flavors beg to take center stage. It's really all about the sushi at this spot—just look around and you'll find most devotees feasting on sashimi, *unagi*, and maki. If raw fish doesn't float your boat, take a shot at one of the house specialties like *kani nigiri*, a baked king crab concoction. There is also a surfeit of hot dishes, think chicken *togarashi* with spicy, sweet, and tangy flavors. Affable and alert service and a relaxed atmosphere, especially on the front patio, make this a hit with area residents.

Old Oak Tap

A5

2109 W. Chicago Ave. (bet. Leavitt St. & Hoyne Ave.)

Phone: 773-772-0406
Web: www.theoldoaktap.com
Prices: $$

Lunch Tue – Sun
Dinner nightly

Though it may seem like a bar, this classy and cool tavern has the tasty starters and creative sandwiches to give the impressive docket of international and domestic craft beer second billing. Pick a table near the fireplace, under the dramatic oak mirror, or just settle into the bar scene, but by all means arrive hungry for the likes of crunchy, spicy, and sweet *sriracha* wings with wasabi aïoli—so beautifully powerful that they may order an accompanying draft themselves. Other options include homemade soft pretzels, duck confit quesadillas, and the *porchetta* sandwich.

Weekends can be a mob scene behind the huge oak door, with conversations and music loud enough to make the chandeliers swing. The large patio is all the rage during warmer months.

Owen & Engine

A1

2700 N. Western Ave. (at Schubert Ave.)

Phone: 773-235-2930
Web: www.owenengine.com
Prices: $$

Lunch Sat – Sun
Dinner nightly

A lofty, handsomely rustic gastro-tavern in the style of Olde English public houses, Owen & Engine packs 'em in with refined British comfort food and a mind-blowing beer menu. Brew fiends will rejoice at the constantly changing selection of drafts and casks, while the less obsessed will be happily satiated with a choice of carefully crafted seasonal house cocktails like the Kentucky Blackhawk, with Buffalo Trace bourbon, lime, sloe gin, and rosemary-thyme syrup.

The kitchen's preparation of top-notch ingredients shines throughout the menu, which may include pan-seared Cavendish quail with braised local kale and crispy quail egg garnish, bubble and squeak, or goats milk cheesecake with candied kumquats, brown butter, and graham cracker crust.

Piccolo Sogno

D5

Italian ✗✗

464 N. Halsted St. (at Milwaukee Ave.)

Phone: 312-421-0077
Web: www.piccolosognorestaurant.com
Prices: $$

Lunch Mon – Fri
Dinner nightly
Grand (Blue)

In an area better known for its nightclubs than its restaurants, Piccolo Sogno (which means "little dream") stands out as a quaint trattoria. Come on a warm day and enjoy the large and lovely outdoor terrace.

Piccolo Sogno has a straightforward Italian menu that draws a large business crowd at lunch with its selection of Neapolitan-style pizzas and pastas. Thin-crust, prosciutto-strewn pizza especially hits the mark. Evenings lure well-dressed couples who come seeking consistently good and hearty dishes made with fresh ingredients. Potato gnocchi with oven-dried tomatoes, mushrooms, and garlic; or slow stewed rabbit with white wine, rosemary, and lemon are just two delicious choices. End the meal with panna cotta topped with fruit and caramel.

Red Canary

D5

American ✗✗

695 N. Milwaukee Ave. (bet. Morgan & Sangamon Sts.)

Phone: 312-846-1475
Web: www.theredcanarychicago.com
Prices: $$

Lunch Sat – Sun
Dinner nightly
Chicago (Blue)

Billed as a "gastrolounge," the Red Canary is a 1920s-style speakeasy meets the 21st century. Here, diners luxuriate in cushy red booths in the main area or perched in balconies. The Victorian, art deco space is crowned by a giant crystal chandelier.

Sultry ambience and a desirable cocktail menu make this nest a natural choice for post-work drinks and apps. Pair drinks like the "Muckraker Mojito" with some Vienna beef pigs in a blanket or fried green tomatoes; or just hit the comfort food cart with buttermilk fried chicken aside red-skinned mashed potatoes, chicken pot pie, and spring strawberry shortcake. Locals love the expansive ivy-lined large beer garden in the back, which often hosts live jazz among its olive trees and flowers.

Rios D'Sudamerica

B2

Peruvian ✗✗

2010 W. Armitage Ave. (bet. Damen & Hoyne Sts.)

Phone: 773-276-0170 Lunch & dinner daily
Web: www.riosdesudamerica.com
Prices: $$ Damen (Blue)

This sophisticated Peruvian restaurant goes to great lengths to distinguish itself from the many Latin eateries in the neighborhood and in the city. It starts with the ambience: choose between the front area for plush seating, drinks, and small bites; main dining room, with banquettes and murals; or a more romantic second-floor mezzanine.

While the heart of the restaurant is Peruvian, there are also choices of traditional Central and South American dishes to sample. Their excellent *tamal verde* features smooth Andean corn dough with cilantro wrapped around tender cubes of chicken, egg, and chile peppers, steamed in husks. Desserts include a passion fruit cheesecake, a mousse-like twist on the common finale, with an intensely sweet-tart punch.

Roots Handmade Pizza

B5

Pizza ✗

1924 W. Chicago Ave. (bet. Winchester & Wolcott Aves.)

Phone: 773-645-4949 Lunch & dinner daily
Web: www.rootspizza.com
Prices: $$ Division

In a town synonymous with deep-dish, it takes a certain amount of chutzpah to bring a new pizza style to Chicago. Roots does just that and succeeds winningly with Quad Cities-style pizza from the Iowa-Illinois border: a round, hand-tossed pie scissor-cut into rectangular strips with a key ingredient–malt in the crust–that adds a bronzed edge and subtle sweetness.

Quality ingredients abound: finely ground sausage is liberally sprinkled across the signature Quad Cities pie, and fresh mozzarella, hand-pulled each day, arrives in breaded planks for a take on the ubiquitous appetizer. Little touches, like the exclusively Midwestern brews on tap and the plate of warm washcloths that come with the check, make the spot an endearing neighborhood player.

Ruxbin

American

B4

851 N. Ashland Ave. (at Pearson St.)

Phone: 312-624-8509
Web: www.ruxbinchicago.com
Prices: $$

Dinner Tue – Sun

 Division

Eclectic and maybe a tad bizarre, this über-popular Noble Square favorite is as successful as it is freewheeling (note the no-reservations policy). The funky setting is comprised of all things refurbished, reclaimed, and repurposed to fashion a timeless interior (see the cookbook pages decoupaged on the ceiling). Yes, that is a bench made of seatbelts and what's that door leading to the bathroom? It's an old revolving darkroom door.

Discover a comparably assorted offering of American bistro fare made with talent and globetrotting flair. The limited, seasonal menu may include crispy eggplant with roasted beets, cucumber, frisée, and honey-cardamom yogurt; hanger steak with kimchi-potato hash and *guajillo* ketchup; or mussels in a sake-tomato broth.

Sabor Saveur

Mexican

B4

2013 W. Division St. (bet. Damen & Hoyne Aves.)

Phone: 773-235-7310
Web: www.saborsaveur.com
Prices: $$

Lunch Sat – Sun
Dinner nightly
Damen (Blue)

While many have heard of Chef/owner Yanitzin Sanchez's creative dishes, few have tasted anything like them before. Expect to be turned on your head at this BYOB spot, where modern Mexican is kissed by French flavors and techniques. *Chile poblano* is stuffed with walnuts, ricotta, and a flavorful tomatillo sauce; pumpkin seed and *huazontle*-topped filet mignon is served with sweet potato and coconut croquettes. Go for the prix-fixe to sample it all but don't miss the flavorful lettuce cream soup.

Inside, modern minimalism takes center stage with a black-and-white palette, simple furnishings, and dramatic candelabra. The open kitchen showcases the action of Ms. Sanchez and her dedicated staff behind these cross-cultural culinary creations.

Schwa ✿

Contemporary ✗

B3

1466 N. Ashland Ave. (at Le Moyne St.)

Phone: 773-252-1466
Web: www.schwarestaurant.com
Prices: $$$

Dinner Tue – Sat

🚇 Division

nickbhyrtk

Located on a dreary stretch of Ashland, the seedy entrance marked by a graffiti-tagged awning has a liquor store mien. Yet, everybody clamors for a taste of Michael Carlson's Schwa—the willfully eclectic and deeply satisfying anti-restaurant with one of the most frustrating reservation systems in Chicago.

There's acid hip hop blaring from the kitchen, but Carlson's brother Seth keeps the front of the house running and hopeful diners may occasionally reach a real person on the phone when calling for a reservation. Though Carlson and staff might look disheveled, they're nothing but sincere, hospitable, and passionate about their food; and regulars show appreciation by bringing extra BYOB brews and bubbly to share with the staff.

So what is it about this food that makes it worth the hoops? Whether choosing three courses or going full force with the nine-course tasting, additional creations like a passion fruit gelée with violet foam, shad roe beignet, and macerated papaya that uncannily mimics the taste of Froot Loops don't skimp on the kitchen's vision. More traditional dishes like *lardo*-draped roast boar tenderloin paired with huckleberries, parsnips, and consommé totally wow with big flavor.

Seadog

1500 W. Division St. (at Greenview Ave.)

Phone: 773-235-8100
Web: www.seadogsushibar.com
Prices: 💰💰

Dinner nightly

🔲 Division

Serving more than just sushi, this Noble Square newcomer is a fine choice to satisfy that craving for Japanese cuisine. An array of fine quality cuts are prepared by a trio whose smiling faces welcome arriving diners and their brown uniforms match the room's earthy aesthetic. From the counter's polished bronze-hued backdrop, the team sends forth the likes of tuna and jalapeño *temaki*; nine variations of spicy maki; a roster of signature rolls that unveil the little sea monster, constructed from white fish tempura, cream cheese, avocado, and *masago*; and non-piscine morsels such as an *oshinko* roll filled with pickled daikon.

Entrée's from the kitchen supplement the sushi bar selection and include standards like tempura, teriyaki, and *yakisoba*.

Siboney

2165 N. Western Ave. (at Palmer Ave.)

Phone: 773-276-8776
Web: www.siboneychicago.com
Prices: 💰💰

Lunch & dinner daily

🔲 Western (Blue)

In many ways, Cuba's kitchens are an amalgam of the best Spanish, African, and Caribbean traditions. The neighborhood that houses Siboney (named for a city in Cuba) is likewise an amalgam and celebration of its culture. This is a lovely, bright, and tidy corner location graced with many windows for people-watching and a front lounge that hosts occasional music performances.

Siboney captures Cuba's vibrant cuisine by focusing on the country's staples (chicken, pork, lobster, and fish) and preparing them with authenticity, whether raw or stewed. The Cuban-style pork ribs are incredibly tender and sweet; the tantalizing bread pudding is spiked with lots of cognac; and the dark, rich coffee blended with milk and sugar will have you feeling truly *Cubano*.

Smoke Daddy

B4

Barbecue

1804 W. Division St. (at Wood St.)

Phone: 773-772-6656
Web: www.thesmokedaddy.com
Prices:

Lunch & dinner daily

Division

Sometimes you just need to slow down: Southern drawls, slow-cooked barbecue, and blues usually do the trick. Such relaxing influences can be found at this neighborhood joint, with nightly live music and a mouthwatering menu of wood-smoked goods. A corrugated aluminum bar, low lighting, and 1950s-era photographs give "The Daddy" its laid-back, retro vibe.

Whether your tastes run to Memphis, Kansas City, or Carolina barbecue, the trifecta of tabletop sauces gives everyone a taste to crow about. Douse your pulled pork, brisket, or ribs, then buy a bottle of your fave for the home grillmaster. Ribs are smoky and tender, but the chicken a bit dry and not worth the calories. Save those for the pork-studded, smoky baked beans or the gooey macaroni and cheese.

Sushi X

C5

Japanese

1136 W. Chicago Ave. (bet. May St. & Racine Ave.)

Phone: 312-491-9232
Web: www.sushi-x.net
Prices: $$

Lunch Mon – Fri
Dinner nightly
Chicago (Blue)

The *animé* projected on a side wall is your first clue that this is not your average sushi joint. Add in the techno music, small stone tables, low lighting, and twenty- to thirty-somethings from the neighborhood, and you'll have your gut feeling confirmed.

The menu further confirms that this is not a place to come for traditional sushi. The crowds flock in for contemporary rolls loaded up with long lists of ingredients. Among the don't-miss specialty rolls is the unusual "Pollo Loco" with panko-crusted chicken, avocado, jalapeño, daikon sprouts, and *sriracha*. Fusion dishes, like red bacon and eggs (spicy smoked bacon with red pepper sauce and scallions served with rice and topped with a fried egg), are an interesting alternative to sushi.

Takashi ⌘

Contemporary 𝗫𝗫

B2

1952 N. Damen Ave. (at Armitage Ave.)

Phone: 773-772-6170
Web: www.takashichicago.com
Prices: $$$

Lunch Sun
Dinner Tue – Sun
🚇 Damen (Blue)

Tyllie Barbosa Photography

If Takashi were a clothing line, it would have to fight Calvin Klein for the rights to minimalist chic. Discreetly set in a two-story brick bungalow on Damen Avenue in the heart of trend central, the understated but well-appointed dining room plays up the space's residential feel with a bar intimately tucked under a staircase, streamlined place settings, polished wood, and painted brick walls.

Despite a full house, the young, laid-back staff keeps things relaxed but not overly casual. Chef/owner Takashi Yagihashi is visible but unobtrusive in the kitchen, glimpses of which can be seen through the translucent panes lining the rear of the main dining room.

Where the décor is subdued, the flavors on each plate are powerful. Throughout the menu, East meets West with mouthwatering results. A line of plump escargots on a bed of creamy potato mousseline contrasts appealingly with creamy garlic and herb sauce as well as Port wine reduction; caramelized clay pot chicken bubbles happily alongside silky Japanese eggplant and shimeji mushrooms in its ceramic cookware. Sheep's milk yogurt panna cotta topped with yuzu gelée needs only a single buttery green tea shortbread cookie for accompaniment.

Taxim

Greek ✗

B3

1558 N. Milwaukee Ave. (bet. Damen & North Aves.)

Phone: 773-252-1558
Web: www.taximchicago.com
Prices: $$

Lunch Sat – Sun
Dinner nightly
🚇 Damen (Blue)

Sharing a tasty spread of hot and cold dishes is the best way to go at Taxim. So grab a group of gastronomes and head over to the Wicker Park hot spot, where cuisine takes a pan-Hellenic adventure, traversing through islands, villages, and cities of Greece. From *pantzária me karydoskordaliá*—roasted red beets with Thracian-style walnut *skordaliá* and feta; *païdákia me pligoúri*—sumptuous wood-grilled lamb chops; to bulgur and chestnut-stuffed winter squash, the dishes here are exquisitely authentic and fresh.

Inside, arched entryways, exposed brick walls, and richly colored throw pillows on wooden banquettes create an old-world vibe. A lovely list of regional Greek wines adds to the experience.

Thai Village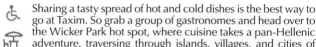

Thai ✗

A4

2053 W. Division St. (at Hoyne St.)

Phone: 773-384-5352
Web: www.chicagothaivillage.com
Prices: ✺✺

Lunch & dinner daily
🚇 Damen (Blue)

The carved wood door and decorative woodwork indicate that you're at the right place when you walk up to this corner storefront. Inside, exposed brick walls, high wooden booths, pressed-tin ceilings painted blue, and Thai-style artwork set the mood.

The menu here is served hot and made to order, with sizzling sounds enticing diners from behind a brick wall. Start with the likes of golden brown fish cakes served warm, with a salad of cucumbers, red chilies, and fresh cilantro, then move on to a delicious curry. The best dessert option is a homemade carrot cake—moist and tender beneath its bright orange glaze. Those with a sweet tooth can also enjoy the traditional Thai iced coffee, strong and dark with a sweet kick from the condensed milk.

Thalia Spice

Asian ✗✗

D5

833 W. Chicago Ave. (at Green St.)

Phone: 312-226-6020
Web: www.thaliaspice.com
Prices: $$

Lunch Sun – Fri
Dinner nightly
🖳 Chicago (Blue)

Cruise into this sexy spot and find an exotic-meets-urban landscape, where locals and free spirits pack a space rocking rustic brick walls, exposed ductwork, and neon colored light installations. Around the corner from Chicago Avenue, the massive carved wooden doors make an impressive greeting, though the actual entrance is a few feet over on Green Street. Now, if you've come here seeking sushi, we'd suggest skipping it. Focus instead on the delectable Southeast Asian specialties—there's even the option to customize a meal according to your country of choice. Savor the Laotian *nom tok* salad—tender chicken tossed with onions, roasted peanuts, ginger, lime, and cilantro; yummy *yaya* noodles; warm Malaysian *roti canai*; or one of five versions of fried rice.

tocco

Italian ✗✗

B4

1266 N. Milwaukee Ave. (bet. Ashland Ave. & Paulina St.)

Phone: 773-687-8895
Web: www.toccochicago.com
Prices: $$

Dinner Tue – Sun

🖳 Division

In a space that is as much an homage to haute couture as it is a trendy Italian restaurant, the only thing thinner than the crust is the clientele. Even the bronzed sunglass-wearing host looks like he'd be more at home on Valentino's yacht in the Riviera. Still hotter than the crowd, the black-and-white dining room dons pink faux-ostrich leather walls, shiny white resin chairs, and hip Italian furniture. Wood-burning ovens churn out cracker-crisp artisanal pizzas (the way to go) in addition to pastas and heartier entrées, like *involtini di pollo*, with prosciutto and rosemary rolled around thinly sliced chicken breasts.

If talk of the latest fashion leaves you feeling empty, enjoy free Sunday yoga lessons in the courtyard during the summer months.

Usagi Ya

C4

J a p a n e s e ✗

1178 N. Milwaukee Ave. (bet. Division St. & Haddon Ave.)

Phone: 773-292-5885 Lunch & dinner daily
Web: www.usagiyasushi.com
Prices: $$ 🚇 Division

Even at lunch, amoeba lights, vibey music, and nearly-naughty paintings give off a nightclub feel that complement the contemporary creative seafood at this funky sushi joint. Fish of paramount quality is handled delicately by the sushi chefs working at the open sake-lined bar overlooking the room.

Beyond the wide selection of rarely boring maki rolls and sushi options, Usagi Ya's menu shines with its unorthodox combinations. Top choices include sticky rice "snowballs" topped with fresh albacore tuna, white truffle soy sauce, and minced scallions; tempura-fried jalapeños stuffed with *unagi*, drizzled with sesame oil and cream cheese dressing; and Thai ocean noodles with plump shrimp, scallops, and squid wading in a spicy lemongrass broth.

West Town Tavern 😊

C5

A m e r i c a n ✗✗

1329 W. Chicago Ave. (at Throop St.)

Phone: 312-666-6175 Dinner Mon – Sat
Web: www.westtowntavern.com
Prices: $$ 🚇 Chicago (Blue)

Comfort fare may elicit simple memories of warm pies and full bellies, but hearty, home-style favorites transcend expectation at West Town Tavern. Sip wine amid loyal locals at the long oak bar; or settle into the warm dining space and peek into the semi-open kitchen.

Start with the likes of wild mushroom chowder–a smoky sensation topped with crunchy blue cheese croutons–then dive into the juicy, braised pork tenderloin served over buttery cannelloni beans, wilted kale, roasted cherry tomatoes, and bits of bacon. Dessert cannot be skipped, as the buttery, flaky pecan pie with its sticky-sweet layer of brown sugar syrup is an impossibly rare treat. Drop in for one of the rotating weekly specials, whether it's Fried Chicken Mondays or Fish Taco Fridays.

Chinatown & South Loop

Chinatown and the South Loop were two neighborhoods that for years didn't have much linking them, besides the north-south running Red Line El. Geographically, they were close, but world's apart in terms of population, architecture, gentrification, and a gastronomic vibe. Recent development here has allowed for the two to meet in the middle. While, they're still very distinct, both neighborhoods have managed to combine their old and new in ways that should appeal to any gastronome residing in the Windy City.

Strolling Through South Loop

One of Chicago's oldest neighborhoods, the South Loop houses a number of buildings that were spared the Great Chicago Fire. Prairie Avenue, in particular, is a concentration of magnificent homes that were built by some of the wealthiest in the city. Glessner House and Clarke House are particular gems.

Glimpses of all sorts of history can be toured through time-tested churches: Willie Dixon's Blues Heaven Foundation, whose main mission is to preserve the blues legacy; National Vietnam Veterans Art Museum; and other impressive landmarks. In previous incarnations, the South Loop (which begins south of Roosevelt Road) housed Al Capone, Chess Records, and other buzzing industrial spaces.

However, in the last 15 years this neighborhood has undergone quite a transformation; and it now includes new condos and shopping, which have helped fuel a rash of fresh restaurants. Also home to Mayor Richard M. Daley, Columbia College, Museum Campus, and Soldier Field, almost anything (or anyone) can be found in the South Loop.

Magnificent Munching

Nurse your sweet tooth at **Canady Le Chocolatier Ltd**. Want a glimpse of the way real natives eat? Nearby **Manny's Coffee Shop and Deli** is ground zero for local politicians. Pastrami, corned beef, and potato pancakes are solid here, and the speedy staff keeps the line moving. So follow suit, glimpse your pick, and grab it! Come to watch the wheeling and dealing, or just eat a giant pastrami on rye. Either way, you will feel satiated.

Revered as one of Chicago's most classic Italian markets, **Panozzo's** creative produce and talent brings a host of locals and tourists alike. A welcoming landmark in Chicago's vibrant South Loop, this glorified Italian deli's well-stocked shelves are arranged with carefully prepared foods. From cold and hot sandwiches and faithful entrées, to classic salads and feshly-baked breads, they personfiy the art behind Italian home-style cooking. Looking to while away an afternoon? Visit the striking **Three Peas Art**

Lounge which is an art gallery, coffee shop, and cupcake bakery united.

PRINTERS ROW

These historical printing lofts were converted into a hotel, condos, and related retail spaces (such as browse-worthy used bookstores) before the rest of the area was gentrified. Now this multi-block strip is bustling with restaurants, offices, and shops, and a Saturday farmer's market June through October.

Just north of the district is the looming Harold Washington Library Center, which serves as a city resource and boasts a beautiful glass-top garden on the ninth floor. On the south end is the landmark Dearborn Station, the oldest remaining train depot in Chicago. It is now a multi-use space for retail stores, both small and large offices, and the like.

CHINATOWN

Chicago is home to the U.S.'s fourth largest Chinatown, with a population of about 15,000 ethnic Chinese, and offers a good combination of original Chinese-American history and contemporary Chinese-American life.

At Wentworth Avenue and Cermak Road, you'll find the Chinatown Gate, an elaborate, ornate, older icon for the neighborhood. Outdoor mall **Chinatown Square** is *the* hub for much of the commercial activity. This two-story extravaganza houses restaurants, retail spaces, boutiques, and banks. While strolling through this neighborhood, don't miss St. Therese Chinese Catholic Church, an edifice that points to the area's pre-Chinatown Italian roots.

Much of the food served in restaurants here is classic Chinese-American fare, which is usually an amalgam of Sichuan, Cantonese, and Chinese-American favorites, mostly of the Midwest. Crab Rangoon anyone?

Stellar Sweets and Spicy Eats

Locals come here, not just to eat out, but to stock up on a gamut of good eats in order to dine in. **Hong Kong Noodle Factory** is, in fact, a factory, and the place to go for wonton wrappers. **Mayflower Foods** also has one of the largest selections of fresh noodles; and **Ten Ren Tea** is lauded for its extensive tea selection and unique tea-making gadgets. To top off a day of fun feasting, don't forget to quench the adventure with a fresh-baked treat from **Golden Dragon Fortune Cookies**, or sweets from **Chiu Quon Bakery**. This Chinatown pearl shows a range of baked goods, dim sum, and desserts...gooey sesame balls anyone?

Those who need guidance can pick up a cookbook from the Chinese Cultural Bookstore and all the necessary gear at **Woks 'n' Things**. After these ethnic delights, saunter over to U.S. Cellular Field, home of the Chicago White Sox—the rare baseball park that serves veggie dogs and house-made potato chips.

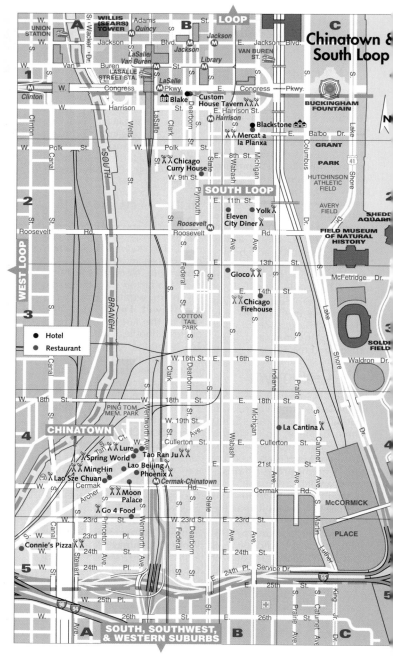

Chicago Curry House

 B2

Indian ✗✗

899 S. Plymouth Ct. (at 9th St.)

Phone: 312-362-9999 Lunch & dinner daily
Web: www.curryhouseonline.com
Prices: 💰 🎫 Harrison

If you've got curry on your mind but not a lot of money in your wallet, make your way to Chicago Curry House for an affordable and satisfyingly spicy Indian and Nepalese lunch buffet in a white tablecloth setting, just a few blocks west of Grant Park.

The buffet boasts boldly flavored dishes like goat stewed on the bone in a tender, cardamom-inflected curry; and creamy *dal makhani*, black lentils and kidney beans dancing in a fragrant chili sauce. Not into buffets? The roster of dishes on the lunch and dinner menus runs the gamut from Indian favorites like fish *tikka masala* and vegetable samosas, to lesser-known Nepalese specialties like *bhuteko kali*, spiced cauliflower with onion and tomato, and abundant combination plates known as *bhojan*.

Chicago Firehouse

 B3

American ✗✗

1401 S. Michigan Ave. (at 14th St.)

Phone: 312-786-1401 Lunch & dinner daily
Web: www.mainstayhospitality.com
Prices: **$$** 🎫 Roosevelt

The shiny brass fire pole is your second clue (after the restaurant name) that this location was once a working firehouse. Today, the overall vibe is more 1940s sophistication, with cherrywood, leather, subway tiles, and other decorative elements of the era.

But firefighters are known for appreciating a good meal, and here nice work is done on American classics. Sautéed cobia is fresh, moist, and delicious in a cashew vinaigrette and served with root vegetables and Brussels sprouts. A classic onion soup arrives complete with melted Gruyère, both nutty and crispy, and caramelized onions in a rich beef broth with a splash of Port. The wedge of creamy raspberry cheesecake with a chocolate-crumb crust is a lovely finale.

79

Connie's Pizza

A5

2373 S. Archer Ave. (at Normal Ave.)

Phone: 312-326-3443
Web: www.conniespizza.com
Prices: $$

Lunch & dinner daily

 Halsted

Back in 1962, a building with a sign that read "Connie's" was purchased by Jim Stolfe; the name stuck, and in '85, the whole operation moved to its current residence—the huge Archer Avenue spot. Churning out mouthwatering pies for the masses, this Chicago mainstay does most of its biz outside its brick walls, providing catering for professional sporting events (Connie's is the official pizza of the White Sox).

Delish deep-dish is a total Chi-town fave. Bursting with fillings of your choice (try the tender Italian sausage), these stuffed pies are sealed with a buttery bread-like crust and topped with garlicky tomato sauce (also available sans sauce). Call ahead to avoid cooking wait times, and pick up your pizza at the drive-through window.

Custom House Tavern

B1

500 S. Dearborn St. (at Congress Pkwy.)

Phone: 312-523-0200
Web: www.customhouse.cc
Prices: $$

Lunch Sun – Fri
Dinner nightly

 Library

Urban and rustic come together in a cool marriage at Custom House Tavern, which calls to mind a modern, minimalist lodge on the ground floor of the Hotel Blake in the South Loop. Layers of stacked gray stone, multiple levels of banquette booth seating, and polished wood accents create a sleek and calming neutral palette, while diners get a sneak peek at the kitchen's bustling activity through a long pane of glass.

Menu items like fish and chips with malt vinegar fries; roasted farm chicken with mushrooms; or tavern steak with smoked blue cheese butter gently tweak familiar American cuisine staples. Sweet potato soup embellished with a smoky marshmallow and spiced peanuts detours from a typical Thanksgiving side dish to embrace woodsy fall flavors.

Eleven City Diner

Deli 🍴

B2

1112 S. Wabash Ave. (bet. 11th St. & Roosevelt Rd.)

Phone: 312-212-1112
Web: www.elevencitydiner.com
Prices: 💰💰

Lunch & dinner daily

🚇 Roosevelt

What's old is new again at this reprise of the classic Jewish deli. The candy counter is stocked with sweets of yore, like Bazooka Joe, while another counter tempts with hanging salamis, smoked fish, and cured meats ready to eat or to-go. The extensive menu features ample servings of exactly what should be on a diner menu: big salads, burgers, and thick sandwiches piled high. Many dishes are a twist on the regulars, like the "Shappy" sandwich, which features thick-cut salami grilled and served on challah. The beef and pastrami is served grilled with mozzarella cheese on a French roll, making it clear that this is a Jewish-style deli and not a kosher joint.

Revisit your youth with thick malts, phosphates, and other drinks from the soda jerk.

Gioco

Italian 🍴🍴

B3

1312 S. Wabash Ave. (bet. 13th & 14th Sts.)

Phone: 312-939-3870
Web: www.gioco-chicago.com
Prices: $$

Lunch Mon – Fri
Dinner nightly
🚇 Roosevelt

From KDK Restaurants comes this rustic Italian mainstay featuring a pleasant setting and tantalizing fragrance of a wood-fired pizza oven. Exposed, crumbling brick and arches leading to a second, sunken dining room are reminders that the space dates back to the 1890s.

The traditional menu and open kitchen reveal a taste for Tuscan and Umbrian specialties. Pastas include fresh spaghetti—with squared-off tips and a springy texture that boasts their handmade origins—sauced with chunky tomatoes, chili pepper, and very tender octopus. The menu includes a number of starters, pastas, and heartier entrées like *bistecca alla Fiorentina*. Budget-seekers come for the lunchtime special that includes an appetizer, entrée, and dessert for $15.

Go 4 Food

A4

212 W. 23rd St. (bet. Princeton & Wentworth Aves.)

Phone: 312-842-8688   Lunch & dinner Wed – Mon
Web: www.go4foodusa.com
Prices: ⊜◎

 Cermak-Chinatown

Stop by to pick up a fresh, flavorful lunch to-go, or stay awhile at one of the few places in Chinatown where it's actually pleasant to have a sit-down meal. Brilliant red walls offset by dark, sleek furniture and a gleaming stainless kitchen make this a clean, modern neighborhood oasis. With afternoon tea and prix-fixe family-style dinner menus, it's a destination for more than just a quick lunch.

Well-priced and well-portioned Chinese plates like *ma po tofu*, Cantonese-style lobster, and seafood congee back up friendly service. The hundred-spiced chicken in a fiery ginger and garlic sauce is a standout. Are there literally 100 spices in the flavorful gravy? Contemplate it while using a slice of the wok stir-fried chicken breast to sop it up.

La Cantina

B4

1911 S. Michigan Ave. (bet. Cullerton & 18th Sts.)

Phone: 312-842-1911   Lunch & dinner daily
Web: www.lacantinagrill.com
Prices: ⊜◎

 Cermak-Chinatown

Whether taking a seat at the bar, snagging a spot on the patio, or dining indoors, the first order of business at La Cantina is to check the chalkboard for the tasty and thirst-quenching margarita menu.

Dark-tiled floors and terra-cotta-hued walls look straight out of Mexico, while the comprehensive menu of Mexican and Tex-Mex favorites is like a love letter to our neighbor to the south. Close your eyes and imagine a Mexican menu and you'll find it all here: burritos, quesadillas, fajitas, nachos, and tacos. Be sure to try a house specialty, like the steak topped with *charro* beans in the Zamora platter, served with a host of outstanding accompaniments. No matter the choice, plates are brimming with flavorful, well-prepared, and delicious food.

Lao Beijing

 A4

Chinese

2138 S. Archer Ave. (in Chinatown Sq.)

Phone: 312-881-0168
Web: www.tonygourmetgroup.com
Prices: ⊜⊜

Lunch & dinner daily

Cermak-Chinatown

Just finding the door to this restaurant in the heart of Chinatown Square may work up an appetite. The street address brings you to the back delivery entrance—follow the footpath to the opposite side for the front door.

Once inside the red-carpeted den, Lao Beijing offers a rather no-frills space in which to savor a bold and pungent array of Chinese dishes. The ample nine-page menu includes many classics, but the house specials highlighting the cuisine of Beijing separate it from other local restaurants. Dishes are tantalizing, with large pieces of meat or vegetables and distinctive spices, as in the Chengdu chicken made with ginger and fermented black bean paste.

Excellent lunchtime bargains bring in the local Asian business community.

Lao Sze Chuan

A4

Chinese

2172 S. Archer Ave. (at Princeton Ave.)

Phone: 312-326-5040
Web: www.tonygourmetgroup.com
Prices: ⊜⊜

Lunch & dinner daily

Cermak-Chinatown

Devotees of the deliciously lip-blistering, tongue-numbing, sweat-inducing flavors of Sichuan cuisine know where to go: they're all at Lao Sze Chuan, sitting elbow to elbow in the bright red restaurant adorned with images of that crimson pepper.

The entire menu seems to be marinated in chili paste: the floral, lingering spices of Sichuan peppercorns in richly stewed *ma po* tofu make the dish an addictive choice, but just as spicy and an equally crave-worthy contender is the flash-fried dry chili chicken, piled high with fried sliced garlic and handfuls of red chilies. Vegetarians have a place at the table too, as sliced, crunchy cabbage marinated in chili paste gets the same hit of heat as the meaty morsels in the boiled beef with spicy Sichuan sauce.

Lure

2017 S. Wells St. (at S. Wentworth Ave.)

Phone: 312-225-8989
Web: www.lurechicago.com
Prices: $$

Lunch Sat – Sun
Dinner nightly
🚇 Cermak-Chinatown

This Japanese *izakaya* brings a new kind of pub grub to Chicagoans with shareable small plates, sake, and creative cocktails served in a postmodern disco. Prepare to be entertained, as you're surrounded by hypnotic aquatic projections, lights embedded in the floor, and live music that ranges from indie rock to wild drummers late into the night.

Though the fusion-influenced menu offers a wide range of snackable dishes, seafood options are stand out: fatty salmon belly takes on an almost creamy texture after marinating in soy and mirin, then gets a quick sear. *Aji himono* lets the table feast on a whole horse mackerel that's been salted and air-dried overnight before the kitchen grills it over cherry wood, leaving moist and tender flesh for the sharing.

Mercat a la Planxa

638 S. Michigan Ave. (at Balbo Ave.)

Phone: 312-765-0524
Web: www.mercatchicago.com
Prices: $$

Lunch & dinner daily

🚇 Harrison

Swing by this colorful Catalan eatery, tucked into a corner of the Blackstone Hotel. Inside the sweeping dining space—where tables face large windows overlooking Grant Park—deep orange banquettes, mosaics, and a brightly tiled open kitchen give off a cheery vibe, while friendly service keeps things efficient.

The flavorful, fresh menu includes dishes like pork and apple sausages with truffled white beans and carrot escabeche (*butifarra con judias*); seared yellowfin tuna over creamy celery root purée and smoked pine nuts (*atun con apio-nabo*); chicken a *la planxa* with pickled *guindilla* aïoli; and *patatas fritas*, crispy house-cut fries drizzled with a paprika-spiced aïoli. The budget-minded head downstairs to Bodega N.5, where everything is five bucks.

MingHin

A4

Chinese 🍴🍴

2168 S. Archer Ave. (at Princeton Ave.)

Phone: 312-808-1999   Lunch & dinner daily
Web: www.minghincuisine.com
Prices: 💰💰   🚇 Cermak-Chinatown

Get dim sum done right at this Chinatown newcomer that's quickly picking up steam with a hipper crowd than you'd typically see noshing on steamed buns in the neighborhood. Banquet tables of twenty-somethings fill the chic, airy space that gives an understated nod to traditional Chinese décor, with pops of red accents against a neutral, wood- and stone-trimmed dining room.

Piping hot beef noodle rolls; *har gow* with fresh, plump shrimp; and steamed lotus-paste buns are tasty dim sum standouts, offered alongside a multi-page à la carte menu that may include Macau-style roast pork belly; Beijing duck; and live (fresh) seafood. Catering further to its hip and happening patrons, MingHin serves up a late night menu of dim sum and hot pots until 2:00 A.M.

Moon Palace

A4

Chinese 🍴🍴

216 W. Cermak Rd. (bet. Princeton & Wentworth Aves.)

Phone: 312-225-4081   Lunch & dinner daily
Web: www.moonpalacerestaurant.com
Prices: 💰💰   🚇 Cermak-Chinatown

More stylish than your average Chinatown restaurant, Moon Palace also boasts particularly friendly, attentive service, and unexpectedly authentic food. Walk into a room of dark wood furnishings and wainscoting juxtaposed with buttery yellow walls, contemporary paintings, and a modern bar.

While the décor is updated, this Chinese menu has not been adjusted to suit the Western palate. The *kung pao* dishes are seriously spicy—tender pieces of chicken are deeply caramelized in a soy-chili oil glaze with peppers, roasted peanuts, and plenty of fried red chilis. Clearly, hand-made soup dumplings (*xiao long bao*) filled with ground pork, ginger, scallions, and rich broth add to the charm here. The noodle soups are as delicious as they are authentic.

Phoenix

2131 S. Archer Ave. (bet. Princeton & Wentworth Aves.)

Phone:	312-328-0848	Lunch & dinner daily
Web:	www.chinatownphoenix.com	
Prices:	⊜⊜	Cermak-Chinatown

Come to Phoenix armed with an appetite and a fun mix of people. This banquet-style dining room in the heart of Chinatown may lack an inspiring décor, and service may be efficient to the point of feeling rushed, but any shortfalls are forgotten over this tasty dim sum.

The requisite carts may be winding their way through the dining room, but a menu complete with photographs documents the made-to-order offerings. Get ready for a smorgasbord of Cantonese classics, from barbecue pork crêpes bursting with smoky and tasty meat; steamed shrimp and cilantro dumplings packed with flavor; melt-in-your-mouth spare ribs; and crispy fried rice balls coated in toasted sesame seeds. The á la carte menu offered in the evening showcases tasty traditional Chinese dishes.

Spring World

2109 South China Pl. (at Wells St.)

Phone:	312-326-9966	Lunch & dinner daily
Web:	N/A	
Prices:	$$	Cermak-Chinatown

Despite its somewhat contrived appearance, Chinatown Square houses some of the city's most authentic Chinese restaurants, including Spring World, the neighborhood's go-to spot for Yunnanese cuisine.

Tables may begin with the complimentary cabbage appetizer—a sweet, lightly pickled, and wonderfully spicy prelude. The extensive menu is illustrated with photographs to help guide you through the language barrier and find your favorites. Highlights include pepper shrimp; preserved pork with winter melon; spicy scallops marinated with garlic sauce; and Yunnan-style rice noodles. Finally, the Sichuan tea-smoked duck is the perfect blend of spicy and smoky flavors. While the restaurant is BYOB, a liquor store is conveniently located next door.

Tao Ran Ju

A4

Chinese ✗✗

2002 S. Wentworth Ave. #103 (bet. Archer Ave. & Cullerton St.)

Phone: 312-808-1111
Web: N/A
Prices: 😊😊

Lunch & dinner daily

🖳 Cermak-Chinatown

Don't be confused by the sign in the window for "T Tasty House." There's also a sign reading, "Tao Ran Ju," and the servers sport this on their shirts. But you're not in this Chinatown staple to mince words. You're here to eat.

Good choice, too. The chef is said to have come from Din Tai Fung in Los Angeles, a mecca for those juicy, meaty, and delightful soup dumplings. These *xiao long bao* are potentially the best in the city, made with delicate wrappers, fragrant pork soup, and well-seasoned ground pork in the center. Accompanied by the traditional vinegar sauce bobbing with julienned ginger, it's tough to move beyond these and try anything else on the menu. Some skillful dishes from the kitchen should follow the dumplings; just pass on the hot pots.

Yolk

B2

American ✗

1120 S. Michigan Ave. (bet. 11th St. & Roosevelt Rd.)

Phone: 312-789-9655
Web: www.yolk-online.com
Prices: 😊😊

Lunch daily

🖳 Roosevelt

If walking through Grant Park works up your appetite, try Yolk for a solid, budget-friendly breakfast or lunch solution (until 3:00 P.M. daily). This bright and whimsical diner, with its sunny yellow awnings, sits just across from the park, serving up substantial daytime meals as well as carb-loaded desserts. Just about everything on the menu comes in ample portions alongside abundant diced red potatoes and fresh fruit. Favorites may include the "Irish Bennie," a toasted English muffin topped with sautéed tomatoes, grilled corned beef hash, and poached eggs with tangy hollandaise sauce. Nutella fans and newbies alike should order the chocolate-hazelnut nirvana that is a Nutella crêpe, served folded in quarters with powdered sugar, strawberries, or bananas.

87

Gold Coast

Glitz and Glamour

What's in a name? When it comes to the Gold Coast, the name says it all. After all, this posh neighborhood is Chicago's wealthiest and most affluent. From the swanky high-rises dotting Lake Shore Drive, to the glittering boutiques of Michigan Avenue, the Gold Coast is luxury defined.

Whoever said money can't buy happiness certainly hadn't strolled through The Magnificent Mile, because this strip presents a serious challenge to that adage. This "magnificent" stretch of shopping, where millionaires mingle over Manolos and heiresses hunt for handbags, is one of the world's best and most well-known. Oak Street, with boutiques from Barneys to Yves Saint Laurent, runs a close second. If in the market for new wheels, take your pick from billionaire boy toys like Bentleys and Bugattis—both of which have dealerships here.

Historical Homes

It's not just about the glitz and glamour though. This neighborhood, listed on the National Register of Historic Places, is the perfect paradise for architecture buffs.

The mansions and buildings crafted in regal Queen Anne, Georgian Revival, and Richardsonian Romanesque styles are breathtaking. They're all glorious to simply see, even if you're not in the market for a new home.

Applauding the Arts

The stunning Gold Coast takes its history quite seriously, and following this philosophy, area residents host a series of annual events, including the block party extraordinaire, Evening on Astor. This immense event also helps raise money and awareness for preservation. It is home to the Museum of Contemporary Art and the Newberry Library, one of the world's leading research libraries. So it should be of no surprise that the neighborhood celebrates the arts in a big way. The annual Gold Coast River North Art Fair is a must-see celebration of art, music, culture, and food. Whether you're an artist or have constantly dreamed of being one, this is a don't-miss celebration of the visual arts. Culture vultures should rest assured as they are bound to find something edgy and unique at A Red Orchid Theater. Here, an ensemble of artists perform a variety of stunning shows throughout the year.

Boisterous Nights

Just because the Gold Coast is sophisticated doesn't mean this area doesn't know how to party. Visit any of the pubs, clubs, and restaurants along Rush and Division streets to get a sense of how the other half lives it up. Cold winter winds got you down? Pull up a stool at the kitschy-chic tiki bar at **Trader Vic's**. Enjoy a culinary tour of American classics touched with Asian accents. Your tongue will tingle with such whimsical dishes as barbecue spareribs; Malaysian chicken skewers; and Hawaiian ahi *poke*. Locals and patrons flock here for Trader Vic's juicy medley of cocktails, making this a perfect spot for a rockin' night out.

For a rootin'-tootin' good time, stop by the **Underground Wonder Bar**, where live jazz tunes have been played nightly until the wee hours for over two decades. The bar takes up most of the front room at this intimate jazz den—after sipping a stellar cocktail, make your way to the back where the stage is jammed with musicians of all genres including singers, bassists, guitarists, percussionists, and horn players.

Fast (and Fresh) Food

This stylish neighborhood is a capital of white-glove restaurants, but don't think that means there isn't good junk food available here as well. **Mr. Kite's Candies & Nuts** will have you flying on a sugar high with its tempting array of goodies including chocolate-covered smores and the like. Get your fill of gefilte while keeping kosher at no-frills **Ashkenaz Deli**. Other delicacies include belly lox, smoked sable, and smoked white fish. It's been here since the 1970s and certainly isn't fancy, but it's just the spot for bagels with lox.

Dog Delights

Up for a double dog dare or merely a hot dog fanatic? Stop by **Gold Coast Dogs** for one or several of its char dogs. These are made even better and more decadent when topped

with gooey cheddar cheese. Speaking of crowning hot dogs, famed **Downtown Dogs** carries an equally savory spectrum of traditional treats. Regulars, tourists, and others gather here for char-grilled dogs, sumptuous street eats, and hamburgers galore. Need to calm and come down from the hot dog high? Duck into **TeaGschwender**, a lovely boutique where you can lose yourself in the world of exotic teas. And if you don't feel like steeping it on your own, snag a seat at **Argo Tea**. From hot tea drinks topped with whipped cream, to flavorful iced drinks, it's like Starbucks without the coffee.

Heaven on Earth

It is said that God is in the details, and this is most definitely apparent at the famed **Goddess & Grocer**, a neighborhood gourmet store where you can stock up on foods like soups, salads, chillis, gourmet cupcakes, and other delightful desserts just like Mom would make. Homemade in a haute kind of way, this is cupcakes, cheeses, and chocolates galore. To add to the glory, they also cater, so you can pretend like you made those divine and delicate hors d'oevres at the baby's christening all on your own.

For some quintessential old-world elegance, don your Grandmother's pearls for afternoon tea at the refined **Drake's Palm Court**. Sip (not slurp!) your tea while listening to the gentle strains of a harp. Also on the agenda is a tasty selection of sandwiches, pastries, fruit breads, and scones. If it's good enough for Queen Elizabeth, it will certainly do.

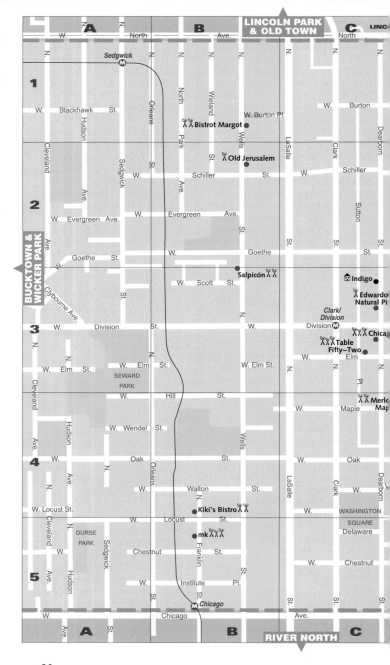

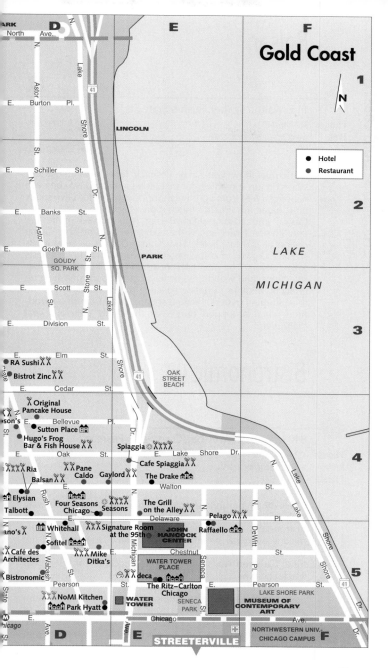

Gold Coast

1

N

● Hotel
● Restaurant

2

LAKE

MICHIGAN

3

D — North Ave.
E. Burton Pl.
Astor
Lake Shore Dr.
LINCOLN
E. Schiller St.
E. Banks St.
E. Goethe St.
GOUDY SQ. PARK
PARK
E. Scott St.
E. Division St.
E. Elm St.
● RA Sushi ✕✕
● Bistrot Zinc ✕✕
E. Cedar St.
OAK STREET BEACH
✕ Original Pancake House
✕✕ ✕son's E.
Bellevue Pl.
✕ Sutton Place 🏨
Hugo's Frog Bar & Fish House ✕✕
Spiaggia ✕✕✕✕
E. Oak St.
E. Lake Shore Dr.
Cafe Spiaggia ✕✕
✕✕✕✕ Ria
✕✕ Pane Caldo
Gaylord ✕✕
The Drake 🏨🏨
Balsan ✕✕
Walton
🏨 Elysian
Four Seasons Chicago
Seasons ✕✕✕✕
The Grill on the Alley ✕✕
Talbott ●
Delaware
Pelago ✕✕✕
ano's ✕
🏨 Whitehall
✕✕✕ Signature Room at the 95th
JOHN HANCOCK CENTER
Raffaello 🏨🏨
Sofitel 🏨🏨
✕ Café des Architectes
✕✕✕ Mike Ditka's
Chestnut St.
WATER TOWER PLACE
✕ Bistronomic
Pearson St.
✕✕ deca
The Ritz–Carlton Chicago
✕✕✕ NoMI Kitchen
🏨🏨 Park Hyatt
WATER TOWER
SENECA PARK
Chicago Ave.
M
hicago
E.
LAKE SHORE PARK
Pearson St.
MUSEUM OF CONTEMPORARY ART
NORTHWESTERN UNIV.– CHICAGO CAMPUS

4

5

D   **E**   STREETERVILLE   **F**

Balsan

Contemporary ✗✗

D4

11 E. Walton St. (bet. Rush & State Sts.)

Phone: 312-646-1400
Web: www.balsanrestaurant.com
Prices: $$

Lunch & dinner daily

 Chicago (Red)

Remember how you savored snack time in kindergarten? Wasn't it fun spreading out that little picnic and maybe even nabbing a bite from your neighbor? Get ready to relive snack time, albeit this time it's much more elegant.

Casual and cosmopolitan Balsan is burrowed inside the chic Elysian Hotel and is the easygoing, casual-chic dining option at this hip hotel. The dining room is as sexy as its sizzling crowd, encompassing everyone from hotel guests to gazetteers. The menu pivots around small plates, raw bar selections, and wood-fired dishes. One person is noshing on gnocchi, another sampling suckling pig croquettes, and the third slurping oysters. Prefer a square meal? Opt for a wood-fired, cheddar-topped burger or the richly delicious veal *blanquette*.

Bistronomic

D5

French ✗✗

840 N. Wabash Ave. (bet. Chestnut & Pearson Sts.)

Phone: 312-944-8400
Web: www.bistronomic.net
Prices: $$

Lunch Tue – Fri
Dinner nightly

 Chicago (Red)

Chefs dream of running a place they want to eat in everyday with friends. That said; Chef Martial Noguier offers Bistronomic. The name evokes the term *bistronomique*, making everyday gourmet Francais okay. Noguier shed the haute cuisine of his Café des Architectes days for a simpler tone. Oxblood walls with slate grey accents are hung with black-and-white gilded prints, while bare wood tables and floors do little to stifle the energy.

Start with cheese and charcuterie, or skip to small and medium plates like fish soup with mussels, tarragon, and saffron; or salmon salad with fingerlings, red onion, and lemon crème fraîche. Large plates may reveal a roast duck *magret* with sunchoke purée and citrus segments. Soon you and your friends will be his friends.

Bistrot Margot

B1

French ✗✗

1437 N. Wells St. (at Burton Pl.)

Phone: 312-587-3660
Web: www.bistrotmargot.com
Prices: $$

Lunch & dinner daily

🚇 Sedgwick

Maybe it's the exposed brick walls and the intimate bistro tables spilling onto the sidewalk, or the feeling that comes from a place named after the Chef/owner's daughter, but there's something particularly charming about Bistrot Margot. This group-friendly Gold Coast spot simply offers amiable service and reasonable prices for quality food. Special promotions are abundant, from half-price wines to lunch and dinner specials. While the menu focuses on French standards like duck confit and steak frites, it caters to the Chicago palate with tasty interpretations. Highlights may include the silky fennel and carrot soup or *pomme de terre farci*, a potato shell stuffed with scrambled eggs, cheese, and bacon topped with horseradish crème fraîche.

Bistrot Zinc

D3

French ✗✗

1131 N. State St. (bet. Elm & Cedar Sts.)

Phone: 312-337-1131
Web: www.bistrotzinc.com
Prices: $$

Lunch & dinner daily

🚇 Clark/Division

Tin ceilings, mosaic tiled floors, peppy yellow walls with framed French posters—it's a whiff of Paris in the heart of the Gold Coast. Bistrot Zinc, named for its handcrafted zinc bar, has that lovable neighborhood restaurant thing down pat. From its décor to its delicacies, it's all very classic French bistro. Even the top-shelf staff (sporting bow ties and rolled up sleeves) smell of charm. Just subtract the fussy accents and frosty demeanors and you're smack dab in the middle of Paris.

Flavorful French comfort food is the house specialty: *croque monsieur*, steak frites, French onion soup, and omelets. The compositions are unfussy, but it's exactly what you wanted. Plus, you can still save some pennies for your piggy bank after a meal here.

Chicago ▶ Gold Coast

Café des Architectes

Contemporary

 D5

20 E. Chestnut St. (at Wabash Ave.)

Phone: 312-324-4063   Lunch & dinner daily
Web: www.cafedesarchitectes.com
Prices: $$$ Chicago (Red)

Tucked inside the sophisticated Sofitel, Café des Architectes is a modern marvel unto itself. Dramatic and contemporary, the restaurant is a fitting tribute to the hotel's dazzling architecture. Vibrant red banquettes, soaring ceilings, huge light fixtures, and an arched glass wall are some of the details that set this place apart—as does the highly professional staff. However, this café is a dining destination in its own right. On the menu, find French-inspired cooking that is as artfully presented as it is prepared. Dishes like walleye pike with rich lobster veloute are worthy of praise, while desserts surprise and delight with the likes of caramel *cremeux*, layering chocolate-caramel ganache with toffee-like crunch and popcorn-flavored sherbet.

Cafe Spiaggia

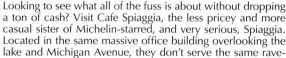

Italian

E4

980 N. Michigan Ave. (at Oak St.)

Phone: 312-280-2750   Lunch & dinner daily
Web: www.cafespiaggia.com
Prices: $$ Chicago (Red)

Looking to see what all of the fuss is about without dropping a ton of cash? Visit Cafe Spiaggia, the less pricey and more casual sister of Michelin-starred, and very serious, Spiaggia. Located in the same massive office building overlooking the lake and Michigan Avenue, they don't serve the same rave-worthy food, but you can still sense the style.

The narrow room feels close, in that charming café way, but the suits and ladies who don't bat a false eyelash at 3-hour lunches seem nonetheless contented. Cozy and elegant, the ambience is the reason to come here, since the food can be overreaching, though tasty as in asparagus with *Prosciutto di Parma* and duck egg. Just sit back, savor a nice glass of Italian wine or a beer, and drink in the scene.

Chicago Q

Barbecue XXX

C3

1160 N. Dearborn St. (bet. Division & Elm Sts.)

Phone: 312-642-1160   Lunch & dinner daily
Web: www.chicagoqrestaurant.com
Prices: $$ Clark/Division

Barbecue goes upscale at this ambitious restaurant in a posh setting. The spacious dining room plays against expectations with industrial lighting, a subway-tiled kitchen, and glass enclosures, surprising moneyed Rush St. guests anticipating a traditional Southern picnic experience.

Start at the bar with small-batch American bourbons and whiskies or a Q Martini adorned with smoked olives. Rich and bold flavors define the menu: silk-tender smoked chicken expertly balances aroma, texture, and spot-on taste in each bite. Braised greens–a trio of mustard, Swiss chard, and collard–simultaneously feel rich and light. Even the baby greens with smoked grape tomatoes and cornbread croutons carry the tastes and textures that make the meal playfully elegant.

deca

Contemporary XX

E5

160 E. Pearson St. (at Water Tower Place)

Phone: 312-573-5160   Lunch & dinner daily
Web: www.decarestaurant.com
Prices: $$ Chicago (Red)

This is surely not what you'd expect of the signature restaurant at the Ritz-Carlton. With an open layout on the 12th floor, deca intentionally feels more like a lobby bar than a dining room. The result? A younger, cooler crowd that you wouldn't normally find at the Ritz-Carlton.

Lunch is somewhat limited, though the DLT (deca lunch trio) is a darling little thing. This three-course meal (served all at once) is a remarkably good value. The menu expands at nighttime to include a variety of seasonal offerings such as venison pâté with pickled vegetables and Medjool dates; cassoulet composed of garlic sausage, duck confit, pork belly, and Tarbais beans; or flatbread topped with fingerling potatoes, wild mushrooms, *fromage blanc*, and truffle oil.

95

Edwardo's Natural Pizza

Pizza ❌

C3

1212 N. Dearborn St. (bet. Division & Goethe Sts.)

Phone: 312-337-4490
Web: www.edwardos.com
Prices: $$

Lunch & dinner daily

Clark/Division

This small Gold Coast outpost is just one of many popular pizza chains that reside in the city and suburbs. A classic kid-friendly pizza joint, Edwardo's does a brisk to-go business, and ships nationwide, should you develop a Chicago-style pizza addiction while in town.

Side dishes such as Buffalo chicken wings are moist and tasty served with the requisite blue cheese and celery. But the real reason to head to Edwardo's is the pizza, and smart diners save room for the hefty stuffed pies, with a flaky pastry crust, gooey cheese, and ample servings of tomato sauce. The spinach soufflé pizza is a healthy favorite. Deep-dishes take at least 45 minutes to bake, so plan accordingly. Lunch combos are friendly on the wallet, but not the waistline.

Gaylord

D4

Indian ❌❌

100 E. Walton St. (bet. Michigan Ave. & Rush St.)

Phone: 312-664-1700
Web: www.gaylordil.com
Prices: $$

Lunch & dinner daily

Chicago (Red)

Offering both Northern and Southern Indian cuisine, Gaylord draws a loyal following for its popular, budget-friendly lunchtime buffet, conveniently located in a spacious subterranean dining room beneath the primo shopping lining Walton Street.

The enormous menu is also vegetarian-friendly, with plenty of *dosas*, *shorbas*, and biryani; as well as other classic options like the peppery chicken *vindaloo* with creamy raita, and freshly baked *roti*. The service staff is warm and efficient, but the kitchen can at times be inconsistent, so be forewarned. Some dishes are terrific while others are a bit off. Complementary *papadams*, chutneys, carrots, and cucumber sticks kick start appetites, and a mango *lassi* nicely cools any burns from the spicy curries.

Gibson's

Steakhouse 🍴

D4

1028 N. Rush St. (at Bellevue Pl.)

Phone: 312-266-8999
Web: www.gibsonssteakhouse.com
Prices: $$$

Lunch & dinner daily

 Clark/Division

There is no better paean to old-school masculinity than Gibson's. Located in the heart of what some call "the Viagra Triangle," this expense account staple is where the power players schmooze, eat, and drink amid dark tables and large portions.

Evoking a sense of the Old World, autographed photos of celebs who have dined here line the walls, and servers in white jackets deliver what is expected: over a dozen different steaks and chops (including W.R.'s Chicago cut ribeye) cooked to order, with classic sides like creamed spinach, asparagus with Hollandaise, and double-baked potatoes. Also sating appetites is a spicy lobster cobb salad and ample desserts. A medley of half-order sizes will keep those lipo'd figures svelte.

The Grill on the Alley

American 🍴

E4

909 N. Michigan Ave. (at Delaware Pl.)

Phone: 312-255-9009
Web: www.thegrill.com
Prices: $$$

Lunch & dinner daily

 Chicago (Red)

Don't dismiss The Grill on the Alley simply because it's part of a multi-state chain. This Chicago outpost brings the best of classic American food in a classic American setting of framed sketches, wood-paneled walls, leather booths, bar, and dining room with a flair for nostalgia. However, its professional service, elegant style, and consistent food are what bring it all to life.

Tucked inside the Westin Hotel in the heart of the Gold Coast, The Grill functions as a high-end cafeteria for the area's power brokers. Here, deals are done over generous portions of familiar American cuisine. Start with oysters on the half shell, before tucking into main courses like blackened ribeye steak with garlic-spinach mashed potatoes or loaded mac & cheese.

Hugo's Frog Bar & Fish House

A m e r i c a n ✖✖

D4

1024 N. Rush St. (bet. Bellevue Pl. & Oak St.)

Phone: 312-640-0999
Web: www.hugosfrogbar.com
Prices: $$

Lunch Sat – Sun
Dinner nightly
Clark/Division

Housed in a sprawling setting adjacent to big brother Gibson's, Hugo's always seems packed. The vast dining room sets white linen-topped tables amidst dark polished wood and pale walls decorated with a mounted swordfish, fish prints, and model ships. Hugo's bar draws its own crowds with abundant counter seating.

The menu focuses on a selection of fish preparations as well as steaks and chops. These are supplemented by stone crab claws, oysters, crab cakes, chowders, and sautéed frog's legs. Speaking of frog's legs, the restaurant takes its name from the nickname of owner Hugo Ralli's grandfather, General Bruce Hay of Her Majesty's Imperial Forces.

Bring a football team to share a slice of the Muddy Bottom Pie, a decadent (and enormous) ice cream cake.

Kiki's Bistro

F r e n c h ✖✖

B4

900 N. Franklin St. (at Locust St.)

Phone: 312-335-5454
Web: www.kikisbistro.com
Prices: $$

Lunch Mon – Fri
Dinner Mon – Sat
Chicago (Brown)

This French cuisine mainstay had been attracting locals and tourists long before the new condos and other construction cropped up. Regulars and newcomers are warmly greeted into the dining room, decorated with candles, fresh flowers, natural light, and rustic wood beams.

The kitchen turns out solid French fare. The French onion soup uses top-notch Gruyère cheese, which is glistening and charred on top. Showing off the chef's skill is the texture of the duck confit with green peppercorn sauce—the meat just falls off the bone and is accompanied by the lip-licking sauce. Also rich and silky is a lime mousse cake with crème anglaise. Owner Kiki himself was once the sommelier at Maxim's of Chicago, so wines are well-paired, although not particularly rare.

Merlo on Maple

C4

Italian ✕✕

16 W. Maple St. (bet. Dearborn & State Sts.)

Phone: 312-335-8200
Web: www.merlochicago.com
Prices: $$$

Dinner nightly

Clark/Division

This *ristorante* houses many floors, but no matter where you sit, the multi-level beauty boasts Victorian touches (hand-carved banisters and leather banquettes), and an informed waitstaff, who deliver the tastes of Emilia-Romagna. Of course, if here on a date, land at the lower level, which–albeit a few feet below–is the most romantic space.

Red sauce isn't exactly their signature, but the amiable kitchen is happy to please a lady. So if you crave the typical tomato sauce, order away. The homemade pastas are lovely, but dishes like *stricchetti verdi* tossed with rabbit ragù; or the *imprigionata alla Petroniana* use top-notch ingredients from Italy's culinary epicenter and are definitely their more unique items.

Mike Ditka's

D5

American ✕✕✕

100 E. Chestnut St. (at Rush St.)

Phone: 312-587-8989
Web: www.mikeditkaschicago.com
Prices: $$

Lunch & dinner daily

Chicago (Red)

Chicago sports legends have a way of becoming restaurateurs at some point, and former Bears coach Mike Ditka is no exception. However, what is an exception is that locals come here not just because of his 1985 Super Bowl win, but because the food is actually quite good (though lighter appetites might be encouraged to man up). Come very hungry and start with Coach's pot roast nachos. Then, move on to the insurmountable meatloaf stack—layered with jalapeño corn bread, meatloaf, mashed potatoes, and fried onion straws. Doggy bags are de rigueur here, but do try to save room for some banana cream pie.

The space is masculine, comfortable, and lined with sports memorabilia—souvenirs are available for purchase on your way out.

mk

American 🍴🍴🍴

B5

868 N. Franklin St. (bet. Chestnut & Locust Sts.)

Phone: 312-482-9179

Web: www.mkchicago.com

Prices: $$$

Dinner nightly

Chicago (Brown)

Local darling Michael Kornick continues to build on his solid reputation with this long-standing, well-run restaurant that brings its share of regulars to the western end of the glittering Gold Coast. Service is happy to please: go ahead and order dishes from the tasting menu if an item beyond the expansive à la carte menu strikes your eye. Upbeat, professional staffers are ready to offer recommendations on personal favorites.

The modern American cuisine mirrors the warm atmosphere and clean lines of the dining room and lounge. The oft-changing seasonal menu showcases simply prepared fresh market ingredients like Tasmanian sea trout with hedgehog mushrooms, haricots, and sunchokes. Desserts are creatively presented enticements to end the evening.

NoMI Kitchen

American 🍴🍴🍴

D5

800 N. Michigan Ave. (entrance on Chicago Ave.)

Phone: 312-239-4030

Web: www.nomirestaurant.com

Prices: $$$$

Lunch & dinner daily

Chicago (Red)

Rising above the Magnificent Mile in the swank Park Hyatt, NoMI Kitchen has emerged from a renovation as a more casual, minimalist version of itself. Though it still offers wowing Michigan Ave. and Water Tower views, in place of Murano chandeliers and white tablecloths are bare wood and pressed-espresso leather tabletops punctuated by smoky gray water glasses, along with an open kitchen that boasts a Benton's country ham station and a cobalt Molteni oven.

The kitchen's focus has shifted to American cuisine, featuring ingredients such as Lake Superior walleye and Laura Chenel goat cheese. Desserts are menu standouts, worth the trip up the elevator for a plate of *gianduja*-dotted blueberry mousse resting upon a delicate sable cookie and a glass of good Port.

Old Jerusalem

B2

1411 N. Wells St. (bet. North Ave. & Schiller St.)

Phone: 312-944-0459

Web: www.oldjerusalemrestaurant.com

Prices:

Lunch & dinner daily

Sedgwick

Set on a charming and centrally located stretch of Old Town, this family-run Middle Eastern favorite has been eagerly accommodating its happy customers since 1976.

The menu focuses on Lebanese-style classics, such as tabbouleh with cracked wheat, scallions, tomatoes, seasoned with lemon, olive oil, and plenty of crisp, green parsley. Hummus arrives rich with tahini, perhaps accompanying the likes of grilled chicken kebabs and traditional flatbreads. Finish with flakey-sweet baklava.

While the décor may not impress, Old Jerusalem manages to make its well-worn looks feel cozy and comfortable for everyone. Very reasonable prices, family-friendly service, and generous portions make this the neighborhood go-to spot, whether dining in or taking out.

Original Pancake House

D4

22 E. Bellevue Pl. (bet. Michigan Ave. & Rush St.)

Phone: 312-642-7917

Web: www.originalpancakehouse.com

Prices:

Lunch daily

Clark/Division

Disputes run rampant about whether or not this little house is the original location of the Original Pancake House in Chicago. Maybe not, but it is something to think about while you wait in the inevitable weekend lines.

This is an all-day breakfast joint and people flock here for the warm service, easy setting, and, of course, the pancakes. The Dutch baby is a decadent oven-based treat, with whipped butter, lemon, and powdered sugar that will have you rolling out on a short-term sugar high. The skillets are big enough to serve a hungry Viking, and egg plates come with pancakes instead of toast, if you prefer (go for it). In addition to classic staples, the menu includes more sides like turkey sausage or chicken hash…to go with, of course, more pancakes.

Pane Caldo

D4

Italian

72 E. Walton St. (bet. Michigan Ave. & Rush St.)

Phone: 312-649-0055 Lunch & dinner daily
Web: www.pane-caldo.com
Prices: $$ Chicago (Red)

Shop until you almost drop and then head straight for Pane Caldo. This intimate Northern Italian restaurant is just across the street from Bloomingdale's, but it feels light years away from the flurry and hubbub of nearby Michigan Avenue. The wood floors, mustard yellow walls, and tables dressed in crisp linens are the very essence of smart casual, as is the good looking crowd that frequents this spot.

The staff, dressed in white aprons and black bow ties, is old-school Italian and you might even elicit a groan or two when placing an order. But don't let the gruff waiters detract from what's ahead: simple and straightforward principles guide the kitchen, turning out pizzas (at lunch), homemade pastas, osso buco, and risotto.

Pelago

E5

Italian

201 E. Delaware Pl. (at Seneca St.)

Phone: 312-280-0700 Lunch & dinner daily
Web: www.pelagorestaurant.com
Prices: $$$ Chicago (Red)

Understated romance is the name of the game at this well-dressed restaurant just off the lobby of Hotel Raffaello. In a setting ideal for impressing dates without going overboard, modern splashes of aqua throughout the serene espresso- and cream-toned rooms keep the Italianate décor on the side of contemporary rather than rustic.

Artisan pastas and seafood take center stage in updated renderings of dishes sourced from Italy's tip to toe, such as the midnight-black tagliolini tossed with shrimp, zucchini, and diced tomato that gets a savory punch from melted herb butter. Prospective Romeos and Juliets should make reservations for the desirable upper dining room; walk-ins may need to content themselves with a less-than-intimate bar table.

Pizano's

Pizza

864 N. State St. (bet. Chestnut St. & Delaware Pl.)

Phone:	312-751-1766
Web:	www.pizanoschicago.com
Prices:	

Lunch & dinner daily

Chicago (Red)

While Chicago may be hailed as home of the deep-dish pizza, the thin-crust pies at Pizano's have justly earned their own devoted following. Of course, the crowds come for the crust—here it is flakey, buttery, thin (by local standards), and perfectly crisp. As unexpected as it sounds, this pizza is truly some of the best in town.

Still, it should be no surprise, as pizza has long been the family calling: owner Rudy Malnati's father founded Pizzeria Uno. The thinner offspring at Pizano's sates its growing fan-base from three locations, and even ships to those who are only Chicagoan at heart. This refreshing and cozy local spot recalls Italo-American style without feeling like a chain-restaurant cliché. The service staff's genuine warmth is palpable.

RA Sushi

Japanese

1139 N. State St. (at Elm St.)

Phone:	312-274-0011
Web:	www.rasushi.com
Prices:	$$

Lunch & dinner daily

Clark/Division

From the same people that brought you the razzle-dazzle knife throwing, food flipping chefs of Benihana, comes RA Sushi. This location—one of three in Chicago—belongs to a nationwide chain of fun, upbeat, and neoteric sushi joints that are part nightclub, part restaurant.

The chefs behind the sushi bar may not be Japanese, but rest assured because the stuff here is really quite good. It's whimsical and casual food—you'll even find funky versions of chips and salsa (spicy tuna tartare alongside wonton chips); and delicate creations like RA-ckin' shrimp served with creamy ginger teriyaki sauce. The rice crispy treats served here are certainly no Kellogg's invention; instead, they are soy paper hand rolls filled with crunchy rice balls and fiery tuna.

Chicago ▲ Gold Coast

Ria ✿ ✿

Contemporary 𝄞𝄞𝄞𝄞

D4

11 E. Walton St. (bet. Rush & State Sts.)

Phone: 312-880-4400
Web: www.riarestaurantchicago.com
Prices: $$$$

Dinner Tue – Sat

🚇 Chicago (Red)

Elysian Hotel

The elegance and sophistication associated with the Elysian Hotel comes to its peak on the third floor at Ria. Inside, rolling champagne carts echo the shimmering fabrics, luscious pillows, and hand-stitched window coverings—everything looks as if moonlight is bouncing from glass to silvery chair to gold curtain and back again. The large room is ideal for celebrations, yet carries a refined European sensibility, which marries well with its contemporary bill of fare.

While considering the focused à la carte offerings or seven-course seasonal tasting menus, take time to peruse the very unique offering of exceptional wines. On the plate, each course arrives as a gorgeous display of technical mastery and exquisite taste, immediately clear in such starters as fine tubes of leek filled with king crab salad dressed in light and tangy lemon vinaigrette. A delicate hand and understanding of pure, balanced flavors shine in the perfectly poached Dover sole stuffed with parsley purée and kissed with Calvados velouté, tender mushrooms, and root vegetables.

The impeccable service team and Chef Danny Grant's excellent kitchen brigade maintain a standard to which other restaurants must now aspire.

Salpicón

B3

Mexican ✖✖

1252 N. Wells St. (bet. Division & Goethe Sts.)

Phone: 312-988-7811
Web: www.salpicon.com
Prices: $$

Lunch Sun
Dinner nightly
🚇 Clark/Division

Priscila Satkoff is this town's unsung hero of contemporary Mexican cuisine. A native of Mexico City, Priscila and her husband Vincent opened Salpicón (named after a typical Mexican dish) in 1995. The colorful décor and lively Mexican soundtrack lend a warm, yet elegant, vibe to the dining room; and though dinner is always popular, brunch is a worthy affair.

Feast on outstanding dishes like *queso fundido con camarones* and *chuleta de Puerco en manchamanteles*—a grilled pork chop served in chile ancho *mole* with grilled pineapple, sweet potato, and plantains.

It's hard to look away from the 120-plus tequilas on offer, but husband and co-owner Vincent Satkoff runs an impressive wine program which pairs an award-winning list perfectly with the menu.

Signature Room at the 95th

E5

Contemporary ✖✖✖

875 N. Michigan Ave. (bet. Chestnut St. & Delaware Ave.)

Phone: 312-787-9596
Web: www.signatureroom.com
Prices: $$$

Lunch & dinner daily

🚇 Chicago (Red)

Riding the elevator up to the 95th floor of the iconic John Hancock Center your ears might pop. This should be your first clue that the "location, location, location" mantra applies to restaurants as well as real estate. While there is both a restaurant and a lounge (on the 96th floor) here, people really come for the views first, the food second. The floor-to-ceiling windows show off 360-degree views of the city skyline and, of course, magnificent Lake Michigan.

The menu is continental in style, taking influences from around the world and toning them down. A good selection of seasonal monthly specials adds to the sizeable choice. Desserts are a strong point here, though stick to the classics like a slice of cheesecake or a crème brûlée.

Seasons ⽊

D4

Contemporary ✗✗✗✗

120 E. Delaware Pl. (bet. Michigan Ave. & Rush St.)

Phone: 312-649-2349   Dinner nightly

Web: www.fourseasons.com/chicagofs

Prices: $$$$ 🚇 Chicago (Red)

Lara Kastner

Fine dining at the Four Seasons does carry a certain weight: carved wood paneling, gold-framed artwork, padded leather armchairs, and views of imposing skyscrapers echo with formality. The large room can feel stuffy, even lonely. But once that gilded charger is removed, by white-jacketed and shoulder-tasseled servers working in lock-step synchronicity, and replaced by Chef Kevin Hickey's contemporary cooking, a certain brightness emanates from the plate.

In fact, the level of creativity arrives as a pleasant surprise with each new course, and does much to enliven its otherwise very classical persona. To begin, the crustacean might be exalted with a perfectly cooked soft-shell crab, its crunchy panko crust and succulent interior set over a circle of Thai red curry, finished with plump green almonds and cilantro-tamarind vinaigrette. Crisp-skinned duck breast over wilted kale is elevated by foie gras and duck confit tamales as well as a superb black plum *mole*. Desserts might include goat cheese semifreddo with magenta hibiscus "ice" and *pâté de fruit*.

A word to the wise walk-in—specify where you want to dine. The lounge is spacious and highbrow, but not of the same caliber as Seasons.

Spiaggia ✿

Italian XXXX

980 N. Michigan Ave. (at Oak St.)

Phone:	312-280-2750	Dinner nightly
Web:	www.spiaggiarestaurant.com	
Prices:	$$$$	🚇 Chicago (Red)

Jeff Kauck

Discreetly positioned on the second floor of One Magnificent Mile, Spiaggia swoops guests out of the corporate milieu into a grand wall of windows, theatrical red marble columns, and deep u-shaped booths for a little bit of romance. Though the ceilings soar, the sunken dining room feels luxuriously intimate—glasses clink in honor of anniversaries and celebrations, and men look sharp in their required jackets, adding to the formal but sociable atmosphere.

Chef Sarah Grueneberg and team (e Tony Mantuano) show their polish both on the floor and through the kitchen's glass walls, their capable hands and minds leading guests on a regional Italian tour. Artisanal foodstuffs flown in from Italy rub shoulders with local produce in rustically inspired dishes, presented elegantly and explained eloquently.

Dinner choices may include a moist fillet of roasted cod strikingly topped with a thin, crunchy layer of squid ink-stained breadcrumbs; or a dramatically presented veal chop still attached to its foot-long rib bone, direct from the wood-burning oven atop silky braised Tuscan kale. A refined pumpkin brioche bread pudding gets a lift from toasted dollops of meringue and cinnamon ice milk.

Table Fifty-Two

Southern 🍴🍴🍴

C3

52 W. Elm St. (bet. Clark & Dearborn Sts.)

Phone: 312-573-4000
Web: www.tablefifty-two.com
Prices: $$$

Lunch Sun
Dinner nightly
Ⓜ Clark/Division

Chef Art Smith's drawl floats overhead like a warm breeze as he chats up guests inside Table Fifty-Two's cozy white row house, a stately survivor of the Great Chicago Fire. Southern charm permeates every inch of the room, from the pressed copper ceiling to the white sideboards to a wood-burning oven churning out the restaurant's signature biscuits.

The meal might get started with an amuse-bouche of deviled eggs topped with pickled mustard seeds, and if it's a Sunday or Monday, the famous fried chicken will be making an appearance on many plates. Plump fried green tomatoes and thick pork chops are on order, but for a true down-home taste, get a tall wedge of hummingbird cake, fragrant with banana and pineapple and slathered in cream cheese frosting.

Do not confuse 🍴 with ⸙ ! 🍴 defines comfort, while ⸙ are awarded for the best cuisine. Stars are awarded across all categories of comfort.

Humboldt Park & Logan Square

Albany Park · Irving Park

This collection of vibrant north side neighborhoods is the heart and soul of where locals live and eat. While the area may lie a few blocks off the beaten path, it is great for anyone seeking that perfect dessert, ethnic grocer, hidden bodega, or quick falafel. Plus, any trip through these up-and-coming neighborhoods is sure to be heavenly with tree-lined streets, quaint architecture, and affordable, trendy stops. Begin your adventure in Chicago's Koreatown, a commercial thoroughfare spanning miles along Lawrence Avenue, from Cicero to California Avenue.

HUMBOLDT PARK

The core of the city's Puerto Rican community is found here. If there's any confusion as to exactly where it begins, just look for the Paseo Boricua, the flag-shaped steel gateway demarcating the district along Division Street. These storefronts are as much a celebration of the diaspora as the homeland, with their impressive and delicious selection of traditional foods, hard-to-find ingredients, and authentic *pernil*.

LOGAN SQUARE

An eclectic mix of cuisines (from Cuban and Mexican, to Italian) combined with historic buildings and boulevards,

attract a crowd of hipsters, working-class locals, artists, and students to this quarter. Within this community, locally-minded at-home cooks and foodies flock to the **Dill Pickle Food Co-op** for bulk groceries. Visitors opt for Sunday's **Logan Square Farmer's Market** on Logan Blvd., with stalls hawking everything from artisanal soaps and raw honey to organic zucchini. Adults and kids have been saving their allowances for a trip to **Margie's Candies**, for its homemade chocolates, toffees, and hot fudge sundaes. A melting pot of global foods, Albany Park offers every gastronomic delight at budget-friendly prices. Highlights include **Al Khayyam Bakery**, a Middle Eastern grocery with cheeses, olive oils, and flatbreads. For dessert, lull at **Nazareth Sweets** and bite into brittles and pastries like walnut or baklava. **Charcoal Delights** is a time-tested, unique burger favorite with such dishes as chicken delight, cheesesteak, and hot dogs with "the works" rounding out the menu.

You will be in good hands at **The Fishguy Market**, which supplies restaurants and home-cooks with quality seafood and service. The nearby **Independence Park Farmer's Market** is also worth a trip. This fast-growing market will satisfy with its array of produce, plants, and baked goods.

Humboldt Park & Logan Square

Accanto

Italian X̃X̃

 C4

2172 N. Milwaukee Ave. (at Francis Pl.)

Phone: 773-227-2727   Dinner Wed – Mon
Web: www.accanto-chicago.com
Prices: $$ California (Blue)

In a hip but understated dining room tucked among the gritty warehouses of North Milwaukee Avenue, Accanto serves contemporary Italian with creative global touches that often surprise the palate. Small but notable details, like a television looping silent clips from Cinecittà film classics and mod half-dome light fixtures, echo the mix of old- and new-world cuisine.

Mull over the menu while snacking on a straight-from-the-oven *piadine* liberally sprinkled with sumac and *za'atar*, but here's a tip: the dish to order is a sophisticated and sublime risotto using *carnaroli* rice. Other menu items may include pistachio-crusted turbot with foie gras jus; venison chop with taleggio polenta; or dessert napoleons with caramelized pears and Chantilly cream.

Al Dente

Contemporary X̃X̃

 A2

3939 W. Irving Park Rd. (bet. Pulaski Rd. & Springfield Ave.)

Phone: 773-208-9539   Lunch Sat – Sun
Web: www.aldentechicago.com   Dinner nightly
Prices: $$

 North/Clybourn

Chef Javier Perez started out washing dishes shortly after emigrating from Mexico City in 1990. He's been working his way around Chicago's kitchens ever since, before launching his own baby, Al Dente, with wife Maria. Walk inside and you may think the name is al *verde*—the palette evokes the green shades of an avocado. Booths, chairs, and napkins are tinted brown, possibly symbolic of the avocado's heart.

The split room is flooded with chatter. Driving the open kitchen is the chef in his lime green coat, expediting contemporary Latin American dishes like *guajillo*-marinated calamari steaks with buttery mushrooms and habanero aïoli; adobo-crusted salmon over spicy chorizo; and fluffy tiramisu finished with a dusting of cocoa and flecks of gold leaf.

Arun's

B1

Thai ✗✗

4156 N. Kedzie Ave. (at Berteau Ave.)

Phone: 773-539-1909
Web: www.arunsthai.com
Prices: $$$$

Dinner Wed – Sun

🔲 Kedzie (Brown)

Chef/owner Arun Sampanthavivat oversees every detail at this culinary mainstay, which has been serving a well-dressed and moneyed crowd since 1985.

No need to bring your reading glasses, since you won't need to fuss with a menu at Arun's. Instead, this upscale Thai restaurant treats its visitors to a 12-course prix-fixe of six appetizers, four entrées (served family-style), and two desserts. The dishes change regularly, but expect creations like diced spicy pork served inside a grilled sweet pepper; or Panang beef curry in coconut milk. Carved vegetables shaped like butterflies and fish are memorable flourishes.

From the elegant setting and white-jacketed servers to the bountiful feast, it's no wonder people return so often for the princely experience.

Azucar

B3

Spanish 🍽

2647 N. Kedzie Ave. (bet. Milwaukee & Schubert Aves.)

Phone: 773-486-6464
Web: www.azucartapasrestaurant.com
Prices: $$

Dinner Wed – Sun

🔲 Logan Square

There is no dearth of small plate spots in the city, yet this dinner-only tapas and cocktail bar across from the Logan Square El is worth seeking out. The narrow room is outfitted with dark wood, exposed brick, mosaic tiles, and glass ceiling pendants.

Ingredients are all-important here, where the kitchen makes its own chorizo, and a wide selection of Spanish cheeses is served with honey, fig jam, and almonds. On the menu, find the likes of *gambas a pil-pil*—sautéed spiced jumbo shrimp with garlic-butter sauce; and Manchego, sliced pear, Serrano ham, and walnut-topped *coca*—crispy Spanish-style flatbread. True to its name (azucar means sugar), sweets feature *rosquillas*—cinnamon and sugar doughnuts served with warm chocolate ganache.

Bonsoirée ❄

Contemporary 🍴🍴

C4

2728 W. Armitage Ave. (bet. California Ave. & North Point St.)

Phone: 773-486-7511
Web: www.bon-soiree.com
Prices: $$$

Dinner Tue – Sun

🚇 California (Blue)

&

Bonsoirée/Bo Streeter

Keep your eyes peeled as you walk along Armitage Avenue. As a nod to Chef Shin Thompson's beginnings when he hosted underground dinner parties, Bonsoirée presents no signs or beacons to let diners know they've found the restaurant. The server presents neither menu nor wine list, adding to the evening's mysteriously alluring anticipation.

Despite the toned-down décor–powder blue and slate pass for flashy colors here–when the room is full, it's buzzing. Foodies snap rampant smartphone pictures, and otherwise blasé urban daters get a little giddy. Eavesdropping between the sardine-packed tables becomes part of the fun.

The eight-course prix-fixe menu is equal parts whimsy and serious technique. A single quail thigh, frenched into lollipop form, may start off the evening with a dip into sour orange Thai curry and a dusting of lime salt. The chef's signature *motoyaki*, a Japanese spin on Coquilles St. Jacques that mixes scallops, peekytoe crab, and ponzu aïoli, could pop up. And you're a lucky diner if the night ends with a profusion of miniature chocolates like a *ras al hanout* brownie and cocoa-star anise marshmallows. Diners hungry for more should reserve the 13-course menu in advance.

Brand BBQ Market

 B4

Barbecue

2824 W. Armitage Ave. (at Mozart St.)

Phone: 773-687-8148
Web: www.brandbbqmarket.com
Prices:

Lunch & dinner daily

Western (Blue)

Tender pulled duck sandwich with a side of bourbon creamed corn? Check. Venison sausage stuffed with Gorgonzola and wrapped in bacon atop fried onions and brandy cherry sauce? Check. Old-fashioned barbecue getting a mouthwatering makeover? Double check. Amp up those 'cue cravings and step into this wooden oasis where wood banquettes and thick varnished tables adorn the space; while aromatic woods like apple and hickory, smoke those juicy meats. A retail area selling chunks of wood entices the ambitious to recreate the experience at home.

Sample the selection of savory sauces on the table, from smoky chipotle to tangy-sweet brown sugar-cayenne. Vegetarians, you won't feel left out with meaty smoked tofu and portobello mushrooms, but don't forget to BYOB.

Chicago Kalbi

A1

Korean

3752 W. Lawrence Ave. (bet. Hamlin & Lawndale Aves.)

Phone: 773-604-8183
Web: www.chicago-kalbi.com
Prices: $$

Dinner Wed – Mon

 Take me out to the ballgame—or the Korean barbecue joint where a ballplayer would feel right at home, as the case may be at this quirky spot. Autographed baseballs line walls and shelves, while photographs and posters of ballplayers paper the walls; but the cluttered décor doesn't deter locals from frequenting this modest but welcoming space.

Gas grills at each table give off an intoxicatingly savory perfume as patrons take their time searing their choice of well-marbled marinated beef, including the always-popular *bulgogi* or *kalbi*, and cool their mouths with a traditional array of *banchan*. For those who prefer their meat off the grill, a beef tartare takes an interesting twist of flavor when folded with Asian pears, sesame seeds, and sesame oil.

Chilapan

C4

2459 W. Armitage Ave. (at Campbell Ave.)

Phone: 773-697-4374
Web: N/A
Prices: $$

Dinner Mon – Sat

Western (Blue)

It's a rip-roaring scene in Chilapan's kitchen, where blaring beats keep a lively team of young cooks (and one revered elder) on their toes, as they spin out plate after plate of soulful scrumptiousness. This sure ain't your average taco stand; and though the space is snug and the El may be raging directly above, the flavor-packed menu will grab every ounce of your attention.

Savor the orange *guajillo*-glazed wild salmon, an ample fillet grilled to perfection, served atop sweet potato purée and mango salsa; tender skirt steak stuffed with spinach and *arbol* tomato salsa; or *empanada potosina*, loaded with *chihuahua*, *epazote*, and mushrooms, and served with tomatillo salsa. Close with warm chocolate cake oozing with cinnamon cream, and never look back.

Fat Willy's

Barbecue

C3

2416 W. Schubert St. (at Artesian Ave.)

Phone: 773-782-1800
Web: www.fatwillys.com
Prices: $$

Lunch & dinner daily

Fat Willy's telegraphs an authentic and messy barbecue experience by luring all with its wafting scent of smoke, hickory, and apple wood piles stacked at the entrance. This is only further teased by homemade sauces and paper towel rolls poised atop kraft paper-protected tables. With customers' doodles from the tables plastering the walls, it's a sign everyone comes and leaves happy here.

Crack through the charred surface on baby back and St. Louis-style rib slabs to devour the pink-tinged center, an indication of superior smoking. Brisket might verge on the dry side, but pulled pork sandwiches are juicy, while corndogs are hand-dipped and fried. Root beer from Milwaukee's Sprecher Brewery adds a little Midwest taste to the bona fide Southern flavor.

Flying Saucer

C5   A m e r i c a n

1123 N. California Ave. (at Haddon Ave.)

Phone: 773-342-9076   Lunch daily
Web: www.flyingsaucerchicago.com
Prices:

The Flying Saucer may look retro, like a 1950s-esque diner complete with a Formica counter, but there's nothing "Leave It To Beaver" about this anti-establishment gathering place. A well-pierced and tattooed crowd enjoys breakfast all day in this spot where the walls are lined with local artists' work. The kitchen created a homey diner menu with a twist, popular with vegetarians and locavores. Try the *huevos volando*, two eggs (organic for a few cents more) cooked your way and smothered in a homemade, spicy and smoky salsa, *guajillo* sauce, and *chihuahua* cheese over warm corn tortillas. A side of organic black beans accompanies, and bright cilantro and sweet chopped onion finish the dish. Wash it all down with a Flying Saucer blend coffee.

Fuego Mexican Grill

C4   M e x i c a n

2047 N. Milwaukee Ave. (bet. Campbell & Maplewood Aves.)

Phone: 773-252-1122   Dinner Wed – Sun
Web: www.fuegomexicangrill.weebly.com
Prices: **$$**   Western (Blue)

Entering Fuego is like setting foot in a theater lobby. Twin sweeping staircases lead to an upstairs nightclub and separate the dancers from the diners. The main dining room with its lengthy bar is ready to pour a litany of flavorful tequila-laced cocktails and sees a constant crew. Slate walls with decorative tile inlays and rust-colored booths lend a sultry vibe—*no mas mariachis aqui*.

Aside from meat and seafood, hit their multitude of *moles*. Before things get crazy at the weekend nightclub upstairs, fill up on moist *tamalitos surtidos* (chicken and mushroom tamales with *mole poblano* and *mole Amarillo*); *camarones al mole blanco*; and pechuga *huitalacoche* (a tender grilled chicken breast stuffed with poblano chilies and Oaxaca cheese).

(k)new

Contemporary ✗✗

C4

2556 W. Fullerton Ave. (at Rockwell St.)

Phone: 773-772-7721   Dinner Mon – Sat
Web: www.knewrestaurant.com
Prices: $$

Though its nondescript façade on a busy stretch of West Fullerton might give you pause, a dreamy setting awaits through the doors of (k)new. Blonde wood furniture and white linens set off by veneered aqua blue walls and exposed ceiling beams whisper "cozy-romantic-casual," a feeling that's amplified by accommodating service.

Chef/owner Omar Rodriguez presents an eclectic menu that builds on unexpected flavor pairings and smartly done glazes and reductions. The rack of two succulent, generously cut venison chops, drizzled with a red wine-fig reduction over sweet mashed potatoes, is straightforward and deliciously executed. *Cavatappi* with lobster, shrimp, and mascarpone sparks with a bold combo of tarragon, mint, and basil for a pleasantly novel dish.

Kuma's Corner

American ✗

B3

2900 W. Belmont Ave. (at Francisco Ave.)

Phone: 773-604-8769   Lunch & dinner daily
Web: www.kumascorner.com
Prices: ⊜⊜

Dig out your old Metallica t-shirt and you'll fit right in at this heavy metal-themed burger joint and dive bar serving locally made beers. It's racy and raucous with head-banging music, so leave Grandma and the kids behind. Forget about any conversation, since Iron Maiden will be pounding in your ears, but in a place with burgers this good, your mouth will be otherwise engaged.

Keeping with the unconventional theme, each burger is named for a heavy metal band from Megadeth to Black Sabbath. Juicy and delicious, these heavenly burgers are the clear draw, as in the Lair of the Minotaur, served on a pretzel roll piled high with caramelized onions, pancetta, creamy Brie, and bourbon-soaked pears.

La Encantada

Mexican

3437 W. North Ave. (bet. Homan & St. Louis Aves.)

Phone: 773-489-5026   Lunch & dinner daily
Web: www.laencantadarestaurant.com
Prices:

Run by the gracious Enriquez family, this *encantada* (enchanted) spot lives up to its name. Inside, royal blue, golden yellow, and exposed brick walls are hung with bright, gallery-style artwork (much of it for sale), while contemporary Latino tunes waft through the air, creating a quixotic vibe. Culinary inspiration begins in the family's hometown, Zacatecas, but pulls from all around the country, with seriously delectable results.

Dig into the rich and cheesy *quesadilla de huitlacoche*; or the divine *chile en Nogada*, poblano peppers stuffed with ground beef, squash, fruit, and walnuts, topped with a creamy walnut sauce and pomegranate seeds. Pair these delicacies with such decadent sides as chipotle whipped potatoes.

Lula Café

American

2537 N. Kedzie Ave. (off Logan Blvd.)

Phone: 773-489-9554   Lunch & dinner Wed – Mon
Web: www.lulacafe.com
Prices: $$ Logan Square

Husband-and-wife owners Jason Hammel and Amalea Tshilds (also of Nightwood) turned this offbeat eatery into one of the city's leading organic and sustainable restaurants. They are serious about the locavore movement, but don't take themselves too seriously. The staff here is young, hip, and relaxed; the diners are regulars.

Following their 2011 renovation, the fan base has expanded as much as their inventive menu. But faves keep locals returning to this quirky dining room decorated with images of organic farming, Busy Beaver buttons, an upright piano, and picture window. Entrées include a pork belly carbonara with escarole, mushroom *soffritto*, and pecorino; while moist carrot cake provides a perfect finish. Monday nights are not-to-be-missed farm dinners.

Longman & Eagle ⌘

Gastropub ✕

B3

2657 N. Kedzie Ave. (at Schubert Ave.)

Phone: 773-276-7110

Web: www.longmananandeagle.com

Prices: **$$**

Lunch & dinner daily

Logan Square

Clayton Hauck

Though a few percentage points spiffier than the usual humble corner tavern, Longman & Eagle's worn-in counters and sturdy dishware are doing their darndest to direct your attention right to the food. And what attention it gets; every meal had here elicits audible *oohs* and *ahhs* when plates are delivered to the table.

Come with a friend, so one of you can order a sandwich like the wild boar sloppy joe, spicy meat paired with beef-fat fries; and the other can get smoky pastrami-cured sweetbreads matched with aerated Gruyère for dipping those fries. Pescatarians are well remembered among the gastropub offerings here with the likes of flaky pan-roasted cod with pungent brandade and mushroom ragoût. The enthusiastic staff is overwhelmingly bearded, flannel-shirted, and puts on no airs while graciously accommodating diners spanning the generations, filling rustic seats and retro barstools. The scene here can get raucous, so if you're bringing the parents, a gentle warning beforehand might be in order.

If you've indulged in one too many of their cocktails or whiskey tasting flights, check to see if any of the six rooms in the upstairs inn—each with unique design and décor—are available.

Maiz

C5 Mexican

1041 N. California Ave. (bet. Cortez & Thomas Sts.)

Phone: 773-276-3149   Dinner Tue – Sun
Web: www.maizchicago.com
Prices: 🍴

 An authentic Mexican restaurant in the heart of Humboldt Park isn't a surprise. Faithful Mexican-American life is what this area is all about. But even here, Maiz Antojitos Y Bebidas is a standout.

The menu is a celebration of corn and its common variations found as Mexican snacks, as the name suggests. Try anything corn-heavy like the *elote*, served street-style slathered with butter, mayo, cheese and chile powder; or the *tamal de elote*, two uniquely corn-flavored tamales served simply with lettuce and tomato. The *corundas*, a heavenly street food from Michoacan, are a delightful find here bathed in a dark *mole* with onions, crumbled cheese, and *crema*. Get a little green mixed in with your yellow by adding the *nopales*, a salad of diced cactus paddles.

Mirabell

B2 German

3454 W. Addison St. (bet. Kimball & St. Louis Aves.)

Phone: 773-463-1962   Lunch & dinner daily
Web: www.mirabellrestaurant.com
Prices: $$ 🚇 Addison (Blue)

 Looking for a taste of the Old Country without leaving your leafy environs? Head straight for Mirabell, where locals have been raising their steins since 1977. From the dirndl-clad waitresses, the accordion and Alpine music, to the pastoral German murals and shaded *biergarten*, this place is Bavarian from head to toe.

Wursts, schnitzels, spaetzle, sauerkraut, and spicy beef goulash—it's enough to bring a tear to the eye of even the steeliest *frau*. Mirabell is meat lover's paradise, so save the date with your veggie friend for another day (though there are some sandwiches and salads, but why bother?). It might not be fancy, but it sure is flavorful; and the traditional food is complemented by an almost exclusively German list of brews.

Noon-O-Kabab

Persian ✗✗

4661 N. Kedzie Ave. (at Leland Ave.)

Phone: 773-279-9309
Web: www.noonokabab.com
Prices: 💰💰

Lunch Mon – Fri
Dinner nightly
Kedzie (Brown)

Noon-O-Kabab is that great little neighborhood spot you hit up for its good food, reasonable prices, and über friendly service. Tucked into arched alcoves, the tile floors and wood furnishings may be simple, but its walls are adorned with beautiful tile murals of dancing figurines.

Delightful Persian specialties are the order of the day. Swing by for a comforting bowl of *ghormeh sabzi*—a stew of lamb, red beans, spinach, fenugreek, and cilantro; or *joujeh koubideh*—skewers of juicy, saffron-flavored ground chicken, served with dill-lima bean basmati rice, and the traditional charbroiled whole tomato. Their bustling catering business a few doors down (also the spot for pick-up and delivery), sells the best *bastani* (Persian gelato) in sunnier months.

Pork Shoppe

Barbecue ✗

2755 W. Belmont Ave. (bet. California & Washtenaw Aves.)

Phone: 773-961-7654
Web: www.porkshoppechicago.com
Prices: 💰💰

Lunch & dinner Tue – Sun

Belmont (Blue)

Step into this den of macho–boasting boutique barbecue–and thank your stars the men are brilliant behind the smokers, as they certainly make for dull decorators. The stoic dining room (imagine wood floors, a rusted communal bar, tables, and chairs) is barely enriched by framed mirrors and relics of old farming equipment.

But, pork is Prada here and shoppers have perfected the routine: place an order, take a number, a wad of brown towels, and sauce (sweet, tangy, and wicked) up! A sammy with smoked pork belly pastrami may steal the show, but window-shop your way through other items like Texas brisket tacos, crunchy and fragrant with onion and cilantro; and oversized chocolate chip cookies. Best with your barbecue is beer, wine, and…bourbon.

Real Tenochtitlan

B3

2451 N. Milwaukee Ave. (bet. Richmond St. & Sacramento Ave.)

Phone: 773-227-1050
Web: www.realtenochtitlan.com
Prices: $$

Lunch & dinner daily

California (Blue)

Memorable *mole* awaits at Real Tenochtitlan, which delivers a polished take on the Mexican fine-dining experience. Details like a wood-coffered ceiling and draped red fabric give the large room an inviting and elegant hacienda feel that's nothing like the typical mom-and-pop joint.

Moles are justifiably the house specialty: the stunningly complex *mole blanco*, with white chocolate, roasted almonds, pine nuts, and chiles, is a revelation; but those who want to sample more sauces have their work cut out for them with *verde, chichilo, rojo coloradito, negro,* and *manchamanteles* variations. For a simpler but no less satisfying dish, homemade tortillas, wood-grilled onions, and woodland mushrooms take the *enchiladas de hongos* far beyond run-of-the-mill.

Rootstock

B5

954 N. California Ave. (bet. Augusta Blvd. & Walton St.)

Phone: 773-292-1616
Web: www.rootstockbar.com
Prices: $$

Lunch Sun
Dinner Mon – Sat

This vibrant, funky wine bar gaining a steady following on the western edge of un-touristy Humboldt Park makes its focus known at first glance: patrons sit down to a bare table, laid only with the wine list—actually a thick, bound book with meticulous descriptions of each well-chosen selection.

Agreeable staffers know their way around the wines and the small plates menu, which showcases house-made charcuterie. Highlights may include an alluringly rustic presentation of silky rabbit rillettes with pickled vegetables and blackberry verjus; or sublimely tender confit duck sporting a chewy, crispy skin. A small but friendly bar makes an appealing option for solo dining, while sizeable portions and a low-key vibe are perfect for catching up with friends.

Semiramis

Lebanese ✗

B1

4639 N. Kedzie Ave. (bet. Eastwood & Leland Aves.)

Phone: 773-279-8900   Lunch & dinner Mon – Sat
Web: www.semiramisrestaurant.com
Prices: ෬   🚇 Kedzie (Brown)

This Lebanese café outshines the competition in an ethnically diverse area filled with Middle Eastern eateries, Korean restaurants, and halal meat shops.

Inside the pleasant space, where colorful tapestries brighten the walls as art, Semiramis offers tasty takes on standards, from refreshing salads to golden brown falafel patties with hints of garlic, sesame oil, and parsley, wrapped in warm and tender flatbread. Have that alongside French fries topped with sumac and garlic for a serious non-burger-and-fries treat. With its focus on good, simple, fresh Lebanese food made from quality ingredients, Semiramis does it right, while providing an inviting place to sit and eat. Both eat-in and to-go orders are filled quickly by the friendly staff.

Smoque BBQ 😊

Barbecue ✗

A2

3800 N. Pulaski Rd. (at Grace St.)

Phone: 773-545-7427   Lunch & dinner Tue – Sun
Web: www.smoquebbq.com
Prices: ෬   🚇 Irving Park (Blue)

City-dwellers and suburbanites alike flock to this Irving Park spot just off the Kennedy for one good reason: righteous Texas-style barbecue. The counter service is friendly and the ambience energetic, but people really come here for the applewood-smoked meats.

And what dreamy meats: smoky, juicy, sauce-splattered barbecue perfection. Smoked for 12 hours, the result is tender and sweet with those divine bits of crispness. Options include pulled pork, brisket, chicken, Texas sausage and meaty ribs—both baby back and St. Louis-style. Even the slaw and cornbread are done just right—a further testament to the owners' dedication to the craft. The peach cobbler is a must add-on to any tray. Sure you're full but who doesn't have room for a little more goodness?

Taqueria Moran

B4 Mexican 🍴

2226 N. California Ave. (bet. Lyndale St. & Milwaukee Ave.)

Phone: 773-235-2663   Lunch & dinner daily
Web: N/A
Prices: 💰💰   🚇 California (Blue)

Here, in the shiny, wide-open stainless steel kitchen, Guadalupe Moran whips up lip-smacking Mexican eats all day long—yep, that's breakfast, lunch, and dinner. Hop into this beloved neighborhood taqueria–practically hiding under the Blue Line–and find a spanking clean and colorful room replete with terra-cotta ceilings and a bright mural depicting a bucolic, south of the border scene.

Tuck in a napkin and brush up on your *español* as you tackle the vast, delicious menu (having a decent hold on the language helps; not all the friendly servers are English speaking). Whether it's juicy pork *adobado* tacos; cilantro packed *carne asada*; or sizzling *fajitas mixtas* (chicken, shrimp, or beef with beans, tortillas, and veggies), food here seriously satisfies.

Telegraph

B3 Contemporary 🍴🍴

2601 N. Milwaukee Ave. (at Logan Blvd.)

Phone: 773-292-9463   Dinner nightly
Web: www.telegraphwinebar.com
Prices: $$ 🚇 Logan Square

Sipping and staring are equally relaxing pursuits at this urbane, stylish wine bar with banks of expansive windows facing Logan Square Park. Charcoal and deep teal walls and dark, chunky wood tables throughout the restaurant let intimate moments unfold among the industrial fixtures.

Slink onto a tawny leather barstool and leaf through the compact but well-chosen wine list, stocked with wines by the glass from all corners of the world. To go with that *vino*, nibbles range from petite to hearty plates in bold flavor combinations, and might include a creamy cannellini bean tartine with ribbons of summer squash, decked out with a fried squash blossom for good measure; or a daring combination of grilled lamb saddle with oysters and cherries.

Urban Belly

Asian ✗

3053 N. California Ave. (bet. Barry Ave. & Nelson St.)

Phone:	773-583-0500
Web:	www.urbanbellychicago.com
Prices:	🪙🪙

Lunch & dinner Tue – Sun

🚇 Belmont (Blue)

Set on an otherwise dreary block, Chef/owner Bill Kim welcomes diners into a space that reeks of that hip cafeteria look (think Chinese Elmwood communal tables and chunky stools, plus artifacts from salvaged Indonesian ships). Just remember to order at the counter before choosing your perch. With dumpling combos like Asian squash and bacon, duck and *pho* spices, and the always reliable lamb and brandy, bring friends and order for them at this Asian-with-strong-Korean influences spot.

Pan-Asian seasonings and interesting pairings such as pork belly fried rice with pineapple *brunoise*, tempt some to abandon the chopsticks and just pick up a fork. Noodle lovers know this is a good place to get their slurp on with a variety of soba, udon, and ramen bowls.

Bib Gourmand 🙂
indicates our inspectors'
favorites for good value.

Lakeview & Wrigleyville
Roscoe Village

"Peanuts! Get your peanuts!" When the Cubs are playing, expect to hear the call of salty ball-game snacks through the north side's best-known neighborhood, though locals may actually be stopping into **Nuts on Clark** for some pre-game caramel corn. Lakeview is the umbrella term for the area north of Lincoln Park, including Wrigleyville (named after its iconic ball field) and Roscoe Village.

Enter Eastern Europe

Even when the beloved Cubs finish their season at Wrigley Field (as sadly happens each October), American summertime classics continue to shape the area's cuisine, yet for historic reasons. Thanks to their large Eastern European immigrant population, an abundant variety of sausages and wursts can be found in casual eateries and markets located on a number of blocks. Showcasing these juicy and tender specialties is the beloved **Paulina Meat Market**, where expected items like corned beef, lamb, veal, and turkey are offered alongside the more novel offerings such as ground venison, loin chops, and "baseball bat summer sausages." The local Swedish population knows to come here for tried and true favorites such as pickled Christmas hams and cardamom-infused sausages. Paulina's incredible growth and steadfast commitment to quality makes this not just a local institution, but perhaps one of Chicago's biggest (and most popular) meat markets.

Classic Chicago

Equally important and comparably carnivorous is Chicago's love for the humble hot dog. Here, chefs, foodies, and touristas stand in lines that may wraparound the block at **Hot Doug's**, the lunch-only purveyor of creatively encased meats in combinations named either to celebrate sultry starlets (like the spicy "Keira Knightly"), or maybe immortalize their friends. Fridays and Saturdays are particularly crowded, because that's when Doug (the bespeckled gentleman at the counter) serves duck fat fries. **Byron's Dog Haus** isn't as gourmet, but both their hot dogs and burgers are classic Chicago and very tasty. Note that the location near Wrigley only has outdoor picnic tables and no inside seating.

Baking in Bavaria

Even Chicagoans can't live on hot dogs alone. When they crave something else, they have their choice in Lakeview. Bavarian baked goods have been a mainstay of **Dinkel's Bakery** since 1922 (and in its current locale since 1932). Originally opened by a master baker who hailed from Southern Bavaria, the business is still family run and remains famous for its traditional renditions of strudels, butter kuchen, and, stollen (items can be purchased fresh, but are also available frozen for shipping). Also praiseworthy is Dinkel's Burglaur (a big breakfast sandwich), and their decadent donut selection is addictive and all the rage.

Sweet Indulgences

For a different type of sweet, stop in for the globally-influenced, Chicago-based **Mayana Chocolates** in flavors as accessible as cookies n' cream and raspberry-dark chocolate, or the more exotic Turkish coffee and hazelnut and coriander praline. At her **Bittersweet Pastry Shop**, Chef/owner Judy Contino is well-known for her wedding cakes, pastries, and other delights like breakfast breads, cheesecakes, brownies, and cupcakes. She's been sculpting these sweet treats for almost two decades now. Those seeking a more local, sustainable (and punk-rock) experience should head to the **Bleeding Heart Organic Bakery** for cakepops, bars, and cupcakes that are listed as either Plain Jane (as in chocolate raspberry), or the Fancy Schmancy (ginger-mint mojito maybe?). They also boast an array of breakfast and dessert items

Another laudation (even if they come in buttery and sugary packages) to Chicago's neighborhoods, is **City Caramels**. Walk in to this sanctum of sweet to be greeted by simple, lip-smacking treats. Eat your way through Bucktown (think coffee-inspired caramels with chocolate-covered espresso beans); Lincoln Square (toasted hazelnuts anybody?), and Pilsen (fragrant cinnamon, ancho chili, and *pepitas*)

with their respective caramel and candy cuts. However, Chicagoans who prefer to end their meals with a bite, should linger at **Pastoral**—hailed as one of the country's top spots for cheese. Their selection of classic and farmstead cheeses as well as fresh breads and olives is a local favorite, as are their weekend classes and tastings.

Fascinating Food Finds

An offbeat, quirky vibe is part of what makes Lakeview thrive. Testament to this is **The Flower Flat**, that cooks up a comforting breakfast and brunch in an actual flower shop. Meanwhile, **Uncommon Ground** is as much a restaurant serving three meals a day, as it is a coffee shop known for its musical acts. During the months between June through September, stop by on Friday evenings to tour America's first certified organic rooftop garden before tasting its bounty on your plate downstairs.

ROSCOE VILLAGE

The Landshark Lager Oyster Festival attracts folks to Roscoe Village each September with Irish and American music, plenty of beer, and a certain mollusk believed to have aphrodisiac qualities. Homesick New Yorkers and transplants take note: This neighborhood is also home to **Apart Pizza**, Chicago's very own homage to the thin-crust pie, though you might be wise to refrain from admitting how much you enjoyed it. Remember, this is a true find and guilty pleasure in deep-dish land.

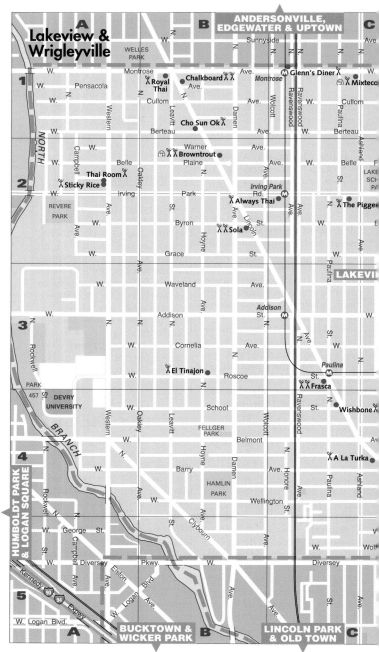

Lakeview & Wrigleyville

ANDERSONVILLE, EDGEWATER & UPTOWN

Royal Thai
Chalkboard
Glenn's Diner
Mixteco
Cho Sun Ok
Browntrout
Thai Room
Sticky Rice
Always Thai
The Pigge
Sola
El Tinajon
Frasca
Wishbone
A La Turka

WELLES PARK
REVERE PARK
LAKEVI
DEVRY UNIVERSITY
FELLGER PARK
HAMLIN PARK

HUMBOLDT PARK & LOGAN SQUARE
BUCKTOWN & WICKER PARK
LINCOLN PARK & OLD TOWN

TRUMAN COLLEGE

D

W. Sunnyside Ave.

CLARENDON PARK

E

41

N

F

Montrose

Montrose Dr.

W. Montrose

Montrose Harbor

1

GRACELAND

CEMETERY

Buena Ave.

WAVELAND AVENUE GOLF COURSE

LAKE

MICHIGAN

Irving Park Rd.

WUNDERS CEMETERY

HEBREW CEMETERY

LUTHERAN CEMETERY

W. Byron St.

TAC Quick

Sheridan

Pizza Rustica

W. Sheridan Rd.

LINCOLN PARK

2

GILL PARK

Hearty

Grace

W. Waveland

WRIGLEYVILLE

Addison

WRIGLEY FIELD

Southport Grocery

Chen's

Addison St.

Majestic

3

Cornelia

Newport Ave.

Home Bistro

Chicago Diner

Roscoe

P.S. Bangkok

Belmont Harbor

Thai Classic

W. Buckingham Pl.

School

Kanela

Aldine

Melrose St.

Belmont

Ann Sather

New Peking

Briar Pl.

Melanthios Greek Char House

izakaya

Barry

Fish Bar

Chilam Balam

DMK Burger Bar

Wellington

Oakdale Ave.

erwin

La Creperie

Willows

4

George St.

Wolfram St.

Surf St.

Pkwy.

Diversey

Diversey Pkwy.

5

Schubert Ave.

LINCOLN PARK

Wrightwood

JONQUIL PARK

Wrightwood Ave.

North Pond

D

E

F

● Hotel

● Restaurant

131

A La Turka

C4

3134 N. Lincoln Ave. (bet. Barry & Belmont Aves.)

Phone: 773-935-6101

Web: www.alaturkachicago.com

Prices: $$

Lunch & dinner daily

🚇 Paulina

Feel like the ruler of your own Ottoman Empire at this beguiling, if somewhat kitschy, Turkish restaurant, where the attentive and accommodating staff treat everyone like a sultan. From the kilim-covered pillows and the Bedouin tent-style curtains to the vivid colors, this lively spot is a true feast for the eyes. There is even a small front area where diners can kick off their heels and sit akimbo among the many silk pillows strewn across the floor.

A La Turka's feast is not just for the eyes, though. The Turkish and Mediterranean cuisine is both authentic and delightful, perhaps including a delicious meze of grape leaves stuffed with currants and pine nuts served alongside fantastic pita bread. Impressive entrées include the tender grilled kebabs.

Always Thai

C2

1825 W. Irving Park Rd. (bet. Ravenswood & Wolcott Aves.)

Phone: 773-929-0100

Web: www.alwaysthaichicago.com

Prices: 🍴🍴

Lunch & dinner daily

🚇 Irving Park (Brown)

Nestled under the Brown Line, Always Thai is more than just Thai. With satay, curries, edamame, tempura, and *shu mai* on the menu, it is a pan-Asian eatery, with a substantial take-out business for neighborhood residents. The room, which seats about 40, isn't fancy, but a colorful mural brightens the scene. *Nam sod* (ginger salad) is served in a fun, footed bowl, with a slightly sweetened lime dressing and is a light, unexpected start to the meal. *Pad kee mao* needs an extra kick from the chili sauce on the table but is a tasty dish of drunken noodles, served with plump shrimp. There isn't a specific regional focus to the menu here, but there aren't many missteps either, making Always Thai a good choice for post-Cubs games or a casual dinner.

Ann Sather

Scandinavian ✕

909 W. Belmont Ave. (bet. Clark St. & Wilton Ave.)

Phone: 773-348-2378   Lunch daily
Web: www.annsather.com
Prices: 💰   🚇 Belmont (Brown/Red)

The cinnamon rolls served at this Swedish bakery and restaurant could rival deep-dish pizza as the iconic Chicago food—that's how strongly locals feel about them.

But those hot, fresh rolls glazed with sugar aren't the only reason breakfast-goers flock here. Despite the large volume of business Ann Sather does, the kitchen still pays attention to every detail. The roast duck comes out greaseless, and topped with the traditional sweet yet tart lingonberry sauce. Meats, pickled herring, Swedish meatballs, homemade sauerkraut with caraway seeds, and excellent spaetzle are all cooked to perfection, so a sampler plate is a good choice for the indecisive. The bottomless cups of coffee are an added bonus, as are a few more of those cinnamon rolls to-go.

Browntrout

B2

American ✕✕

4111 N. Lincoln Ave. (bet. Belle Plaine & Warner Aves.)

Phone: 773-472-4111   Lunch Sun
Web: www.browntroutchicago.com   Dinner Wed – Mon
Prices: $$ 🚇 Irving Park (Brown)

"If you give a man a fish", as the saying goes...Well, Chef Sean Sanders happened upon a memorable fish on his New Zealand honeymoon, and the rest is history. Elegantly easygoing, this darling is adored by locals who may linger at the bar, bare tables, or central communal console.

Everything about this fly-fishing retreat feels crisp, from crimson and espresso walls hung with serene oils to sketched chalkboards listing prix-fixes and tasting menus (offered Sunday to Thursday). Divided into "smalls" and "bigs," this ever-changing menu populated with sustainable and organic products may include dishes like a "small" shaved pumpkin salad with Jack cheese, apples, pistachios, and Concord grape vinaigrette; or a "big" 12-hour roasted pork shoulder.

Chicago ▶ Lakeview & Wrigleyville

Chalkboard

Contemporary

B1

4343 N. Lincoln Ave. (bet. Montrose & Pensacola Aves.)

Phone: 773-477-7144	Lunch Sun
Web: www.chalkboardrestaurant.com	Dinner Wed – Mon
Prices: $$	Montrose (Brown)

Yes, there is a chalkboard (a big one), and it is where to go for the details on the contemporary Americana fare. Gilbert Langlois lovingly prepares an astonishing array of dishes that can include everything from homemade pâté and refreshing watermelon salad, to blackened catfish and Indiana plum duck. If the wonderfully crunchy and juicy fried chicken, served Southern-style with braised greens and buttermilk mashed potatoes, is available, order it!

The dining room, complete with white-framed mirrors, tiled floors, and striped banquettes, calls to mind a European tea room. No surprise, since afternoon tea is served on weekends. Polite and professional service is complemented by Chef Langlois, who often makes the rounds and chats up customers.

Chen's

Asian

E3

3506 N. Clark St. (bet. Cornelia Ave. & Eddy St.)

Phone: 773-549-9100	Dinner nightly
Web: www.chenschicago.com	
Prices:	Addison (Red)

Almost anything that sits in the shadow of the beloved Wrigley Field could draw a crowd. One of the charms of the neighborhood is that there's always someone out and about. But the twenty- and thirty-somethings who live in the area flock here not just because of its fun, convenient location, but because Chen's serves up solidly satisfying Chinese food. Best-sellers include sesame plates, like the chicken sesame platter with crispy chicken coated in a sweet and spicy glaze of honey, garlic, and pepper, topped with toasted sesame seeds. The hot and sour soup may not be at all authentic, but has the signature punch, thanks to a splash of vinegar and white pepper. There is also a short list of sushi for those who crave a taste of Japan with their Chinese delights.

Chicago Diner

 Chicago ▶ Lakeview & Wrigleyville

E3

Vegetarian ✗

3411 N. Halsted St. (at Roscoe St.)

Phone: 773-935-6696
Web: www.veggiediner.com
Prices: ☜

Lunch & dinner daily

Addison (Red)

This small, tightly packed dining room features retro red tables lined with stainless steel, black vinyl chairs, rustic pine booths, and, when weather permits, a large outdoor garden for dining alfresco.

The garden's luscious and the neighborhood is convenient to Wrigley Field and all manner of North Side attractions. But people come here for the ample vegetarian menu. Since 1983, the kitchen has specialized in dishes with faux meats. This is where former carnivores come to satisfy a craving, such as the gyros seasoned like lamb and served with vegan-friendly *tzatziki*. Other favorites include the Fib Rib and Radical Reuben sandwiches. The Chicago Diner's sumptuous baked goods are available around town.

Chilam Balam

F4

Mexican

3023 N. Broadway (bet. Barry & Wellington Aves.)

Phone: 773-296-6901
Web: www.chilambalamchicago.com
Prices: $$

Dinner Tue – Sat

Wellington

Named after the Mayan prophecy predicting the end of the world in 2012, this may be your last chance to enjoy Chilam Bilam's fabulous food. Chef Chuy Valencia invokes a green and local philosophy at his subterranean hot spot that seems to be always buzzing with a crowd. Chilam Balam is tight, so if you spot a seat, nab it! The surrounding exposed brick is enriched by paints and wall sconces, and *estrellas* hang above noisy groups; but a tiny four-seat bar in the back reveals a semi-open kitchen where ladies in colorful bandanas toil away.

The deal is BYOB, so bring your mezcal to sip alongside seasonal Mexican plates like shiitake mushroom empanadas; *huitlacoche* ravioli with pumpkin seed-cream sauce; and grilled pork ribs with a honey-pasilla pepper sauce.

135

Chizakaya

Japanese

D4

3056 N. Lincoln Ave. (bet. Barry & Wellington Aves.)

Phone: 773-697-4725
Web: www.chizakaya.com
Prices:

Lunch & dinner Tue – Sat

 Paulina

What reads like a standard ramen joint at lunch turns into a hopping *izakaya* at sundown, where an upbeat soundtrack sways the hanging light bulbs and fresh-faced Chicagoans pass small plates up and down the communal tables in the back room. Tilted ceiling panels in the main dining room boast murals featuring modern interpretations of classic Japanese art and iconography, a fitting comparison given the contemporary twists on faithful *izakaya* fare.

Dishes showcase a range of flavors and textures: *takoyaki* with tender octopus meld with spicy mayo and bonito flakes; and skewered *kushi yaki* like chicken gizzards, beef tongue, and Wagyu with wasabi and lime go quickly. Refreshment comes with a tangy strawberry-yuzu sorbet that nicely finishes the savory fare.

Cho Sun Ok

Korean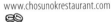

B1

4200 N. Lincoln Ave. (at Berteau Ave.)

Phone: 773-549-5555
Web: www.chosunokrestaurant.com
Prices:

Lunch & dinner daily

 Irving Park (Brown)

Cho Sun Ok is not just OK, it's one of those places you either love or hate. The lovers are here for their flavorfully authentic Korean food, while haters can't get past the gruff service. But really, who cares when you can grill your own meat and pair it with the best of their *banchan*, like spicy kimchi, seaweed salad, and glazed roasted potatoes?

Honey-toned floors and furnishings impart a cozy feel and couple harmoniously with their highly regarded soups and stews. Between the small smattering of tables, find big flavors in delicacies like *maduguk*, a peppery beef soup bobbing with tender *mandu*, dried seaweed, and scallions; *suhn dubu*, a soft tofu stew with mixed seafood; and *nakji bokkeum*, octopus stir-fried with vegetables in a fiery sauce.

DMK Burger Bar

A m e r i c a n

E4

2954 N. Sheffield Ave. (at Wellington Ave.)

Phone: 773-360-8686

Web: www.dmkburgerbar.com

Prices:

Lunch & dinner daily

🚇 Wellington

Want a stellar burger? Hit DMK Burger Bar, brainchild of David Morton (of steakhouse fame) and Michael Kornick (mk). Grab a seat at the lengthy bar or cop a squat on an old church pew and admire concrete floors contrasting chocolaty-purple pressed-tin ceilings. What this place lacks in comfort, it makes up for in comfort food.

Follow the locals, and order by number. Perhaps #11: sheep's milk feta, olive tapenade, and *tzatziki* atop a grass-fed lamb patty; or go for #3: beef topped with pastrami, Gruyère, sauerkraut, and remoulade. Cross over to the bad side and pair your sammie with hand-cut gourmet fries. And for a fine finale, slurp up a cold brew or homemade soda.

If you're in a seafood state of mind, lil sib Fish Bar next door will sate that ache.

El Tinajon

G u a t e m a l a n

B3

2054 W. Roscoe St. (bet. Hoyne & Seeley Aves.)

Phone: 773-525-8455

Web: N/A

Prices:

Lunch & dinner daily

🚇 Paulina

A mainstay of the residential Roscoe Village neighborhood, El Tinajon offers authentic Guatemalan dishes. The bright, friendly décor includes Mayan handicrafts throughout the storefront. Bring an appetite and focus on the well-made dishes. Perhaps start with the *yucca con ajo*, tender cassava in a rich garlic butter sauce. Do not skip the *jocon cobanero*, a soulful and tart green chicken and potato stew with elegant tomatillo flavor. Each element of the stew is cooked perfectly and sided with colorful rice; it's a positively lovely dish. *Rellenitos* make a unique and enjoyable finish of rich plantains stuffed with cinnamon and chocolate sweetened black beans.

The appealing breakfast menu provides a promising start to any gray, winter day.

erwin

American ✗✗

American ✗✗

E5

2925 N. Halsted St. (bet. George St. & Oakdale Ave.)

Phone: 773-528-7200
Web: www.erwincafe.com
Prices: $$

Lunch Sun
Dinner Tue – Sun
 Wellington

Former public school teachers turned restaurateurs, husband-and-wife team Erwin and Cathy Drechsler have been earning top marks for their charming American café since 1994. This duo knows how to make everyone feel welcome—even the birds tempted by the eclectic birdhouses in the front window are greeted with smiles.

The gourmet comfort food perfectly complements this cozy restaurant, where a mural of blue skies and Chicago rooftops gives the impression of perpetual summer. Meanwhile, the kitchen offers a scrumptious slice of Americana with a caramelized onion tart filled with blue cheese, walnuts, and sage; cornmeal-crusted whitefish with quinoa and sweet potatoes; or a duck confit and basil sausage over parsnip purée with bacon, cabbage, and apples.

Fish Bar

Seafood ✗

E4

2956 Sheffield Ave. (at Wellington Ave.)

Phone: 773-687-8177
Web: www.fishbarchicago.com
Prices: $$

Lunch & dinner Tue – Sun

 Wellington

Sidled up next to its sibling, the DMK Burger Bar, this good-time seafood shack does it up right. The atmosphere is light and casual: old metal stools line a long wooden bar, strips of weathered wood panel the walls, and a table is set beneath the polished hull of a canoe.

Daily seafood dishes come raw (tartares, ceviches, and carpaccios), grilled, and fried; while soups, bisques, and chowders warm the belly. Tasty sandwiches run the gamut from lobster roll to fried oysters to crab cake. Dive into a plate of crispy rock shrimp, lightly breaded and tossed in a spicy *sriracha* mayo and fresh *tobiko*; or a Ball jar loaded with a refreshing ceviche of corvine, pineapple, Serrano chilies, avocado, cucumber, lime and cilantro, served up with warm crackers.

Frasca

C3 Italian 🍴🍴

3358 N. Paulina St. (at Roscoe St.)

Phone: 773-248-5222
Web: www.frascapizzeria.com
Prices: $$

Lunch Sat – Sun
Dinner nightly
🚇 Paulina

Frasca isn't your usual pizza place. There are no red checkered tablecloths, and no guys in white tees hurling dough in the air—this respite wears a refined country-casual look. On warm nights, the patio is packed with patrons, while the comfortable dining room beckons during colder months. With nine varieties and a comprehensive toppings menu, Frasca is at its core a pizzeria and wine bar, but entrées and pastas supplement the typical menu. Diners can tick off their choices on the farmer's table menu, which spotlights cheeses, cured meats, and bruschette. This gem doesn't take itself too seriously, and in fact, offers such capricious takes on the holidays as Guinness crust pizzas on St. Patrick's Day and Mexican-topped pizzas on Cinco de Mayo.

Glenn's Diner

C1 American 🍴

1820 W. Montrose Ave. (bet. Ravenswood & Wolcott Aves.)

Phone: 773-506-1720
Web: www.glennsdiner.com
Prices: $$

Lunch & dinner daily

🚇 Montrose (Brown)

Find this oddball diner nestled under the Brown Line, with its alfresco tables, and interior cereal box décor. Glenn's aims to be an affordable, neighborhood haunt uniting two groups that don't usually mingle in the same circle—fresh seafood and cold cereal anyone? To further illustrate this, blackboards throughout display daily seafood specials.

On most days the menu proffers more than 25 kinds of cereal (Trix to Cheerios), and 16 fish forms from barramundi to crab cakes. Dining on a budget? Come during the week for all-you-can-eat specials; savory eggs and sweet baked goodies (pies perhaps?) help complete the menu on those days when neither cereal nor fruits from the sea will do. The restaurant is BYOB, so bring a bottle to pair with the Fruity Pebbles.

Hearty

American XX

E2

3819 N. Broadway (bet. Grace St. & Sheridan Rd.)

Phone:	773-868-9866	Lunch Sun
Web:	www.heartyboys.com	Dinner Wed – Sun
Prices:	$$	🚇 Sheridan

Dan Smith and Steve MacDonagh, affectionately known as the Hearty Boys, aren't out sleuthing and solving mysteries. Instead of chasing crimes, these two are mixing mayhem in the kitchen. Their food revisits American trailer park classics—these dishes aren't anything you've torn from *Good Housekeeping*. Rather, they advertise a ramped up and gourmet repertoire. Start with playful spins on deviled eggs or shrimp and grits, then move on to the beer-braised pork belly with pumpkin spaetzle and caraway roasted Brussels sprouts. It might have German roots, but it's all Hearty Boy flair.

From the repurposed soda cans fashioned into flowers to the black wood floors and aquamarine tiled mahogany bar, Hearty's edgy mien is perfect for the swank crowd.

Home Bistro

American XX

E3

3404 N. Halsted St. (at Roscoe St.)

Phone:	773-661-0299	Dinner Tue – Sun
Web:	www.homebistrochicago.com	
Prices:	$$	🚇 Belmont (Brown/Red)

Home Bistro (HB for those in the know) is a chipper American bistro fixed up with orange faux-finished walls cradling framed mirrors, artwork, and painted quotes. In keeping with this ideal, the staff is particularly hospitable and kind. The tight-knit team is proud of their bistro, and loyal fans keep returning to this delicious den where everybody knows your name—as well as the names of servers and kitchen staff, all printed on the menu.

Here, comfort foods may have Euro flair but translate into all-American dishes like white anchovies atop a mound of arugula with creamy Yukon Golds; handmade fettuccine ribbons woven around deliciously seasoned duck sausage and Parmesan sprinkles; and a piping hot fruit bread pudding trickled with whipped cream.

Kanela

E4

A m e r i c a n ✕

3231 N. Clark St. (bet. Belmont Ave. & School St.)

Phone: 773-248-1622
Web: www.kanelachicago.com
Prices:

Lunch daily

Belmont (Brown/Red)

With an array of options devoted to the most important meal of the day, Kanela helps its Lakeview neighbors break the fast every morning and afternoon. Its mellow java brown interior is a haven for the unhurried, but speedy patrons can grab a quick jolt at the tiled bar in the corner, proudly pouring Austria's Julius Meinl coffee.

Whether starving for savory bites like freshly griddled homemade chicken sausage flecked with herbs and spices, or sweeter plates like banana split crêpes with strawberries, bananas, and Nutella—or a little of both—Kanela delivers. A double stack of French toast stuffed with blueberry-studded Greek yogurt and topped with apple-jalapeño chutney simultaneously sates every craving with just the right amount of heat.

La Creperie

F5

F r e n c h ✕

2845 N. Clark St. (bet. Diversey Pkwy. & Surf St.)

Phone: 773-528-9050
Web: www.lacreperieusa.com
Prices:

Lunch & dinner daily

Diversey

One of the world's greatest culinary pleasures can be found in the simple crêpe, marrying your favorite sweet or savory ingredients and a paper-thin pancake in perfect, melted bliss. La Creperie knows the value of this French specialty and has been serving them since 1972. Family-run, this place feels comfortably lived-in with its weathered plank flooring and retro French travel posters.

The menu includes a selection of appetizers, sandwiches, and brunch items, but the crêpes are really why everyone is here. There is a dizzying array of choices from the simple chicken and goat cheese in a buckwheat crêpe, to more unusual, like coq au vin or bœuf Bourguignon. Just don't forget dessert, perhaps filled with chocolate, coconut, or crème caramel.

Melanthios Greek Char House

Greek ✗✗

F4

3116 N. Broadway (bet. Barry Ave. & Briar Pl.)

Phone: 773-360-8572
Web: www.melanthiosgreekcharhouse.com
Prices: $$

Lunch & dinner daily

You won't have any trouble finding such an anchor on this stretch of Broadway—just look for the building that appears as if it were transplanted from Greece. It's an all-around good time at Melanthios, where high spirits reign and the staff makes you feel like *en famille*. Whether you dine outside, or retire indoors–where whitewashed walls, ceiling fans, and a brick fireplace exude a rustic air–brace for a gleeful affair.

One glance at this menu, and it's enough to bring tears to your *yia yia's* eyes. Oldies but goodies like moussaka, *saganaki, taramasalata,* and spanakopita; as well as the glistening goodness of the rotisserie-cooked gyros feature among a gamut of traditional Greek dishes. Come on weekends for whole roasted lamb or pig.

Mixteco Grill

Mexican ✗

C1

1601 W. Montrose Ave. (at Ashland Ave.)

Phone: 773-868-1601
Web: N/A
Prices: 💰💰

Lunch Sat – Sun
Dinner Tue – Sun
🚇 Montrose (Brown)

Set on a stretch of Montrose that houses everything from a retro electronics store to a pilates studio, Mixteco lives up to its name, offering a delightful mix of Mexican specialties. This grill isn't about burritos and quesadillas. Instead, Mixteco dishes up fab regional Mexican cooking that hungry diners lap up as if it were going out of fashion.

The easygoing 'tude and warm flavor make this resto a favorite of neighborhood denizens and deal seekers. Choose from a plethora of deliciousness including *cochinita pibil*—a slow roasted pork with achiote and sour orange juice; *sopes di pollo*, corn masa boats floating with chicken, *mole*, and sesame seeds; or sinful *crepas de cajeta*—that is if you haven't already gorged on the tortilla chips.

New Peking

F4

Chinese ✗

3132 N. Broadway (bet. Barry Ave. & Briar Pl.)

Phone: 773-528-1362
Web: N/A
Prices:

Lunch & dinner daily

🚇 Belmont (Brown/Red)

 Looking for a low-key evening chowing on cheap Chinese? Swing by this casual Lakeview spot for tasty Beijing specialties, steamy soups, and homemade noodles. The well-kept space is small–with seating for about forty–spotlighting glass-topped tables, and black framed chairs with turquoise cushions atop a grey carpet.

Subtle flavors punctuate a plentiful menu: start off with a sizzling rice soup (listen to the puffed rice crackle when the server pours a flavorful broth into the bowl), swimming with whole pea pods, pounded white chicken, super fresh shrimp, and served with a zingy chili sauce. Offerings include your pick of protein in popular dishes such as lobster sauce, plum sauce, *kung pao*, or Hunan black bean sauce. Service is friendly and attentive.

The Piggery

C2

American ✗

1625 W. Irving Park Rd. (at Marshfield Ave.)

Phone: 773-281-7447
Web: www.thepiggerychicago.com
Prices: $$

Lunch & dinner daily

🚇 Irving Park (Brown)

 If the name isn't obvious enough, vegans should steer clear of The Piggery, a gastronomic temple to all things porcine. Kitschy pig paraphernalia on walls and shelves throughout the sports bar compete for attention with multiple flat screen TVs; even the striated wood floors could pass as bacon-inspired if you look long enough.

Pick your piggy poison from the ample menu. Firecrackers, a house specialty of cream cheese-stuffed and bacon-wrapped jalapeños, are manageably spicy and offer more than greasy heat. Slabs of tender ribs basted in house-made barbecue sauce are heady without any cloying sweetness, but if a few green leaves are needed, a pulled pork salad might do the trick. Take a break from the salt with a slice of sweet apple pie for dessert.

Pizza Rustica

P i z z a ✗

3913 N. Sheridan Rd. (bet. Byron & Dakin Sts.)

Phone:	773-404-8955	Lunch & dinner
Web:	www.pizzarusticachicago.com	Wed – Mon
Prices:	⬤⬤	🚇 Sheridan

Before hitting a Cubs game, stop at Pizza Rustica just blocks from Wrigley Field. Golden curtains dress the front windows, and local artistry adorns the walls along with chalkboards touting the days specials. Regulars saddle up to the black tiled bar; follow suit or pull up an aquamarine upholstered chair to your table.

This BYOB serves up rectangular Roman-style pizza. Skip the overdressed salad and head straight for a four-sided pie; orders come by the slice, half, or whole pie. The half is a hefty portion, and the whole is a crowd pleaser. Try the Half Tutta, affectionately called "Garbage Pizza," topped with sausage, pepperoni, mushrooms, black olives, and blue cheese, piled on their signature buttery crust.

A move across the street is in the works.

P.S. Bangkok

Thai ✗✗

3345 N. Clark St. (bet. Buckingham Pl. & Roscoe St.)

Phone:	773-871-7777	Lunch & dinner Tue – Sun
Web:	www.psbangkok.com	
Prices:	⬤⬤	🚇 Belmont (Brown/Red)

In the bustling heart of Lakeview–not far from the Dunkin' Donuts parking lot which is a 24-7 underage hippie magnet–the warm and clean dining room of P.S. Bangkok has been welcoming patrons for more than 25 years. Disciples of this Thai treasure get matching floral upholstery, soft rock music, and enticing aromas.

Fresh ingredients are a hallmark of the kitchen, which churns out a range of Thai-American classics like spring rolls and noodle dishes. But if bodacious, don't turn away as the menu also showcases more unusual items like red corn curry and lotus blossom curry floating with coconut milk and cabbage petals cradling seafood. The green papaya salad (dressed in lime and green chilies) pops in your mouth with carrot and green bean strips.

Royal Thai

B1

Thai ✗

2209 W. Montrose Ave. (bet. Bell Ave. & Leavitt St.)

Phone: 773-509-0007 Lunch & dinner Wed – Mon
Web: www.royalthaichicago.com
Prices: 🍪🍪 🔲 Western (Brown)

Royal Thai has long been a family-run standby that is inviting, cordial, well maintained, and very friendly. Glass-topped tables are dressed with silk runners embroidered with elephants and padded menu binders—their orangey hues match the assortment of plump goldfish swimming through the room's towering fish tank.

The cooking here sticks to the classics, and although the menu does not reveal uncommon regional specialties, it is all tasty and spiced to your liking. *Som tum* arrives as a fresh and crunchy green papaya salad that is mouthwateringly sweet, tart, and pungent; *tom yum* soup is bracingly seasoned with lemongrass, lime, and chili; and a crisped and golden brown deep-fried fillet of Idaho trout is dressed with a brightly flavored tamarind sauce.

Sola

B2

Contemporary ✗✗

3868 N. Lincoln Ave. (at Byron St.)

Phone: 773-327-3868 Lunch & dinner daily
Web: www.sola-restaurant.com
Prices: $$ 🔲 Irving Park (Brown)

Chef/owner Carol Wallack was known and admired for Deleece, the Irving Park eatery where she cooked before Sola. Here she brings a more southern Californian/Hawaiian vibe to the city's north side (note: the address is on Lincoln, but the entrance is on Byron.)

Virtual travel to the tropics is possible through the Sola menu. Try the scallops, served with apple-crab risotto, beans, and apple-curry butter. Or the Kahlua potstickers, which are stuffed with slow-cooked pork and served with mango salsa. Even the cocktails are adventurous. The Wicked Whahini, for example, sounds far out with its fruit juices, vodka, star anise, and ground black pepper, but it works. For a deal, try the ingredient-themed prix-fixe menus offered during the week.

Southport Grocery

American ✗

D3

3552 N. Southport Ave. (bet. Addison St. & Cornelia Ave.)

Phone: 773-665-0100
Web: www.southportgrocery.com
Prices: ⊜⊜

Lunch daily

⊞ Southport

Open for breakfast and lunch, this sleek neighborhood bistro also offers (as the name suggests) enough homey dishes for take-away and extensive top-of-the-line ingredients to keep even the most finicky foodie happy. Locals love this place, which occasionally leads to long lines on weekends and lots of high-energy conversations inside.

The made-from-scratch vibe is apparent in all the dishes, providing a welcome alternative to greasy spoon breakfasts. The chopped salad with herbed buttermilk dressing is a meal unto itself. Sandwiches may include the roast beef melt, with pickled vegetables, smoked Swiss, and crispy shallots. Save room for the grilled coffee cake, stuffed with cream cheese and grilled until gooey—it's as decadent as it sounds.

Sticky Rice

Thai ✗

A2

4018 N. Western Ave. (at Cuyler Ave.)

Phone: 773-588-0133
Web: www.stickyricethai.com
Prices: ⊜⊜

Lunch & dinner daily

⊞ Irving Park (Blue)

Lots of heart went into decorating this hipster hangout, focused on the regional cuisine of Northern Thailand. Bright yellow and orange paint, huge wood carved flowers and screens make it the brightest Thai joint around. The same degree of heart goes into the food, prepared lovingly (and slowly) by the kitchen.

The menu stands out, and as one would hope given the name, the sticky rice is fantastic. A daily special might include super-tender baby cuttlefish with crispy tentacles accented by Thai basil, onions, ginger, and lemongrass. Their *larb* is piquant, made here with ground pork instead of the more commonly found chicken. Save room for desserts featuring guess what—more sticky rice—perhaps accompanied by some funkadelic durian.

TAC Quick

Thai ✗

E2

3930 N. Sheridan Rd. (at Dakin St.)

Phone: 773-328-5253   Lunch & dinner Wed – Mon
Web: www.tacquick.net
Prices: 🚇 Sheridan

It's a two-menu operation here at TAC Quick. One lists all the familiar Westernized favorites from beefy *nam tok* to soups, noodles, and spicy Chinese broccoli with slices of crispy pork belly, jalapeño, and garlic. And the second...well, it's a secret (sort of, given that it's posted on the website), but this is where Chef Itti really struts his stuff and garners a loyal following.

Fiery, wonderfully traditional, and infinitely adventurous dishes like Thai beef jerky; Issan fermented pork and rice sausage; "mouse ear" salad; and Kari curry with squid, shrimp, onions, and coconut milk are whipped up with aplomb. The word is out, so hop off the train one stop shy of Wrigley and join the heat-seekers for some Thai Authentic Cuisine.

Thai Classic

Thai ✗✗

E4

3332 N. Clark St. (bet. Buckingham Pl. & Roscoe St.)

Phone: 773-404-2000   Lunch & dinner daily
Web: www.thaiclassicrestaurant.com
Prices: 🚇 Belmont (Brown/Red)

Spotless and pristine, Thai Classic has remained a staple of this vibrant area of Lakeview for over 20 years now. Large windows anchor the dining room allowing for streams of natural night, and of course, plenty of people-watching opportunities. The menu chronicles not just Thai typicals like spring rolls, *satay*, salads, curries, rice and noodle dishes, but ventures beyond the classics with an array of special entrées. *Gai yaang* is a house specialty made with boneless Thai barbecued chicken, pounded flat and marinated in coconut milk and an enticing reserve of herbs and spices.

Another home run is the jungle curry, bathing with chicken, crisp vegetables, and spicy chili oil. The weekend offers an afternoon buffet perfect for bodies on a budget.

Thai Room

Thai

A2

4022 N. Western Ave. (at Cuyler Ave.)

Phone: 773-539-6150
Web: www.thairoomchicago.com
Prices: ⬤⬤

Lunch & dinner Tue – Sun

🚇 Irving Park (Blue)

Despite her old age, this Thai fixture is still pretty, prim, and proper. With such vibrant frills (burgundy carpets, dark wood-panels, and intricate woodwork), it is only fitting that the "room" tones it down with white-clothed tables topped with woven fabric and clear glass.

Upon entering, notice a sign (warning?) on the front door announcing a limited availability of mango sticky rice. Make a dash for it, and pray that the elderly entourage saved some for you. To the hum of soft music, glide through tasty Thai food like *sai gioong e-san*, sausages filled with ginger and cashews; *luuk chin tod*, meatballs licked with sweet 'n spicy sauce; and the house specialty, Thai Room catfish, flaky and fried, crowned with sautéed vegetables and green curry.

Wishbone

American

C4

3300 N. Lincoln Ave. (at School St.)

Phone: 773-549-2663
Web: www.wishbonechicago.com
Prices: ⬤⬤

Lunch daily
Dinner Tue – Sun
🚇 Paulina

From the wraparound counter with glimpses of a bustling kitchen to the booths and ample tables topped with comforting, all-American food, this place is just plain fun. Competence and comfort extend to the lightning-fast service, making it a favorite for larger groups and families.

Walls adorned with unusual artwork and a vast collection of chickens and roosters gives the place a quirky vibe. It's Southern with a twist and unique takes on American favorites. The counter is filled with regulars on a first-name basis, enjoying a limited all-day breakfast menu. Dinner offerings may include specials like smoky and spicy Cajun salmon served alongside perfect collard greens with smoked turkey. Or, get your Southern on with some shrimp and grits.

Lincoln Park & Old Town

LINCOLN PARK

History, commerce, and nature come together in these iconic Chicago districts. The eponymous park, running along the Lake Michigan shore, offers winter-weary Chicagoans an excuse to get outside. And to add to the outdoor fun, famed Lincoln Park keeps its patrons happy and frolicking with a splendid spectrum of outdoor cafés, restaurants (ranging from quick bites to the city's most exclusive reservations), and takeout spots perfect for assembling a picnic.

Populated by post-college roommates, young families, and affluent yuppies, Lincoln Park is a favorite amongst locals and visitors, no matter the time of the year. It includes more than a handful of designated historic districts, pre-Great Chicago Fire buildings, museums, shopping, music venues, and the famous (and free) Lincoln Park Zoo.

Delicious Dining

Well-heeled foodies make reservations to come here for some of the most exclusive restaurants in the city (**Charlie Trotter's**, **Alinea**, and **L20**, to name a few). During the weekend, the area is hopping, thanks to a combination of the theater, bar scene, and scores of apartment buildings that cater to the twenty- and thirty-somethings crowd. On Wednesdays and Saturdays in summer, the south end of the park is transformed into hipster-chef-foodie central during the **Green City Market**. With the objective to elevate the availability of top-notch produce, and to improve the connect between farmers and local producers to restaurants and food organizations, this market aims to educate the masses about high-quality food sourcing. (In winter it is held inside the Peggy Notebaert Nature Museum). Additionally, the market draws long lines thanks to its fresh meats, cheeses, and crêpes.

Best of Bakeries

Fans of the sweets made from local ingredients by **Floriole Café & Bakery** have reason to rejoice—Floriole now has a Lincoln Park storefront showcasing a lunch menu paired with daily specials. Also luring a pack of visitors are their perfect pastries, breakfast delights, sandwiches, salads, cookies, and sweet treats. Those with an affinity (or addiction) for all things baked, can now get them even when Green City is closed.

For other stomach-filling options outside of the market, try the heartwarming **Meatloaf Bakery**, where meat loaf and mashed potatoes are crafted into all manner of dishes, such as a cupcake-shaped "loaf" (with mashed potato icing). Other treats may include the *mother loaf, a wing and a prayer loaf, loaf-a-roma,* and the *no buns about it burger* *loaf.* Don't let the quirky titles fool you, because this may just be some of the best and most gratifying food in town. Lincoln Park is also a great place to satisfy that Chicago hot dog craving. Like many foods (Juicy Fruit, Cracker Jack, and Shredded Wheat, for example), it is said that the Chicago-style dog may have originated at the Chicago World's Fair and Columbian Exhibition (in 1893), although that provenance is not definitive. Others credit the Great Depression for its birth. One newcomer is the chef-driven **Franks 'n' Dawgs**. Bustling at most hours, this Lincoln Park gem employs fresh and locally-sourced ingredients featured in their fun and fine food. Look forward to delectable gourmet sausages, hand-crafted hot dogs, and artisan breads.

The Wieners Circle is as known for its late hours (as late as 5:00 A.M.) and purposefully rude service, as for its tasty repertoire of dogs and fries. Lincoln Park is one of the dog-friendliest areas around, but then what else would you expect from a neighborhood named after a park? Satisfy Fido's appetite as well as your own, with a stop at **Three Dog Bakery**, where the chef caters to canine customers.

A Perfect Quench

Wash down all that tasty grease at **Goose Island Brewery**, makers of the city's favorite local beers. Loop the Goose Canoe Tours (offered during the summer) gives you a view of the Chicago River island from which the brew is named. If you're still parched, visit the friendly and relaxed **Webster's Wine Bar**. Nab a seat on their streetfront patio, where you can enjoy a glass or two from their winning and expansive wine selection.

Healthy and Heavenly

It is a whole different ballgame at **Karyn's Fresh Corner and Raw Café**, a restaurant with a full vegan and raw menu. The adjacent **Fresh Corner Market** sells meals to-go, plus fresh juices and supplements. "Meatballs" are made from lentils, and "sloppy Joes" from soy protein, and the raw food experience is unlike anything else you've seen.

OLD TOWN

The Old Town quarter sports a few quaint cobblestoned streets that house the Second City comedy scene (now with a Zanies, too, for even more laughs); June's annual must-see (and must-shop) Old Town Art Fair; the Wells Street Art Fair; and places to rest with beers and a groovy jukebox, like the **Old Town Ale House**, which will bring back memories of your gran's living room. Wells Street is the neighborhood's main drag, and is where browsing should begin. Any epicurean shopping trip should also include the **Old Town Oil** for infused oils, aged vinegars, and excellent hostess gifts.

Finally, **The House of Glunz**, opened in 1888, is one of Chicago's oldest wine merchants. Prefer a sweeter vice? **The Fudge Pot** tempts passersby with windows full of toffee, fudge, and other house-made chocolaty goodness. Whether you smoke or not, the **Up Down Cigar** is worth a peek for its real cigar store Indian carving.

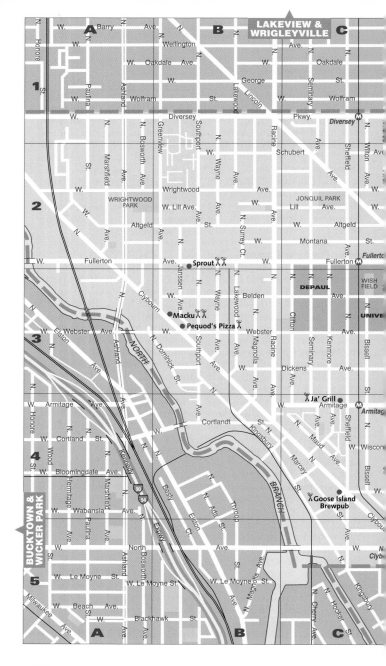

Hotel
Restaurant

D E F

1
2
3
4
5

W. Wellington Ave.
Oakdale Ave.
W. Surf St.
LINCOLN PARK
W. Diversey Pkwy.
Hai Yen
W. Schubert Ave.
Taj Darbar
attoush
W. Wrightwood Ave.
Del Seoul
Wrightwood Ave.
Frances' Deli
LINCOLN
Orchard
Deming
North Pond
PARK
Arlington Pl.
esta Mexicana
Ponzu Sushi
Bourgeois Pig Cafe
Fullerton
Aquitaine
a D'Citta
W. Belden Ave.
L2O
Mon Ami Gabi
W. Grant Pl.
Webster Ave.
LINCOLN PARK ZOO
Dickens Ave.
Riccardo Trattoria
Gemini Bistro
harlie otter's
Armitage Ave.
Rustic House
Wisconsin St.
South Pond
ka
Willow St.
Perennial Virant
inea
Menominee St.
LINCOLN PARK
OLD TOWN
Twin Anchors
Eugenie St.
Adobo Grill
no Wood Fired
Mizu
CHICAGO HISTORY MUSEUM
North Ave.
North Blvd. North Ave.
Sedgwick
Blackhawk St.
Burton Pl.
E. Banks St.
GOLD COAST
SANDBURG VILLAGE

LINCOLN PARK

NOTEBAERT NATURE MUSEUM

CONSERVATORY

THEATRE ON THE LAKE

LAKE MICHIGAN

NORTH AVENUE BEACH

North Pond

Diversey Harbor

Lake Shore Dr.

Broadway
Sheffield St.
Lake Shore Dr.
Clark
Lakeview Ave.
Stockton Dr.
Cannon Dr.
Lincoln Park West
Stockton Dr.
Cannon Dr.
Lake Shore Dr.
Geneva Terr.
Howe
Hudson
Cleveland
Larrabee
Mohawk
Orchard
Burling
Vine St.
Sedgwick
Wells
Wieland
Park
LaSalle
Clark
Dearborn
State
Astor
Pkwy.

OZ PARK

153

Adobo Grill

E5

1610 N. Wells St. (bet. Eugenie St. & North Ave.)

Phone: 312-266-7999
Web: www.adobogrill.com
Prices: $$

Lunch Sat – Sun
Dinner nightly
🔲 Sedgwick

Fun, festive, and flavorful, Adobo Grill is celebrated as a longtime Old Town favorite for good reason. Housed within a small building, it is at once cozy and lively. Everyone from local denizens to kids with their parents comes to this jamming place.

First, order a lip-smacking margarita with fresh lime and just a touch of Triple Sec. After a few sips, flag down one of the guacamole carts trolling the dining room. This house classic is made tableside and prepared with just the right amount of heat to suit your mild or wild taste buds. Terrific entrées are made even better alongside rich and smoky *frijoles puercos* and homemade tortillas for sopping up the extra sauce.

Aquitaine

D3

2221 N. Lincoln Ave. (bet. Belder & Webster Aves.)

Phone: 773-698-8456
Web: www.aquitainerestaurant.com
Prices: $$

Lunch Tue – Sun
Dinner nightly
🔲 Fullerton

According to Chef/partner Holly Willoughby, this elegant spot inherits its name from Eleanor of Aquitaine, queen consort of England and France in the 12th century. French-influenced dishes spruce up the mostly American, seasonally changing menu. The brooding, sexy interior is styled in charcoals and reds, with ornately designed wallpaper and a large, welcoming bar.

Get started with a *petite* tarte—a fluffy egg quiche loaded with portobello mushroom, sun-dried tomato, and goat cheese tucked into a crisp, buttery shell; and then dig into a pretzel roll, stuffed with roasted chicken, tomato, arugula, and truffle-lemon dressing. End with a tantalizing dessert, like amber cake, layers of lemon madeleines and custard topped with caramel and pistachio.

Alinea ✿✿✿

Contemporary ✗✗✗✗

1723 N. Halsted St. (bet. North Ave. & Willow St.)

Phone:	312-867-0110	Dinner Wed – Sun
Web:	www.alinea-restaurant.com	
Prices:	**$$$$**	🚇 North/Clybourn

Lara Kastner

Maybe it's easiest to think of Alinea as one part restaurant, two parts culinary art installation of mind-blowing ingenuity, challenging every sense with an unparalleled interplay of science and expectation. Or maybe—amid young couples and lengthy instructions—it just feels new, like sitting at the children's table at some impossibly sleek family event. Whether you approach Chef Grant Achatz's storied modernist cuisine with avant-garde intellect or whimsy, you will likely leave here claiming to have seen the future. And it was beautiful.

This exciting and delicious experience exists nowhere else in America and isn't for everyone; the staff's tendency to guide diners through each taste and technique is either welcomed or a bit too intrusive for some gourmands. Yet there is so much that the unsuspecting palate might miss.

Halibut is a study in white when paired with garlic, lemon, and parsnip; but add other spectacularly present elements stripped of their hues (vanilla, pepper, coffee, licorice) for a dish that is a phenomenon, nuanced and magical. The chocolate finale is a performance starring glass tubes, silicone sheets, liquid nitrogen, unadulterated pleasure, and maybe Grant himself.

Boka

Chicago ▶ Lincoln Park & Old Town

1729 N. Halsted St. (bet. North Ave. & Willow St.)

Phone:	312-337-6070	Dinner nightly
Web:	www.bokachicago.com	
Prices:	$$$	North/Clybourn

Jeff Kauck

Wind your way through the courtyard entry edged by flowing water where couples might fork up nibbles on a balmy night, to arrive at the exposed-brick front bar and its smattering of leopard print-covered chairs. Take note of the clever cell phone nook near the hostess stand for hungry but busy clientele who just *have* to take that call. Under a tent of billowing white fabric, like a Frank Gehry building turned inside out, is the main dining room where dinner awaits.

And that dinner will be a parade of envelope-pushing ingredient pairings and creatively composed plates courtesy of Giuseppe Tentori, a chef eminently capable of coaxing big flavors out of restrained cooking. The small details are showstoppers throughout: amaranth, that hippie-dippie whole grain staple, becomes elegant when paired with braised baby artichokes and homemade *halloumi* cubes. *Vadouvan*-poached prawns steal the show from pan-roasted halibut with smoky bacon *espuma*; while a layer of toasted marshmallow fluff marries caramel ice cream and rich cashew-studded cake.

Degustation menus allow the chef to reprise some off-menu but all-time favorites, with the added bonus of a discount off the reserve wine list.

Bourgeois Pig Cafe

D2

Deli

738 W. Fullerton Pkwy. (at Burling St.)

Phone: 773-883-5282

Web: www.bpigcafe.com

Prices:

Lunch & dinner daily

Fullerton

Set in an old brownstone, "the Pig" (as locals call it) is steps away from DePaul University and the Children's Memorial Hospital, thereby luring a plethora of students, doctors, and neighborhood moms. Large chalkboards display a litany of delicious sandwich, panini, and dessert options; and given its bookish theme, it is only fitting that literary allusions are behind the dish names at this character-driven café in the heart of Lincoln Park.

Make sure you pick one of their new takes on old classics. Order at the cash register and your "Great Gatsby" will be delivered to your table upstairs. This twist on a club sandwich features focaccia filled with turkey, pesto, mayo, bacon, tomatoes, and Swiss grilled in a panini press to marry the flavors.

Del Seoul

D2

Korean

2568-2570 N. Clark St. (bet. Deming Pl. & Wrightwood Ave.)

Phone: 773-248-4227

Web: www.delseoul.com

Prices:

Lunch & dinner daily

Diversey

The Korean "street" food craze has hit the nation, but Del Seoul's moan-worthy delights are far beyond some passing fad. Thank the Jeon family for whipping up those intoxicating flavors into a menu of addictive fusion specialties, as well as *bulgogi* and *bahn mi*. Savory "Seoul style" dumplings are made from a 100-year old recipe, and *gamja* fries are smothered in kimchi, pork belly, and melted cheese.

And the tacos... oh, the tacos. Grilled white corn tortillas stuffed with chicken, spicy pork, braised beef *kalbi*, or sesame-chili shrimp, then crowned with cilantro-onion relish, chili-garlic salsa, and a secret slaw. Luckily, tacos are not too big, so try a variety. Order at the counter from the overhead video screen, take a number and grab a seat.

Charlie Trotter's ✿ ✿

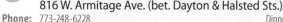

D4

Contemporary 𝗫𝗫𝗫

816 W. Armitage Ave. (bet. Dayton & Halsted Sts.)

Phone: 773-248-6228
Web: www.charlietrotters.com
Prices: $$$$

Dinner Tue – Sat

🚇 Armitage

Kipling Swehla

For the past quarter-century, Charlie Trotter's has been one of Chicago's great dining destinations. From its quaint townhouse in a swanky neighborhood, the restaurant exudes an understated elegance that smartly draws everyone's attention back to the plate. The gracious staff follows suit, as consummate professionals whose greatest wish is to better read your mind and please your palate. The clientele seems distinguished, as if everyone is rising to the occasion of dining here.

One may consider the multi-course menu to be an event—with notes of theatricality that ebb and flow and arc, leaving descriptions behind as they recall emotion. Shimmering layers of Belgian endive with pine nuts and green cardamom are pure and suddenly exotic. *Chawan mushi* marries Asian pear, dashi, quail egg, and tomato confit with the unbearable lightness of ethereal egg custard. A block of bison tenderloin is perfectly cooked to medium, dressed with ebony- and ivory-hued garnishes like candied espresso beans for an intense jolt. To end, let the blood orange sorbet return you to childhood—creamsicles anyone?

This kitchen has an incredible understanding of ingredients and the rare talent to elevate them to greatness.

Fattoush

Lebanese

D2

2652 N. Halsted St. (bet. Diversey Pkwy. & Wrightwood Ave.)

Phone: 773-327-2652
Web: www.fattoushrestaurant.com
Prices:

Dinner Wed – Mon

Fullerton

Blocks from DePaul University–amidst mega stores and bars–emerges this rare find of a place, where fresh, fragrant fare draws chowhounds craving an authentic Lebanese meal. In the main dining room, colorful walls display quaint depictions of pastoral life; while plain white paper covers a dozen plus tables. Prefer to park it on the floor? Take a seat downstairs in the sultry "souk," where lush carpets, pillows, and cushions surround a large table.

From tender vegetarian grape leaves (rice, basil, parsley, tomatoes, and chickpeas in a creamy dressing), to tasty gluten-free spinach pie (that's right, gluten-free!) offerings here are made to order, and with plenty of TLC. The lovely chef makes regular rounds and can be seen smiling and socializing.

Fiesta Mexicana

Mexican

D2

2423 N. Lincoln Ave. (bet. Fullerton Ave. & Halsted St.)

Phone: 773-348-4144
Web: www.fiestamexicanachicago.com
Prices:

Lunch & dinner daily

Fullerton

A long-time hangout for the twenty-somethings and young families living in Lincoln Park, Fiesta Mexicana lives up to the party-style atmosphere its moniker promises. The recently renovated space features a bar and a number of dining rooms, with a large mural of a Mexican mountain scene done in bright colors welcoming diners.

Guests are greeted with tasty chips and salsa and an expansive menu offering a cross-section of Tex-Mex, traditional Mexican, and Mexican-inspired fare. The combination platters are a solid way to sample the Tex-Mex choices; while chile poblano-spinach and artichoke *fundido* shows off the kitchen's creative juices. Opt for a starter rather than a dessert, as these are the weakest link.

Good value specials are offered at lunch.

Frances' Deli

D2

2552 N. Clark St. (bet. Deming Pl. & Wrightwood Ave.)

Phone: 773-248-4580
Web: www.francesdeli.com
Prices:

Lunch daily
Dinner Sat – Sun

Lincoln Parkers love this deli/diner with good reason. Snug and inviting in a well-worn sort of way, Frances' may be short on looks but is long on satisfaction. The line is out the door on weekends with a mix of students, locals, and young professionals.

Everyone flocks here for crowd-pleasing, gut-busting meals. The burgers, triple-decker sandwiches bursting with quality meats, and yummy breakfasts like challah French toast and omelets, could cure any hangover. Potato pancakes and blintzes are better than grandma's. You definitely won't have room, but milkshakes, malts, and sundaes are musts. That thick, icy, and exactly-as-it-should-be chocolate-peanut butter milkshake is seriously the bomb, though you'll need to lie down later.

Gemini Bistro

E3

2075 N. Lincoln Ave. (at Dickens Ave.)

Phone: 773-525-2522
Web: www.geminibistrochicago.com
Prices: $$

Dinner Tue – Sun

🚉 Armitage

An unfussy attitude meets a gleamingly chic design in this white-tiled flatiron building just off Lincoln Avenue's main drag. Ease a likely wait at the no-reservations spot with a cocktail like the margarita-esque Heater or Gemini lemonade over at the marble bar. Early birds can snag the prix-fixe menu along with a coveted sidewalk patio table.

Loosely inspired by its Mediterranean neighbors, Gemini's menu might unveil a generous fillet of flaky pan-roasted halibut napped in lobster sauce alongside fava bean and corn succotash; or pea-studded risotto accented with mint, black pepper, and a healthy dose of Parmigiano Reggiano.

One tip: consider the reasonable valet instead of risking a parking ticket in this permit-heavy neighborhood.

Goose Island Brewpub

C4

Gastropub

1800 N. Clybourn Ave. (at Willow St.)

Phone: 312-915-0071
Web: www.gooseisland.com
Prices:

Lunch & dinner daily

North/Clybourn

Microbreweries aren't a rarity these days, but for over 20 years, Goose Island has had both the brewing and the cooking down. Amid large kettles and brewmasters in boots fielding questions from novice beer makers, the focus here is obvious. Locals come for more than 20 beers on tap, but stay for serious snacks like spicy *sriracha* chicken wings, cheddar-jalapeño pretzels, and fried oysters.

The pork sausage sandwich is prepared with a fun twist, served with German Dusseldorf mustard and caramelized onions on a pretzel roll. That chocolate bark, too, has a surprise: it is made with dark Belgian chocolate, sea salt, bacon, and spent grain from the brewing process.

Responsible drinkers may want to grab a Green Line Growler of their favorite brew to-go.

Hai Yen

D1

Vietnamese ... (icons)

2723 N. Clark St. (bet. Diversey Pkwy. & Schubert Ave.)

Phone: 773-868-4888
Web: www.haiyenrestaurant.com
Prices: (icons)

Lunch Fri – Sun
Dinner nightly
Diversey

This friendly, attractive Vietnamese restaurant has all the traditional musts on its large menu. But the most fun dish that distinguishes Hai Yen from others is their signature, *bo la lot*. Listed under the "wraps" section of the menu, flavorful sausage-like rolls of ground beef and pork are enveloped in an aromatic leaf and then grilled. They arrive on a platter of fresh herbs, rice paper, and a bowl of hot water. Wet the rice paper to soften it, wrap up herbs and meat together, dunk in *nuoc cham*, and eat. Tasty, delicious, and fun!

There are plenty of other goodies to follow, such as the *cua rang muoi*—Vietnamese-style Dungeness crab stir-fried simply with caramelized onions, salt, pepper, and garlic.

A second location resides on West Argyle.

161

Ja' Grill

Jamaican ✗

 C4

1008 W. Armitage Ave. (bet. Kenmore & Sheffield Aves.)

Phone: 773-929-5375
Web: www.jagrill.com
Prices:

Lunch Fri – Sun
Dinner nightly
🚇 Armitage

 It is more than 1,700 miles from Chicago to Jamaica, but paradise feels right next door at Ja' Grill. Tucked into the upscale shopping mecca of Armitage Avenue, Ja' Grill welcomes visitors with Bob Marley belting from the speakers, a colorful décor with painted murals, and a large orange-lit bar proffering hair-raising drinks. The Jamaican flag shows this is the right place to make everything "cook and curry."
Jerk pork, served juicy, sweet, and tender with coconut-cooked "rice and peas" (peas equal kidney beans in Jamaica), cabbage, carrots, and plantains, is a standout. To spice it up, request the wonderfully hot pepper sauce. Watch your tongue on the delicious beef patties, which may burn you up as if delivered straight from the microwave.

Macku

Japanese ✗✗

B3

2239 N. Clybourn Ave. (bet. Greenview & Webster Aves.)

Phone: 773-880-8012
Web: www.mackusushi.com
Prices: $$

Dinner nightly

Sushi fans fall into two camps: east and west. There are those who love their westernized maki (spicy tuna anyone?) and those who go the traditional nigiri route. Whether you're a newbie or an aficionado, Macku has you covered.
This contemporary Japanese restaurant literally lays out every option; its neat display of fresh fish at the sushi bar is an enticing sign of what's to come. Start with the straightforward sushi favorites, like salmon, tuna, and yellowtail; or choose from the nice selection of specialty rolls, like the spicy spider roll with soft shell crab, *kanikami*, chili oil, avocado, and cucumber.
The menu may have it all, but this modern and stylish restaurant is small with just a sprinkling of tables and seats at the sushi bar.

L2O ❀

E3

2300 N. Lincoln Park West (bet. Belden Ave. & Fullerton Pkwy.)

Phone: 773-868-0002   Dinner nightly
Web: www.l2orestaurant.com
Prices: $$$$

Katherine Bryant

With the departure of Chef Laurent Gras, L2O is reincarnated as a new and very different restaurant, now helmed by Chef Francis Brennan. The shifts and modifications have been gradual, moving from intense creativity to a more approachable experience. Today's crowd is more lively than stuffy, with few suits in sight. The physical space itself is unchanged, with frosted glass panels, white leather chairs, inviting alcoves of crushed velvet and onyx tables all lending a sense of muted luxury and romance.

As the kitchen continues to evolve, it aims to operate at a very high level. Menu descriptions can sound straightforward, but that *tagliolini* may arrive as a beautiful twirl atop lobster-uni emulsion, beneath a dollop of osetra caviar. Desserts might feature a dramatic presentation of fresh raspberries, tapioca pearls, mascarpone sorbet, and a fluttering sheet of gold, swirled with warm yuzu "consommé."

Yet the road to reinvention can be bumpy, with service that is either well-informed and jovial, or flops into pretentiousness. This new kitchen may not thrill with the ingenuity of its former self, but is nonetheless pleasing with graceful renditions of refined contemporary cuisine.

Mizu

E5

Japanese

315 W. North Ave. (at Orleans St.)

Phone: 312-951-8880
Web: www.mizurestaurant.com
Prices: $$

Dinner nightly

 Sedgwick

This Lincoln Park Japanese restaurant is a real find. Chocolate brown banquettes line the walls, while white orb chandeliers cast a soft glow over the beige tiled floors of this contempo-chic gem. For the ultimate *izakaya* experience, visit the tatami room, located behind sliding wooden doors—it's the real McCoy, complete with the shoes-off sensibility, and mats for sitting on the floor.

The extensive menu lures all by offering a little bit of this (yakitori, their specialty) and a little bit of that (traditional and westernized sushi and sashimi). Oyster shooters, grilled squid, *gyoza*, soba—you name it, and they have it. Maki like the New Mexico with tuna, yellowtail, *tobiko*, avocado, and jalapeño, show the sushi chefs' creative touch.

Mon Ami Gabi

E3

French

2300 N. Lincoln Park West (at Belden Ave.)

Phone: 773-348-8886
Web: www.monamigabi.com
Prices: $$

Dinner nightly

Inside the historic Belden-Stratford (also home to L2O), Mon Ami Gabi is Lettuce Entertain You Enterprises' take on the classic French bistro. It is in fact the very picture of Paris–with a cozy, dark room displaying closely packed tables, vintage mirrors, and tiled floors–and recalls those quaint salons sitting across the Atlantic.

Up to five diners can choose to eat at the bar where they might opt for the delicious trout *Grenobloise*, a golden fillet topped with tangy capers, lemon supremes, and crusty cubed croutons. The menu is also chock-full of well-executed classics and may unveil such sumptuous dishes as macaroni gratin married with creamy béchamel and topped with a heavy cap of Gruyère; and an apple tarte Tatin with vanilla whipped cream.

North Pond

Contemporary ✗✗

E2

2610 N. Cannon Dr.

Phone: 773-477-5845
Web: www.northpondrestaurant.com
Prices: $$$

Lunch Sun
Dinner Tue – Sun

Originally built as a shelter for Lincoln Park ice skaters, the charming Arts and Crafts bungalow housing North Pond now warms its guests with an elegantly pastoral setting for all seasons. Expansive windows throughout the several dining rooms play up the worthy view, and a roaring fireplace heightens the romance in colder months.

The menu puts the restaurant's ingredients-first philosophy front and center, with two-item titles for each dish that highlight the sustainable and seasonal produce on offer. Plates like "Monkfish, Fennel" feature a grilled center-cut monkfish steak alongside both braised and shaved raw fennel and a bouillabaisse reduction, a commendable example of the layers of complementary flavor and textural contrast found in each dish.

Pequod's Pizza

Pizza ✗

B3

2207 N. Clybourn Ave. (at Webster Ave.)

Phone: 773-327-1512
Web: www.pequodspizza.com
Prices: $$

Lunch & dinner daily

 Armitage

Ditch your diet, grab your fellow Blackhawk fans, and head into this Lincoln Park stalwart for some of the best pie in town. Christened in 1970 for Captain Ahab's whaling ship, Pequod's sails a smooth menu of bar food apps, hearty sandwiches (try the tender Italian beef with melted cheese and hot peppers), and fantastic pizzas.

Crusts range from thin- to deep-dish, but the specialty is the pan pizza, with its cake-like crust and halo of caramelized cheese that sticks to the sides of the pan. Toppings like spicy sausage and pepperoni are heaped on with abandon, as if the pizza makers are whipping up a pie to take home for themselves. Pequod's stays open till 2:00 A.M. most nights, so stop by for a late night nosh and ponder the great white whale.

Perennial Virant

E4

1800 N. Lincoln Ave. (at Clark St.)

Phone: 312-981-7000
Web: www.perennialvirant.wordpress.com
Prices: **$$**

Lunch Sat – Sun
Dinner nightly

Chef Paul Virant, of Western Springs' Vie, brings his reputation as Chicago's premier pickler and canner to do double duty at this convivial urban farmstead on the fringes of Lincoln Park. Tartan- and t-shirt-clad servers amble around oak tables, and Ball jars packed tight with preserves line the walls. One or two Currant Cobblers, with Buffalo Trace bourbon and oloroso sherry, and you'll join the boisterous crowd spilling from the lounge.

Tangy treasures abound in each dish: pickled peppers pep up laughing bird shrimp; smoked Sungold tomatoes crown *brûléed* walleye; and pickled snow peas blend with sweet onion vinaigrette on crispy *carnaroli* rice cakes. Live by the house motto and "eat what you can, can what you can't"—or just bring a doggy bag home.

Ponzu Sushi

E2

2407 N. Clark St. (bet. Arlington Pl. & Fullerton Pkwy.)

Phone: 773-549-8890
Web: www.ponzuchicago.com
Prices:

Lunch Mon – Thu
Dinner nightly
Fullerton

Tiny Ponzu Sushi seats just 36 people in its dining room, with room for just five more at the sushi counter. Yet, it is free of any complexes about being small. Colored walls, tablecloths, and napkins exude big personality and brighten the room.

What Ponzu lacks in size, it makes up for in selection. The menu is built around a foundation of sushi and rolls—including classic maki and many signature and specialty rolls. Custom maki are available (except on Friday and Saturday) as well as what they call *tsumiki*, their version of block-style sushi. Try the dragon roll; an inside out roll with shrimp tempura, avocado, and *tobiko* topped with slices of freshwater eel.

Non-sushi eaters dine on dishes from the kitchen like *gyoza*, tempura, donburi, or ramen.

Raj Darbar 😃

D2

Indian ✗

2660 N. Halsted St. (bet. Schubert & Wrightwood Aves.)

Phone: 773-348-1010   Dinner nightly
Web: www.rajdarbar.com
Prices: $$ 🔲 Diversey

This stretch of Halsted has seen its share of change, from college-kid hangouts to upscale boutiques to what was the world's first two-story Home Depot. Amidst this odd mix of retail you will find Raj Darbar, with its drab décor but seriously talented kitchen.

Alu tikki are a wonderful way to start: smooth and creamy (yet textured) seasoned potatoes create a casing for a chili-rubbed pea filling all dipped in chickpea batter and crisply fried. Tender *jheenga tandoori* is incredible; the shrimp is marinated in a mixture of yogurt, garlic, and ginger with the addition of spices then perfectly roasted in the tandoor. *Biryani*, *pudina paratha*, and *dum ki gobhi* are solid choices while *rasmalai* makes for a competent, creamy ending to a fragrant feast.

Riccardo Trattoria 😃

E3

Italian ✗✗

2119 N. Clark St. (bet. Dickens & Webster Aves.)

Phone: 773-549-0038   Dinner nightly
Web: www.riccardotrattoria.com
Prices: $$

Chef/owner Riccardo Michi's family is best-known for its swanky Bice restaurants. When Michi struck out on his own he brought along the family know-how, but he eschewed the fancy for the fuss-free. The result? The highly popular, yet casually chic Riccardo Trattoria.

Friendly, flirty waiters feed the charming vibe. Perfect for date night or group dinners, it offers a menu of authentic and reasonably priced Italian dishes, along with a well-edited wine list. Daily and seasonal specials vary, but dishes might include a black mussels Livornese in white wine and spicy tomato broth; or orecchiette with wild boar sausage, rapini, sun-dried tomatoes, and pecorino. Other nights might offer rich veal sweetbreads *scaloppine* with porcini and truffle sauce.

Rustic House

D4

American ✗✗

1967 N. Halsted St. (bet. Armitage Ave. & Willow St.)

Phone: 312-929-3227
Web: www.rustichousechicago.com
Prices: $$

Dinner Tue – Sun

 Armitage

Rustic House takes its name pretty seriously, marking its walls with burlap, building its bar with weathered barn planks, and hanging iron wheel chandeliers lit by pillar candles. But as befits its setting in a historic building, there's an edge of refinement to the rusticity, tweaking familiar tropes with a glamorous update.

The menu follows the same polished comfort food path; you'll find a juicy free-range organic chicken turning on the rotisserie each night, sometimes joined by a rack of veal or suckling pig.

Snack on thin kettle chips and homemade onion dip before spooning up chicken pot pie draped with a fluffy puff pastry blanket. Sauternes-soaked blueberry peach pie in an iron casserole is the perfect marriage of down-home and elegant.

Sono Wood Fired

D5

Pizza ✗✗

1582 N. Clybourn Ave. (bet. Halsted St. & North Ave.)

Phone: 312-255-1122
Web: www.sonowoodfired.com
Prices: $$

Dinner nightly

 North/Clybourn

Check out the curvaceous, Italian import attracting all that attention over there: she's quite a stunner. Of course, we're talking about the restaurant's eponymous centerpiece—that colorfully tiled, wood fired oven is the reason for all the buzz. Sono's space is styled in bare wood, latte colored walls, and exposed brick, with a lively, full service bar.

But the best spot in the house is at the six-seat wooden counter near the fiery gal herself. Bubbling hot, thin-crust pizzas are the name of the game—whether topped with spinach, garlic, goat cheese; or spicy *soppressata, mozzarella di bufala,* and charred onions.

Bookend this pizza indulgence with tender, fried artichoke hearts aside crispy sage, to start; and a creamy tiramisu, to finish.

Sprout

B2

Contemporary 〽〽

1417 W. Fullerton Ave. (bet. Janssen & Southport Aves.)

Phone: 773-348-0706
Web: www.sproutrestaurant.com
Prices: $$$

Lunch Sun
Dinner Tue – Sat
🚉 Fullerton

Top Chef fans might flock to see All-Star favorite Dale Levitski, but even those who eschew reality TV will find top-quality eats at this casually intimate spot. A white linen dining room and bar opens to a front stone-lined patio that doubles as an alfresco destination or a cozy, enclosed respite from Chicago winters.

Sprout describes its menu as "flavor math" and offers a three-course prix-fixe with soup and cheese courses to bookend the meal. Diners choose from brief lists of ingredients for each course. Bold and flavorful plates may include octopus with chorizo, piquillo pepper purée, and picholine olives that seamlessly meld tenderness, sweetness, and heat; or cassoulet-inspired seared lamb tenderloin fanned over white beans and sausage.

Twin Anchors 😊

E4

Barbecue 〽

1655 N. Sedgwick St. (at Eugenie St.)

Phone: 312-266-1616
Web: www.twinanchorsribs.com
Prices: $$

Lunch Sat – Sun
Dinner nightly
🚉 Sedgwick

Chicago may have been Frank Sinatra's kind of town, but Twin Anchors was his kind of restaurant. This Sinatra sweetheart is a local institution, and has been dishing out barbecued ribs since 1932. It is definitely the kind of place where everybody knows your name—when you visit, ogle the list of regulars who frequent this easygoing establishment. Regulars and regular Joes line up (there are no reservations) for a taste of the tender and smoke-flavored barbecued ribs, chicken, and pulled pork. It's a go big or go home kind of place; so pass by the burgers, steaks, and sandwiches and go for the ribs with a side of fries and zesty baked beans.

Come dressed for a mess since the vibe is unfussy; and if you can't stomach the long wait, opt for take-out.

Loop

The hustle and bustle of Chicago's main business district is named after the El train tracks that make a loop around the area. Their clickety-clack noise is an instrinsic part of the soundtrack of the Windy City.

Today's Loop

This neighborhood has a culinary soundtrack as well, one that is constantly evolving with the region. It wasn't that long ago that the Loop locked up at night. When offices, housed in the great iconic Chicago skyscrapers, closed at 5:00 P.M., so did the surrounding businesses, and the area remained quiet and deserted. However, thanks to a revitalized Theater District, new residential living, hotels, and student dorms, there are now renewed restaurants, thrilling wine shops, and gorgeous grocery stores open past dusk. Local foodies and visitors with queries can now contact the Chicago Cultural Center's "culinary concierges" with any food tourism-related question.

Sensational Spreads

Start your voyage and begin exploring at Block 37, one of the city's original 58 blocks. It took decades of work, and several political dynasties, but the block is now home to a new five-story atrium with shopping, restaurants, and entrances to public transportation lines. Here, you'll find Japanese cream puff sensation **Beard Papa**, with its *mochi* ice cream, *fondant au chocolat*, mango showers, and vanilla-filled baked obsessions. Probiotic **Starfruit** with a spectrum of delicious frozen yogurts also has an outpost here, as does **Andy's Frozen Custard**, a more decadent choice for travelers thirsty for a treat.

There are several quick food options on the Pedway level that are popular for office lunches. (The Pedway system of tunnels links crucial downtown buildings underground, which is essential during those cruel Chicago winters.) In the same vein, for a quick, grab and go lunch, **Hannah's Bretzel** (131 S. Dearborn St.) is ideal. Lauded as "über sandwich makers," their version of the faithful is usually fashioned from freshly-baked German bread and features ultra-fresh fillings. While their menu may resemble that of an average diner, one bite into their decadent sandwiches (perhaps the grass-fed sirloin special spread with showers of nutty Gruyére, vine tomatoes, field greens, onions, and spicy horesradish aïoli), and find yourself in sandwich nirvana.

Chicago Chocolate Tours gives two-plus hour tastes of downtown's candy and baked icons' sites on Thursdays and Fridays. These delicious walking tours leave from Macy's State Street location. Another (popular) preference is **Tastebud Tours** which has a Loop option on its daily tour menu. Stops include hot dogs, pizza, and **The Berghoff**—the city's oldest restaurant. Check out the historic Berghoff bar for lunch, dinner, dessert, and of course, steins of beer. Also terrific is Berghoff's pre-theater, prix-fixe menu that may reveal such juicy eats like *sauerbraten*, potato pierogies, and Thai codfish cakes. Their bevy of beers (think: the Berghoff Seasonal Special, Prairie Lager, and Sundown Dark) will keep you boisterous and quenched; and if you're in the mood for something lighter, root for the root beer.

When strolling these grounds, don't miss the range of public art that pops up in many of the government plazas and other open spaces across the Loop. Summer brings a mélange of musical performances to Millennium Park, Grant Park, and the Petrillo Music Shell, that is just begging for a picnic *en plein air*.

Market Carousing

During warmer months, several farmers' markets cater to the downtown crowd, including the ones at Federal Plaza on Tuesdays and Daley Plaza on Thursdays. Concession carts freckle the streets of various locations in nearby Millennium Park, and are simply perfect for grabbing a snack whilst sauntering. Some years ago, produce options increased dramatically with the opening of **Chicago's Downtown Farmstand**, a locally-focused vegetable purveyor on Randolph Street, that showcases a wide selection of colorful produce.

Lake Street's **Pastoral Artisan Cheese** (a favorite of both *Saveur* Magazine and locals alike) is the go-to, made-to-order sandwich spot for the Loop's lunch crowd. The city is filled with

caffeine addicts as well as coffee connoisseurs; and sightseeing is tiring, so make sure you get a pick-me-up at **Intelligentsia Coffee**, a local coffee chain with an emphasis on direct trade. Locations can be found all over town, but the **Millennium Park Coffeebar** is particularly convenient. Outfitted with an industrial-style decor, it perfectly reflects the architecure of nearby Millennium Park. Caffeine junkies also appreciate the several **Torrefazione Italia** locations dotting maps of the Loop.

No trip to Chicago, much less the Loop, would be complete without munching on **Garrett Popcorn**. Head to one of the three Loop locations (follow the aroma for directions) for cheese, caramel, pecan, and other enticingly flavored popcorn.

Taste of Chicago

The Taste of Chicago is one of the city's biggest events. This 10-day summer fête in Grant Park draws hordes of hungry diners and food gourmands from near and far. (The park itself was incorporated before the city was founded.) For the last 30 years, local restaurants have set up scores of food booths that feature delicacies from around the globe. The place is packed for the 10-day duration, thanks to the great food and live music, but come July 4th weekend, it's a bit of a madhouse!

This free festival is now the second-largest attraction in the state; and the beloved (local) **Eli's Cheesecake** is the sole remaining original Taste of Chicago exhibitor. In 2010, it celebrated its 30th anniversary with a giant, creamy cheesecake.

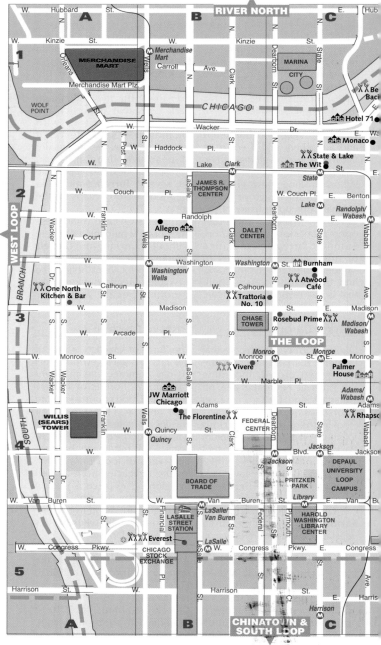

RIVER NORTH

W. Hubbard St. **A** **B** E. (Hub

W. Kinzie St. W. Kinzie St. E.

MERCHANDISE MART

Merchandise Mart
Carroll

Ave. Clark

MARINA CITY

XX Be Baci

Merchandise Mart Plz.

WOLF POINT

CHICAGO

Hotel 71

W. Wacker Dr. Wa

Monaco

Haddock Pl.

Lake Clark St.

XX State & Lake
The Wit

State

W. Couch Pl. E. Benton

Randolph/Wabash

Randolph

Allegro

DALEY CENTER

Washington Washington St. Burnham

One North Kitchen & Bar

Atwood Café

Trattoria No. 10

CHASE TOWER

Rosebud Prime

THE LOOP

Madison/Wabash

Vivere

Monroe Monroe Monroe

Palmer House

Adams/Wabash

JW Marriott Chicago

The Florentine

FEDERAL CENTER

Rhapso

WILLIS (SEARS) TOWER

Quincy Quincy

Jackson Jackson

BOARD OF TRADE

PRITZKER PARK

DEPAUL UNIVERSITY LOOP CAMPUS

Van Buren St. Van Bu

LASALLE STREET STATION

LaSalle/Van Buren

HAROLD WASHINGTON LIBRARY CENTER

Everest

CHICAGO STOCK EXCHANGE

Congress Pkwy. Congress

Harrison St. Harrison St. Harris

A **B** **C**

CHINATOWN & SOUTH LOOP

WEST LOOP

NORTH BRANCH

SOUTH BRANCH

172

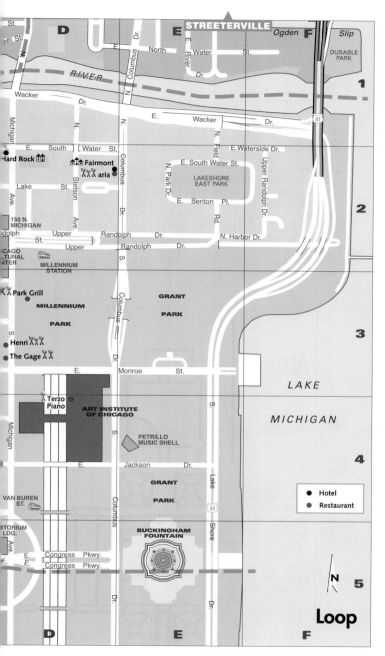

aria

D2

Asian XXX

200 N. Columbus Dr. (bet. Lake & Water Sts.)

Phone: 312-444-9494
Web: www.ariachicago.com
Prices: $$$

Lunch & dinner daily

🚇 Washington

Au courant and luxurious, aria (the hotel restaurant in the Fairmont) satiates guests with a parade of breakfast, lunch, and dinner items. But, thanks to the mighty modern sushi bar, dinner may be your best bet at this Asian-inspired arena.

The lounge is a great place for a signature drink—maybe a take on the classic Tom (chive and pepper) Collins? But, leaving aside her tried-and-true blends, aria's selection of spirits (and bar service) is purely premium and keeps fabulous company with her carte of delicious dishes. The menu has upped the fusion ante and now serves such delicacies as duck breast with coconut polenta; cold buckwheat soba twirled with vegetables; seared *madai*; and "almond joy" topped with three squares of coconut "panna cotta."

Atwood Café

C3

Contemporary XX

1 W. Washington St. (at State St.)

Phone: 312-368-1900
Web: www.atwoodcafe.com
Prices: $$

Lunch & dinner daily

🚇 Washington

Gold-curtained windows, sculptural sconces, and warm wood accents leave a striking impression at Atwood Café. The refined setting plays up its location in the Reliance Building–one of the first modern skyscrapers that now houses the Hotel Burnham–with art deco flourishes that heighten its historic grandeur. Attentive service keeps pace with the business lunch scene, State Street shoppers, and dinner guests making the most of a prime pre-theater location.

The turn-of-the-century setting gives way to a contemporary Mediterranean-influenced menu that features dishes such as shrimp chowder with feta cheese and crispy *tasso* ham garnish; pan-roasted lake trout with celery root purée, toasted almonds, and arugula; or slow-roasted rabbit with date gastrique.

Bella Bacinos

Italian

C1

75 E. Wacker Dr. (bet. Michigan Ave. & State St.)

Phone: 312-263-2350
Web: www.bellabacinos.com
Prices: $$

Lunch & dinner daily

State/Lake

Deep-dish, thin-crust, or stuffed, Chicagoans love their pizza no matter how it is sliced and Bella Bacinos, one of four in the city, dishes up some fantastic pizza with top ingredients. It all started over 30 years ago when Dan Bacin decided to throw a curve ball into pizza making. No more canned ingredients and sauces. Instead, Bacin used the freshest meats, cheeses, and vegetables he could find. The result? Some of the best pizza in town.

You can have it any way you want it at Bella Bacinos, but the stuffed pizza is always a pleaser. This location, in the landmark Mather Tower, has a swanky décor with a lively bar. It's more than just pizza (hearty pastas and entrées round out the menu), but really, why would you want anything else?

The Florentine

Italian

B4

151 W. Adams St. (bet. LaSalle & Wells Sts.)

Phone: 312-660-8866
Web: www.the-florentine.net
Prices: $$

Lunch & dinner daily

Quincy

A grand circular staircase sets the scene for fine dining at The Florentine, the BLT Restaurant Group's Italian offering at the JW Marriott within the historic walls of the Continental & Commercial Bank Building. Ascend from the lobby to a spacious aerie that takes a playfully modern wink at Italian design with an eye-catching marble-countered central bar, walnut flooring, and sienna leather seating.

Wines available by the quartino are attractive options for diners sharing small plates from the creative antipasti selection, such as mozzarella *fritta* with golden raisins and pine nuts. Be sure to sample fresh pastas like squid ink *spaghetti alla chitarra* balanced with roasted cherry tomatoes, thinly sliced garlic, and hints of chilies and mint.

Everest ✿

French 🍴🍴🍴🍴

B5

440 S. LaSalle St. (bet. Congress Pkwy. & Van Buren St.)

Phone: 312-663-8920   Dinner Tue – Sat
Web: www.everestrestaurant.com
Prices: $$$$ 🚇 LaSalle/Van Buren

Everest

The name makes perfect sense, once you have ascended the forty floors (remembering to change at the 39th) and navigated the hallways and steps up to this dramatic view of the Chicago skyline. As expected, window tables are prime real estate on a clear night. The contemporary room is not large, though mirrors give the illusion of space; while billowing fabrics, white columns, and tabletop sculptures fashion a look that, depending on your age and stage, is either timeless or dated. But no one is complaining, as the mood is always just right for celebrations.

The classic Alsatian menu is a pleasant departure from the city's more ubiquitous cuisines. Dishes showcase the region's intermingling of Franco-Germanic ingredients and flavors, as in succulent lobster with gewürztraminer butter delicately infused with ginger. For dessert, the baba–based on an 18th century Alsatian recipe–packs a fantastically boozy punch with fluffy, rum-soaked cake served with pineapple-raisin ice cream. Not to be outdone, the lovely selection of mignardise shine with the likes of peppermint marshmallows glazed in dark chocolate and anise macarons.

Take your eyes off the view to peruse the excellent wine list.

The Gage

Gastropub ✗✗

D3

24 S. Michigan Ave. (bet. Madison & Monroe Sts.)

Phone: 312-372-4243
Web: www.thegagechicago.com
Prices: $$

Lunch & dinner daily

🚇 Madison

Superbly situated on Michigan Avenue opposite Millennium Park, with tables spreading onto an impressive patio offering views across the expanse, it is no wonder that The Gage is permanently packed, regardless of the food. To The Gage's credit, it doesn't rest on its location's laurels alone. This massive place pleases (and draws) locals and tourists alike, with its solid gastropub menu, reasonable prices, and popular post-work bar.

Snack on crispy pork belly, duck fat nuts, or scoop up the to-die-for N-17 "fondue" of Butter Kaase, Brie, and spinach. Chomp the upmarket "Gage" burger with local Camembert and melted onion marmalade on a toasted malt roll; or dig in to the roasted saddle of elk with a dry cherry reduction.

Henri

Contemporary ✗✗✗

D3

18 S. Michigan Ave. (bet. Madison & Monroe Sts.)

Phone: 312-578-0763
Web: www.henrichicago.com
Prices: $$$$

Lunch Mon – Fri
Dinner nightly
🚇 Monroe

Behind a Louis Henri Sullivan façade facing Millennium Park, this jewel-box restaurant takes its name and design from Sullivan's turn-of-the-century milieu. Elegantly appointed with mohair, velvet, and herringbone, the setting mirrors the polished service and presentation.

Henri's classic French menu sparks with global and contemporary touches, as in dishes like lobster Wellington, with generous chunks of sweet meat and foie gras in golden pastry. An excellent dark chocolate tart ends the meal with simple perfection.

Clever categories–like Teutonic Plates for cold-climate whites, and Black Pine for pinot noir–divide Henri's biodynamic wine list. Also available: a rotating selection of reds and whites by the glass poured from the day's magnum offering.

One North Kitchen & Bar

 A3

1 N. Wacker Dr. (bet. Madison & Washington Sts.)

Phone: 312-750-9700

Web: www.restaurants-america.com

Prices: $$

Lunch Mon – Fri
Dinner Mon – Sat

 Washington

Both on street level and within the USB Tower, One North Kitchen & Bar is a hub of activity, albeit different kinds depending on the time of day. When the clock strikes noon, the ballast is abuzz with financial industry types who come in droves over their lunch hour. Things calm down until pre-theater, after which One North's dinner rush heralds a changed clientele.

FiDi folk love the lunches because they star generously sized sandwiches made with luscious ingredients, sided with pommes frites. Grilled shrimp, pork chops, and macaroni and cheese are some of the other big hits among the nine-to-fivers. For those looking to relax, enjoy a homemade and daring dessert of the day on the terrace, also idyllic for a drink before or after city sightseeing.

Park Grill

 D3

11 N. Michigan Ave. (at Millennium Park)

Phone: 312-521-7275

Web: www.parkgrillchicago.com

Prices: $$

Lunch & dinner daily

 Madison

Located next to the shining Cloud Gate inside Millennium Park, appealing and approachable Park Grill affords views of would-be medalists hitting the winter ice rink and just about every other tourist in town walking by during warmer months. No matter the season, diners find dressed-up American cuisine to please the masses.

The wide-ranging menu has everything from salads big and small to burgers of Kobe beef, salmon, or Berkshire pork. Ambitious dishes like sea scallops with fig vinegar please the sophisticated palate, while contemporary desserts like the peanut butter tart served with roasted banana purée are worth the caloric splurge. Budget eaters like the two-course power business lunch during the week and the children's specials on the weekends.

Rhapsody

Italian ❌❌

65 E. Adams St. (bet. Michigan & Wabash Aves.)

Phone: 312-786-9911
Web: www.rhapsodychicago.com
Prices: $$

Lunch Mon – Fri
Dinner Tue – Sat
🚇 Monroe

Attached to the Symphony Center, Rhapsody is a natural choice for pre- or post-theater dining, but the lovely setting makes it a destination at any time. From its charmingly whimsical exterior and its large patio nestled in a blooming flower garden to its friendly and timely service, Rhapsody delivers a virtuoso performance.

The kitchen is under new direction with Chef Dean Zanella who brings a distinct Italian influence to the contemporary menu that showcases local and seasonal product in items such as buffalo milk ricotta crostini with apple *mostarda*; or his signature Anna's veal meatballs. Pastas bring on *Nonna* Zanella's gnocchi, and nightly specials have offered pan-seared grouper dressed with herbed emulsion over *fregola sarda*.

Rosebud Prime

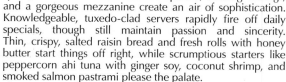

Steakhouse ❌❌❌

1 S. Dearborn St. (at Madison St.)

Phone: 312-384-1900
Web: www.rosebudrestaurants.com
Prices: $$$

Lunch Mon – Fri
Dinner Mon – Sat
🚇 Monroe

Class and elegance drift through the striking bi-level dining space, where luxurious rose banquettes, soaring ceilings, and a gorgeous mezzanine create an air of sophistication. Knowledgeable, tuxedo-clad servers rapidly fire off daily specials, though still maintain passion and sincerity. Thin, crispy, salted raisin bread and fresh rolls with honey butter start things off right, while scrumptious starters like peppercorn ahi tuna with ginger soy, coconut shrimp, and smoked salmon pastrami please the palate.

Slice into a juicy *petit* filet, seared just so and served with a side of jus. Complete the decadence with fresh blueberries, raspberries, and strawberries served with velvety sabayon—whipped with a touch of cream and spiked with Grand Marnier.

State & Lake

C2

201 N. State St. (at Lake St.)

Phone:	312-239-9400	Lunch & dinner daily
Web:	www.thewithotel.com	
Prices:	$$	State/Lake

Its name says it all, so don't fret if you forgot to write down the address of this restaurant before setting sail. State & Lake, nestled into the ground floor of the sleek Wit Hotel, is draped in dark leather-padded walls, cork floors, and intimate, soft lighting that give the space a seductive sophistication. The dining room is perpetually packed with corporates discussing business over lunch, and groups–destined for the nearby Theater District–for dinner.

Start the day with a sausage and egg casserole, break midday for a Reuben, and come dusk, tuck into delicious baby back ribs or a juicy filet. Channel your inner frat boy and go straight for the oblong bar that also boasts frosty taps (literally) pouring around a dozen beers.

Terzo Piano

D4

159 E. Monroe St. (bet. Columbus Dr. & Michigan Ave.)

Phone:	312-443-8650	Lunch daily
Web:	www.terzopianochicago.com	Dinner Thu
Prices:	$$$	Monroe

With a dash of urban sophistication, this luminous space befits its larger digs displaying a crisp minimalist design and outdoor terrace. Tucked into the west wing of the Art Institute of Chicago, this immaculate room shows off towering windows, edgy artwork, and a fantastic view of the park.

Take a break from the galleries and refuel on delicious roasted pike served atop a bed of *farro, cipollini* onions, and aromatic almond and herb purée; or fresh made *ravioletto* stuffed with creamy mozzarella and porcini mushrooms floating in a rosemary-scented broth. Chef Tony Mantuano of Spiaggia is at the helm, spinning out decadent offerings like flatbread pizzas, *antipastos*, and artisanal cheeses. In keeping with museum hours, dinner is served on Thursdays only.

Trattoria No. 10

Italian 𝗫𝗫

C3

10 N. Dearborn St. (bet. Madison & Washington Sts.)

Phone: 312-984-1718
Web: www.trattoriaten.com
Prices: $$

Lunch Mon – Fri
Dinner Mon – Sat
🚇 Washington

Pick up the phone before stepping in to Trattoria No. 10, since reservations are an absolute must at this clubby, cozy, and inviting spot. Located below street level, this charming place feels a world away from the hustle and bustle, but take a look around and you'll find Loop lawyers and other businesspeople brokering deals over grilled calamari and sausage ravioli.

The rustic Italian specialties are what keep this spot on the speed dial of so many area power brokers. From house-made ravioli with butternut and acorn squash in sweet walnut butter sauce, and Berkshire pork osso buco with mascarpone mashed potatoes, to farfalle with duck confit, asparagus, mushrooms, pearl onions, and pine nuts, it's gourmet comfort food defined.

Vivere

Italian 𝗫𝗫𝗫

B3

71 W. Monroe St. (bet. Clark & Dearborn Sts.)

Phone: 312-332-4040
Web: www.vivere-chicago.com
Prices: $$

Lunch Mon – Fri
Dinner Mon – Sat
🚇 Monroe

Simple, old-school charm has been drawing Chicagoans to this restaurant complex since its oldest member first introduced locals to Italian dining in 1927. By those standards, Vivere is quite the newcomer, having served its rustic Northern Italian specialties for merely two decades.

The setting shows more opulence than age, with copper, brass, and caramel tones casting an amber hue through the attractive space that seems to embrace its sexy curves as it travels up the sweeping staircase to the buzzing mezzanine. The menu may feature a crisp Caesar salad, hickory-smoked sea scallops, house-made pasta such as pheasant *agnolottini* in sage-butter sauce, or mustard-encrusted venison. Let the superb staff guide you through the vast wine selection.

Pilsen, Little Italy & University Village

This cluster of neighborhoods packs a perfect punch, both in terms of food, spice, and sheer energy level. It lives up to every expectation and reputation, so get ready for a tour packed with literal, acoustic, and visual flavor. The Little Italy moniker applies to one stretch of Taylor Street. While it abuts the University (of Illinois at Chicago) Village neighborhood, Little Italy is bigger and more authentically Italian than it first appears. The streets are as stuffed with epicurean shops as an Italian beef sandwich is with meat. (Speaking of which, try

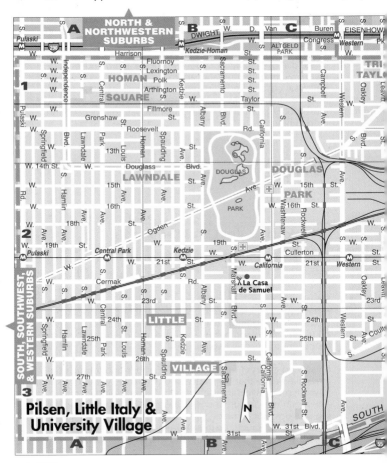

Pilsen, Little Italy & University Village

a prime example of this iconic Chicago sandwich at the aptly named **Al's No. 1 Italian Beef**.) Start with **Conte Di Savoia**, an Italian grocery and popular takeout lunch counter. In June, folks flock here for the Oakley Festa Pasta Vino festival. Wash this down with a frozen, fruit slush from **Mario's Italian Lemonade**. Lemon is the most popular flavor from the cash-only stand, but offbeat varieties like chocolate and banana are also refreshing. While strolling these vibrant grounds, make sure you glimpse the Christopher Columbus statue, which was originally commissioned for the 1893 World's Columbian Exposition.

UNIVERSITY VILLAGE

Like any self-respecting college "town," University Village houses a plethora of cozy coffee

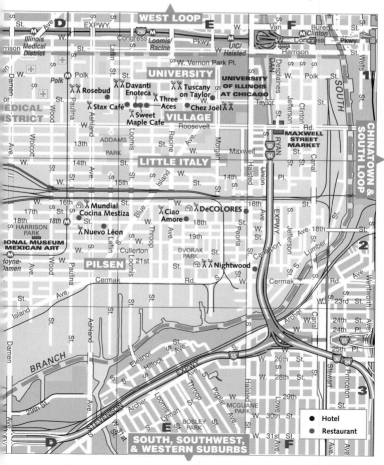

shops and cafés. A population of doctors, medical students, nurses, and others working in the neighborhood hospital contributes to an always-on-the-move vibe. **Lush Wine & Spirits** sells the expected, plus local obsession **Salted Caramel** is famed for its popcorn, especially the bacon-bourbon variety.

On Sundays, the destination is the legendary **Maxwell Street Market**. Relocated to Desplaines Street in 2008, this sprawling market welcomes more than 500 vendors selling produce, Mexican street food including tamales and tacos, and non-food miscellanea. Celebrity chef, Rick Bayless and the like shop here for locally-grown tomatoes and tomatillos; while others buy ingredients for at-home culinary creations (not to mention tires, tube socks, and other flea market fare). Maxwell Street Market is also *the* choice for authentic Mexican delicacies.

PILSEN AND LITTLE VILLAGE

Chicago's large Mexican population (more than 500,000 per the last U.S. Census count) has built a patchwork of regional Mexican specialties, many of which are found in the south side's residential Pilsen and Little Village neighborhoods. Pilsen is home to the free National Museum of Mexican Art, the only Latino museum accredited by the American Association of Museums, as well as an abundance of faithful Mexican taquerias, bakeries, and other culturally relevant businesses. Everyone goes all out for Mexican Independence Day in September, including more than 25 participating area restaurants. The Little Village Arts Festival packs 'em in October.

Stop by sumptuous **Sabinas Food Products** factory for freshly made tortillas and chips to take home, followed by a trip to the Tuesday farmer's market at the Chicago Community Bank. Much of Pilsen's 26th Street is filled with auto chop shops and other workaday businesses. But the large-scale tortilla factories, where three or four women press and form corn tortillas, are an exception. Since 1950, **El Milagro** has offered a unique taste, with a cafeteria-style restaurant (presenting seven kinds of tamales on the menu); and a store that sells burritos, spiced corn chips, maize, and those locally-made tortillas. While feasting, don't forget to fix your eyes upon the mural on the wall! Pork lovers (and, well, that's most Chicagoans) can't resist the siren call of **Carnitas Uruapan**. Close to the pink line El, this storefront serves carnitas by the pound, accompanied by corn or flour tortillas and tangy salsas. Massive *chicharrónes*, fried pork skins, are also available for those craving more artery-blocking goodness.

Pilsen's low rents and eclectic vibe have for long now attracted artists and hipsters. They all congregate at **Simone's Bar**, a certified green restaurant and place-to-be-seen.

Chez Joël

E1   French ✕✕

1119 W. Taylor St. (bet. Aberdeen & May Sts.)

Phone: 312-226-6479   Lunch Tue – Sat
Web: www.chezjoelbistro.com   Dinner Tue – Sun
Prices: $$

A bit of Paris has landed in Little Italy with Chez Joël, the charming, red-brick corner bistro with its Francophile following and tasty fare. Gilded mirrors, pale yellow walls, a stunning crystal-beaded chandelier, and red velvet-draped windows weave an aura of timelessness, while French oldies piping through speakers add to the romance.

Owned and operated by brothers Joël and Ahmed Kazouini, the beloved spot spins out bistro favorites like crocks of French onion soup with a deliciously browned and bubbly lid of cheese; steamed mussels with white wine; crème brûlée; and profiteroles. Cocktails like the Bleu Margarita and the Calvados Royale also have a sexy accent. In warmer weather, snag a seat in the breezy courtyard and dine under the trees.

Ciao Amore

E2   Italian ✕

1134. W. 18th St. (at May St.)

Phone: 312-432-9090   Lunch Tue – Fri
Web: www.ciaoamoreristorante.com   Dinner Tue – Sun
Prices: $$ 🚇 18th

It's a truly American story: a boy is born in Venezuela to a Roman-Pugliese mother before moving to Chicago with his family at a young age. Such is the culinary history of Ciao Amore's owner Cesar Pineda, and the reason for a globally influenced Italian menu that's very much unlike its taqueria neighbors in Pilsen.

Fresh ingredients fill and complement house-made pastas in many dishes. Standouts may include *brascole*, an oddly spelled but flavor-packed traditional Italian braciole stuffed with spinach, prosciutto, and pine nuts nestled alongside ricotta, Asiago, and pesto-filled gnocchi. *Ravioli d'aragosta* wears its Italian-Venezuelan heritage prominently, plunging delicate lobster-stuffed pasta pockets into a devilish jalapeño-laced *arrabbiata*.

Davanti Enoteca

Italian

 E1

1359 W. Taylor St. (at Loomis St.)

Phone: 312-226-5550
Web: www.davantichicago.com
Prices: $$

Lunch & dinner daily

With its warming wood-burning oven, brick arches displaying wine, and robust selection of Italian dishes, Davanti Enoteca knows how to combat Chicago's coldest winters. Sunny windows and French doors that open to the outside world on warmer days assure that this is a lovely spot, no matter the time of year.

The kitchen finds inspiration in classic Italian favorites, yet caters to Chicago's tastes. Irresistible mounds of spaghetti *cacio e pepe* are richer than the traditional Roman dish, but this creamier rendition boasts a luscious, pecorino-based sauce that is nonetheless delicious. While dishes are not often complex, they highlight superior ingredients, as in the seared Nantucket Bay scallops in a hearty, delicate, and fresh cauliflower soup.

DeCOLORES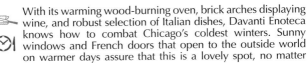

Mexican

E2

1626 S. Halsted St. (bet. 16th & 17th Sts.)

Phone: 312-226-9886
Web: www.decolor.us
Prices: $$

Lunch Fri – Sun
Dinner nightly

Looking for a side of culture with your main course? DeCOLORES is just the right spot. This art gallery-cum-restaurant feeds your soul and your stomach with its unique blend of culture and cuisine. From the unframed torn canvases lining the walls to the bright and festive skull that rests on the bar, art can be found throughout the space. The dining room's cool ambience is punctuated by ethnic reminders (white skulls and red votive candles).

But it's not just about the art—the kitchen also mixes up masterpieces of nouveau Mexican food. From a creamy and silky scallop and crawfish soup; flaky tilapia dotted with olives and paired with a salad of romaine, apples, walnuts, and cranberries; to a velvety, tart cheesecake flan, the meals here are works of art.

La Casa De Samuel

 B2

2834 W. Cermak Rd. (bet. California Ave. & Marshall Blvd.)

Phone: 773-376-7474   Lunch & dinner daily
Web: N/A
Prices: California (Pink)

This Mexican jewel has been tossing tortillas since 1989, and it's still going strong. Packed with everyone from *familias* to couples, La Casa de Samuel draws them in with dishes piled high displaying tasty treats. From the chunky salsa made with toasted chiles to the crêpes flambé prepared tableside and doused with flaming Cointreau for added drama, everything is good from start to finish.

You can go with the usual suspects (chicken enchilada maybe?) or go all out and try something quirky, like grilled rattlesnake, grilled alligator, or marinated venison. No matter the choice, diners are forever rewarded with juicy, flavorful dishes topped with aromatic sauces. The best part? It won't scorch your wallet to feed your face and leave with a full belly.

Mundial Cocina Mestiza

 D2

1640 W. 18th St. (bet. Marshfield Ave. & Paulina St.)

Phone: 312-491-9908   Lunch & dinner Tue – Sun
Web: www.mundialcocinamestiza.com
Prices: $$ 18th

Patient palates will be rewarded at this unassuming and underrated spot that is serious about regional Mexican cuisine and preparing every order from scratch. Sweet meaty aromas wafting from the open kitchen and homemade sangria whet the appetite, while welcoming service matches the exceptional flavors on each plate.

Restorative, filling chicken and tortilla soup studded with vegetables and a cool, lightly pickled nopales salad could make a substantial meal, but that would mean forgoing the *Tampiqueña Sinaloese* with tender marinated steak, sautéed corn, smoky poblano peppers, and a lusciously creamy tomatillo sauce. An over-the-top pineapple cheesecake decked with tequila coconut flakes on a surprising Oreo cookie crust is too good to pass up.

Nightwood

F2

2119 S. Halsted St. (at 21st St.)

Phone: 312-526-3385
Web: www.nightwoodrestaurant.com
Prices: $$

Lunch Sun
Dinner Mon – Sat

Despite its ultra-modern, loft-like vibe, a sense of soulfulness pervades Nightwood, bringing to mind warm thoughts of hearth and home. Clearly proud of the restaurant's commitment to farm-sourced, seasonal ingredients, the staff makes every detail testament to their mission, and the steady stream of customers rewards their effort.

An open bar, kitchen, and shelving throughout the space matches the full transparency of the constantly changing menu, which showcases peak-of-the-season ingredients like spring's fiddlehead ferns presented with a wood-grilled Slagel Farm veal chop. Even potentially curious dishes like smoked trout and creamy cheese wrapped in mortadella and dressed in honey mustard turn out to be gorgeously interesting spreads.

Nuevo Léon

D2

1515 W. 18th St. (bet. Ashland Ave. & Laflin St.)

Phone: 312-421-1517
Web: www.nuevoleonrestaurant.com
Prices:

Lunch & dinner daily

 18th

From the minute your feet step on the clay tiles inside this Mexican eatery, you'll be transported into the cultural ambience for which Pilsen is known. Take in the artifacts like hand-painted plates and murals on the walls, and Mexican music blasting.

Like any good Mexican joint, this local darling has combination platters on the menu, and they're the best way to get a cross-section of the kitchen's best. The *carne a la Tampiqueña* includes simply-seasoned tender grilled beef, tomato-scented rice, beans, and both a tomatillo-lime salsa verde and smoky red chile salsa, which elevate the taste to something extraordinary. The *horchata* is well-spiced and soups of the day vary by season. Large portion sizes mean leftovers for lunch *mañana*.

Chicago ▶ Pilsen, Little Italy & University Village

Rosebud

D1

Italian ❌❌

1500 W. Taylor St. (at Laflin St.)

Phone: 312-942-1117
Web: www.rosebudrestaurants.com
Prices: $$

Lunch & dinner daily

🖥 Polk

It's the original, baby. This is where the Rosebud empire started in the late 1970s. Named for the flower of Sicily, it's the kind of place where wise guys and regular Joes loosen up over heaping plates of pasta. Sinatra is on the stereo and autographed photos of celebrities line the walls. It's a bit cliché, but Rosebud revels in it.

Add a vowel to your last name and leave your carb-hating friends at home. The fresh bread arrives right away, but save plenty of room because this place pours it on. Portions are enormous—even the sausage and peppers appetizer arrives oversized. Tasty and well-priced entrées include classics, like rigatoni alla vodka, veal *braciola*, and chicken Vesuvio. Sweet tooths should save room for tiramisu or *spumoni*.

Stax Café

E1

American ❌

1401 W. Taylor St. (at Loomis St.)

Phone: 312-733-9871
Web: www.staxcafe.com
Prices: 💰💰

Lunch daily

Comfortable seats, fresh juice, and French toast: the perfect recipe for a classic brunch hangout. At Stax, an airy nook near the UIC campus, staffers in t-shirts with cheeky slogans ("We are Breakfast Poets. Oh, how we love thee") swiftly refill coffee mugs and deliver eggs Benedict and burgers to sleepy-eyed eaters.

Breakfast and lunch options are wide-ranging: omelets like the Spanish Harlem, filled with chorizo, roasted tomatoes, poblanos, and *queso fresco*, are beautifully fluffy and light. Ham and cheese crêpes with honey mustard walk the line between sweet and savory; and heavenly ricotta pancakes with strawberry-rhubarb compote sweeten the morning. Eyeing the mini chocolate Bundt cake? Snag it at the start of your meal—desserts sell out early.

Sweet Maple Cafe

E1

1339 W. Taylor St. (bet. Loomis St. & Racine Ave.)

Phone: 312-243-8908   Lunch daily
Web: www.sweetmaplecafe.com
Prices: 🍪

You know that neighborhood breakfast spot where locals grab a cup of coffee *en route* to tide them over while they stand in line outside waiting for a table? In Little Italy, Southern-style Sweet Maple Cafe is definitely that place, with a smidge of Southern charm and hospitality mixed in.

Regulars love the large, fluffy pancakes (with honey, applesauce, butter, and syrup); scrambled eggs served with flavorful country-style pork sausage patties; and, requisite at any place that calls itself "Southern," those flaky biscuits and buttery grits. Sweet Maple Cafe also serves lunch, but breakfast is served through the lunch hour, and with the omelets, home fries, plus the rest of the breakfast treats, why would you even order lunch?

Three Aces

E1

1321 W. Taylor St. (bet. Loomis & Throop Sts.)

Phone: 312-243-1577   Dinner nightly
Web: www.threeaceschicago.com
Prices: $$ Racine

Three Aces turns bar food up to 11 in a gritty but chic space that gives off a serious rock n' roll vibe. In a dim yet inclusive room meant to hold a crowd, the young and tattooed gather under light fixtures nicked from Joliet Prison to order up beer-and-shot combos or cocktails like the Fiery Jalisco, a bracing combination of mezcal, grapefruit, and St. Germain.

In the same vein as the haute-basement décor, the refined menu delivers modern American riffs on Italian classics like lightly crispy *arancini* on a bed of braised short ribs, and inventive flatbread *pizzette* with quality toppings. The signature Hammer of the Gods burger with aged cheddar, bacon jam, *porchetta*, paté, and a fried egg towering atop juicy beef is a one-of-kind showstopper.

Tuscany on Taylor

Italian

1014 W. Taylor St. (bet. Miller & Morgan Sts.)

Phone: 312-829-1990
Web: www.tuscanychicago.com
Prices: **$$**

Lunch Mon – Fri
Dinner nightly
UIC-Halsted

It's easy to fall in love with Tuscany on Taylor. This cushy jewel in the heart of Chicago's Little Italy shares its Italian spirit and warmth with all who enter.

The dining room has an inviting, mood-lifting appeal with cheerful blue-and-white checkered tablecloths, wood floors, and an expansive kitchen. Formally dressed servers anticipate your every need, but after a few bites of Tuscany's homemade pastas, unique wood-fired pizzas, and tender veal, you won't be wanting for much. Pastas can be light (topped with fresh tomatoes) or hearty (topped with Bolognese); while entrées like grilled NY strip steak, roasted chicken, veal medallions with creamy Gorgonzola, and sausage and peppers are guaranteed to leave you feeling stuffed and comforted.

Start your day off right with a brilliant breakfast, wherever you see the symbol .

Chicago ▶ Pilsen, Little Italy & University Village

River North

Art galleries, hopping nightlife, well-known restaurants and chefs, swanky shopping, great views, even a head-turning fast-food chain: almost everything that Chicago boasts is offered here. Perhaps because River North offers so much it also attracts so many. From ladies who lunch to office workers to tour bus-style tourists, most folks who pass through the Windy City make a stop here.

Beyond the Ordinary

River North (which, it stands to reason, is located north of the Chicago River) has no shortage of food and drink attractions. True, as you pull up to Ontario and Clark streets, you might just think, "chain restaurant central," but even the chains in River North have their charm.

Among them is the **Rock 'n' Roll McDonald's**, a block-long, music-themed outpost of the ubiquitous burger chain. One of the busiest **MickeyD's** in the world, this one has an expanded menu, music memorabilia, and bragging rights to the first two-lane drive-through. (Remember: McDonald's is a local chain, still headquartered in the suburbs.)

The Rainforest Café (with its wild range of flesh, fowl, and fish dishes); the forever and boisterous **Hard Rock Café**; and **M Burger** (a new chain rolled out by the Lettuce Entertain You Enterprise) are all quite the hit, and popular tourist draws. One of *the* most beloved burger joints, M Burger is a Michigan Avenue jewel boasting an array of burgers (try the no meat Nurse Betty) alongisde fries and shakes. Speaking of drive-through chains, River North is the flagship location of **Portillo's**, a local, beloved hot dog, burger, and beer chain. Its large exterior belies its efficient service and better-than-expected food.

When it comes to size, few buildings can top the mammoth **Merchandise Mart** (so large it has its own ZIP code). Along with its history, retail stores, boutiques, and drool-worthy kitchen showrooms, it is home to two great food shops. At **Artisan Cellar**, in addition to boutique wines, panini, and specialty cheeses, you can purchase Katherine Anne Confections' fresh-cream caramels. Locals also love **The Chopping Block** for its expertly-taught, themed cooking courses, well-edited wine selections, and of course, their newly stocked and shiny knife lines. (There's another location in Lincoln Square for north side courses.)

Nearby, the Cooking Hospitality Institute of Chicago, known as **CHIC**, has a student-run restaurant where diners can get a glimpse of the next big thing in Chicago kitchens. Beloved by locals in the know, CHIC displays a unique blend of elegance and comfort paired with gracious service and a daily-changing menu.

Open Books, a used bookstore that relies on its proceeds to

fund literacy programs, has plenty of cookbooks on its shelves. Outfit any kitchen with finds from the Bloomingdale's Home store in the 1912 Medinah Temple. You'll smell the **Blommer Chocolate Outlet Store** before you see it. Late at night and early in the morning, the tempting chocolate aroma wreaks down the river beckoning city dwellers to its Willy Wonka-esque confines. This is where to stock up on sweets from the 70-plus-year-old-brand. Blommer's also boasts a specialty cocoa collection ranging from such fabulous (and sinful) flavors as black cocoa, cake-based cocoa powders, and Dutch specialty varieties.

Deep-Dish Delights

River North is as good a place as any to indulge in the local phenomenon of Chicago-style, deep-dish pizza. Also called stuffed pizza (referring to the pie, but it could also refer to the way you'll feel after you snarf it down), deep-dish pizza was created in the Windy City in the 1940s. Closer to a casserole (or, as they say in the Midwest, "hot dish,") than an Italian-style pizza, it is a thick, doughy crust, holding abundant cheese, sauce, and toppings inside.

Some say it is Chicago water in the dough that makes that crust so distinctive. Deep-dish pies take awhile to prepare, so be prepared to wait wherever you go. **Pizzeria Uno** (and its sister **Pizzeria Due**), and **Giordano's** are some of the best known pie makers. If a little indigestion isn't a concern, follow that priceless pizza with another Chicago-style specialty: the Italian beef

sandwich. Very much like a messy, yet über tasty French dip, an Italian beef isn't Italian, but all Chicago. Dating back to the 1930s, it features seasoned, thinly sliced beef on a hoagie roll, with either hot or sweet peppers on top. If you order it "wet," both the meat and the bread will be dipped in pan juices. You could also add cheese, but this isn't Philly! Two of the biggest contenders in the Italian beef wars are in this 'hood: **Al's Italian Beef** and **Mr. Beef**. Both eateries have top-quality sausages and hot dogs on the menu as well.

Get Your Groove On

Nightlife in River North is a big deal, with everything from authentic Chicago Irish pubs, to cocktail lounges for those who like to see-and-be-seen. Nestled in the landmark Chicago Historical Society Building, **Excalibur** is a multi-floor dance club and is all about velvet ropes, house music, and an epic drink list. **Blue Chicago** is a civilized place where you can sit, get a drink, and listen to that world-famous Chicago sound, the Blues.

English, an aptly named British bar, is a popular watering hole for watching soccer and other sports, not usually broadcasted at your typical Chicago sports bar. English is also home to "Top Chef" alumna, Radhika Desai.

Finally, don't skip the **Green Door Tavern**, which gets its name from the fact that its colored front told Prohibition-era customers where to enter for a drink. Order a "famous sandwich" or "Green Door Burger" and you will understand what all the fuss is about.

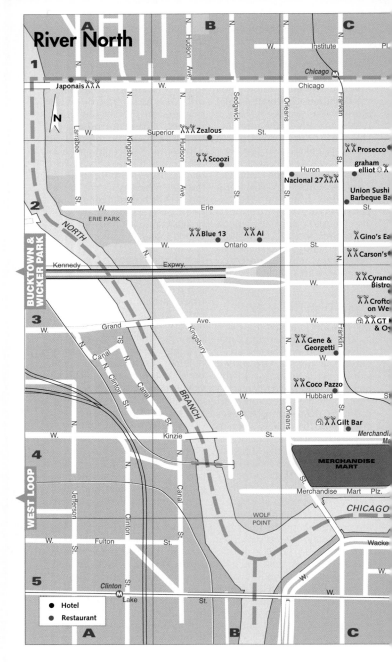

River North

A | B | C

1

Japonais ✕✕✕

N

Superior Zealous ✕✕✕

Scoozi ✕✕

Prosecco ✕✕

graham
elliot ✕

Nacional 27 ✕✕✕

Huron

Union Sushi
Barbeque Ba

Erie

2

ERIE PARK

NORTH

Blue 13 ✕✕   Ai ✕✕

Ontario

Gino's Ea ✕

Carson's ✕✕

Kennedy   Expwy.

Cyrano ✕✕
Bistro

Crofto ✕✕
on We

Grand

GT ✕✕
& O

3

Gene & ✕✕
Georgetti

Coco Pazzo ✕✕

Hubbard

Gilt Bar ✕✕

Merchandi
Ma

MERCHANDISE
MART

4

Merchandise Mart Plz.

CHICAGO

WOLF
POINT

Wacke

W.

Fulton

5

Clinton

Lake   St.

● Hotel
● Restaurant

BUCKTOWN &
WICKER PARK

WEST LOOP

194

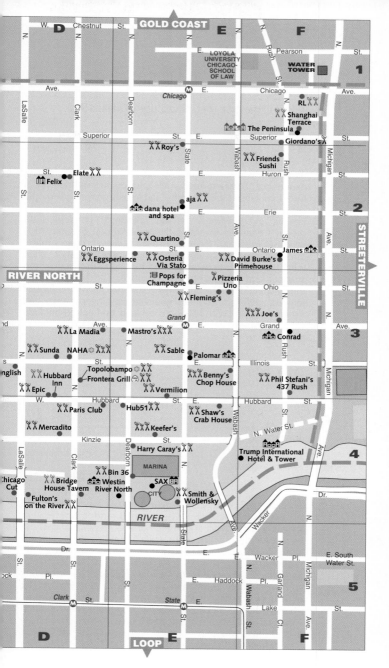

Ai

358 W. Ontario St. (bet. Kingsbury & Orleans Sts.)

Phone: 312-335-9888
Web: www.aichicago.us
Prices: $$

Lunch Mon – Fri
Dinner nightly
🚇 Chicago (Brown)

Ai is A+ when it comes to offering a Japanese dining experience. Bamboo-lined walls and touches of brick warm the room; while tables, booths, and a sushi bar provide ample seating.

Feeling overwhelmed by the seemingly limitless sushi menu? Order the inventive flights of salmon or tuna. Ai is seriously fresh and top-notch sushi, but wait, there's more. The signature *madai* ceviche maki is worth a shot, filled with avocado and cucumber and topped with Japanese red snapper and a piquant ceviche sauce. The kitchen keeps things spirited with a bold lineup that reveals Maine lobster tempura with *kampyo* (dried gourd strips), ginger, mango, and avocado topped with habañero ceviche; and entrées include wasabi-rubbed filet mignon served over Japanese sweet potato.

aja

660 N. State St. (at Erie St.)

Phone: 312-202-6050
Web: www.danahotelandspa.com
Prices: $$

Lunch & dinner daily
🚇 Chicago (Red)

Aja soars over two floors within the dana hotel, dominated by undulating sculpted wood panels and cushy leather seating. A large, well-appointed bar and fireplace accent the windowed main dining room while a stunning staircase leads to an upper-level sushi bar, which is also accessible from the hotel lobby.

Specialty house-made sauces at each table, including sweet brandied hoisin and tart coconut-chili vinegar, let diners personalize the exceptional pan-Asian cuisine. Menu highlights include handmade pork dumplings in a rich wonton soup and perfectly seared tuna with yuzu *chimichurri* over truffled whipped potatoes. Imaginative desserts like a caramel-apple cheesecake-filled spring roll served with five-spice dipping sauce complete the journey.

Benny's Chop House

Steakhouse ✗✗✗

E3

444 N. Wabash Ave. (bet. Hubbard & Illinois Sts.)

Phone: 312-626-2444

Lunch & dinner daily

Web: www.bennyschophouse.com

Prices: $$$

Grand (Red)

From its quiet location tucked into the shadow of the Trump Tower, this contemporary American steakhouse manages to shine. The art deco-inspired décor and casual yet very competent staff may be your first clues that Benny's stands above its many Chicago chophouse brethren, but the excellent food here is everyone's focus.

While many tables are topped with the likes of USDA Prime dry-aged steaks, other offerings are as enticing. Chopped salad is flawlessly rendered, and the only downside to oysters Rockefeller is that the preparation requires cooking such tasty shellfish. Playful, fun, and decadent treats abound in the likes of blue cheese tater tots. Portions are often generous here: the baked Alaska "for two" would more suitably feed an army.

Bin 36

American ✗✗

E4

339 N. Dearborn St. (bet. Kinzie St. & the Chicago River)

Phone: 312-755-9463

Lunch & dinner daily

Web: www.bin36.com

Prices: $$$

Lake

It's a wine store! It's a cheese shop! It's a restaurant! No, it's all three and much more inside this perennially popular downtown spot. The entrance of the cavernous multi-level space doubles as a specialty market with affordably priced bottles and a casual sit-down café with a curving bar. Further back, notice a spacious atrium and communal tables offering additional dining and sipping options from morning coffee to evening tastings and in-depth "Bin School" wine courses.

Though wine and cheese are the main focus at Bin 36, patrons interested in a more substantial nosh than a tasting plate or wine flight can sit down and choose a few of the tasty, generous, and eclectic dishes—including excellent seafood—from the contemporary American menu.

Blue 13

Contemporary Contemporary 𝄪𝄪

B2

416 W. Ontario St. (bet. Kingsbury & Orleans Sts.)

Phone: 312-787-1400
Web: www.blue13chicago.com
Prices: $$$

Dinner Tue – Sun

Chicago (Brown)

Consider this seductive den your rebel with a foodie cause. With exposed brick walls, visible duct work, and patent tattoos on the cooks' arms, Blue 13 puts it all out there and dares you to dis' its sultry look. Dim industrial lighting and mirrors above the banquettes amplify the beautiful people basking in mellow jazz and Tabasco-spiced martinis. The kitchen is focused and daring. Pizza overloaded with lobster is shamelessly decadent, but the gnocchi gratin with Amish chicken, Manchego cheese, and white truffle oil is luscious and restrained. Venison strip loin is perfectly partnered with both tart apple gastrique and woodsy mushroom ragout. By dessert, resistance is futile: try to keep from using your fingers on the buttery crumbs atop mango cobbler.

Bridge House Tavern

American 𝄪𝄪

D4

321 N. Clark St. (on the Chicago River)

Phone: 312-644-0283
Web: www.bridgehousetavern.com
Prices: $$

Lunch & dinner daily

Lake

Take the elevator by the Clark Street bridge down to this riverside dwelling. When the sun is warm, Chicagoans clamor for Bridge House Tavern's spectacular tree-lined patio, exquisitely defined by the hum of cars crossing the bridge above and its compelling skyline vista. Inside, a brew of suits and locals crowd the onyx bar, attractively dressed with flagstone walls.

The service verges on erratic and your order may be wrong, but what a view! Grab your prime patio seat before the happy-hour hordes descend. An endless supply of sautéed Green City Market vegetables provide just the right crunch, while macaroni and cheese with Nueske bacon is pure decadence. The smoked salmon BLT is good, but when served with that bacon milkshake it is a showstopper.

Carson's

Barbecue

C2

612 N. Wells St. (at Ontario St.)

Phone: 312-280-9200
Web: www.ribs.com
Prices: $$

Lunch & dinner daily

 Chicago (Red)

Fear not, barbecue fans. Though this Chicago classic has undergone a face-lift, behind the slightly forbidding windowless brick walls of the Wells Street flagship, the restaurant's Old World sensibility and, most importantly, its recipe for sweet, smoky signature ribs all remain intact.

Steps away from other gut-busting Chicago food institutions like Al's Beef, Gino's East, and Mitchell's Ice Cream, Carson's continues to hold its own as the go-to spot for delectable barbecue. Pit-smoked with hickory wood for hours, the legendary slabs of baby back ribs are worth every messy bite and tender enough to gnaw all the way down to the bone. Travelers and Chicago expats can rest easy knowing that these supremely slathered wares ship overnight across the nation.

Chicago Cut

Steakhouse

D4

300 N. LaSalle St. (at Wacker Dr.)

Phone: 312-329-1800
Web: www.chicagocutsteakhouse.com
Prices: $$$

Lunch & dinner daily

Merchandise Mart

In a town that's fanatically loyal to its meat, Chicago Cut rivals some of the well-tested classics that have "steaked" their claim on the city's bellies for decades. Diners pack the place wall-to-wall from breakfast through dinner, admiring the river views in this glossy modern steakhouse and choosing a bottle from the extensive iPad wine list.

Though it's a menu fixture, the gently charred, wet-aged bone-in filet mignon sells out quickly, so snag the cut if it's available. It wouldn't be a steakhouse without lots of spuds and creamy greens on the side; the house-made hollandaise sauce served with asparagus is a perfect foil for both meat and vegetables. Split the dessert: one order of nutty, spicy carrot cake is large enough to feed a four-top.

Coco Pazzo

Italian XX

C3

300 W. Hubbard St. (at Franklin St.)

Phone: 312-836-0900
Web: www.cocopazzochicago.com
Prices: **$$**

Lunch Mon – Fri
Dinner nightly
Merchandise Mart

Near the mammoth Merchandise Mart, this nearly 20-year-old mainstay attracts a steady crowd for both business lunches and after-work dinners. The rumble of the El and the hustle and bustle of the neighborhood contribute to the energy here with a chatty and buzzy ambience. A simple, unfussy, Tuscan menu explains the repeat business and wide appeal.

Lunch and dinner menus differ slightly, with lunch featuring wood-burning oven pizzas and entrée salads; and dinner skewed toward more satisfying entrées. Try the creamy risotto with spinach and taleggio, or the crispy pork chop Milanese paired with shaved fennel, olives, and citrus vinaigrette.

The wine list has a strong Italian focus and is a good mix of well and lesser known winemakers and varietals.

Crofton on Wells

Contemporary XX

C3

535 N. Wells St. (bet. Grand Ave. & Ohio St.)

Phone: 312-755-1790
Web: www.croftononwells.com
Prices: **$$$**

Dinner Mon – Sat

Grand (Red)

Appropriate to its home in a historic 1920s Italianate building, flashy and trendy has no place at Crofton on Wells. The room is meant for low-key romantics and those seeking timeless comfort among the oxblood and charcoal gray walls, warm brown leather barstools, and wood-framed mirrors that evoke a streamlined American bistro.

Chef/owner Suzy Crofton sticks to the French-American staples, featuring quality ingredients with too-brief flickers of imagination. The signature crab cake with delicately kicky chili vinaigrette never abdicates its spot on the menu, and standards like pan-roasted salmon and beef tenderloin dominate (ask for each medium-rare or risk the consequences). A multi-entrée selection of vegetarian dishes is a thoughtful sidebar.

Cyrano's Bistrot

C3

French ✕✕

546 N. Wells St. (bet. Grand Ave. & Ohio St.)

Phone: 312-467-0546
Web: www.cyranosbistrot.com
Prices: $$

Dinner Mon – Sat

🔲 Grand (Red)

Beyond the vividly painted façade lies a charming French bistro straight out of central casting, complete with vintage French film posters, warm Provençal colors, and roosters in every nook and cranny. On an icy, wet evening, there may be no cozier place to fill both belly and soul than a windowed banquette or a seat at the amiable bar.

Stellar sides like garlicky spinach and blue cheese mashed potatoes elevate a menu of straightforward bistro classics such as a crispy-skinned, roasted half-chicken gleaming with a garlic, mushroom, and white wine reduction. Other delights include a flavorful onion soup; duck terrine studded with chicken liver, pine nuts, and sun dried tomatoes; or lavender-scented crêpes with chocolate sauce and banana mousse.

David Burke's Primehouse

F2

Steakhouse ✕✕

616 N. Rush St. (bet. Ohio & Ontario Sts.)

Phone: 312-660-6000
Web: www.davidburkeprimehouse.com
Prices: $$$

Lunch & dinner daily

🔲 Grand (Red)

David Burke's Primehouse is true to its name and focus: these steaks are sired by a bull named "Prime" raised on Creekstone Farm in Kentucky, before being aged in their Himalayan salt-tiled room, and, finally, wheeled on a cart to your table.

Inside the James Chicago hotel, this is a comfortable, attractive, and suitably masculine space in which to enjoy an impressive steak—perhaps complemented by their two privately labeled bottles, a sauce called 207L, named after Prime's ear tag, and another spicy-sweet variation.

Appetites are whet with fluffy cheese-topped popovers, and then sated with surf and turf dumplings (a mixture of chopped lobster and braised short rib). Skip the sides to leave room for a s'mores-inspired slice of Prime cake.

Eggsperience

E2

35 W. Ontario St. (at Dearborn St.)

Phone: 312-870-6773
Web: www.eggsperiencecafe.com
Prices: 🍪🍪

Lunch & dinner daily

🚇 Grand (Red)

When only a 24-hour diner will do, Eggsperience delights with an egg at the ready. This spacious, dressed-up diner offers a multitude of seating options, including a lengthy counter. Outside, you may find fast-moving lines; inside it is a bright, cheery spot, with natural light and many representations of the almighty egg.

Find it also on the plate, in omelets, skillets, and frittatas, just to name a few dishes. The cast-iron skillets are chock-full of ingredients, such as the "mmmmmushroom skillet" made with mushrooms, spinach, two kinds of cheeses, potatoes, and onions. With that order are sides of pancakes, which are mercifully light and fluffy. Caffeine addicts rejoice: a whole tasty pot of coffee is placed on your table.

Elate

D2

111 W. Huron St. (at Clark St.)

Phone: 312-202-9900
Web: www.elatechciago.com
Prices: $$

Lunch & dinner daily

🚇 Chicago (Red)

Sunny dispositions are de rigueur at Elate in the Felix Hotel—whether the upbeat atmosphere comes from the smile-worthy name, the downtown activity bopping along outside the floor-to-ceiling windows, or the quirky but approachable food, is up to the diner to decide.

The words "Snickers pot de crème" might prove irresistible, and the dessert's taste certainly backs it up, but before sampling one, diners may want to try savory dishes like octopus confit with smoky roasted eggplant and a hit of yuzu; or moist Duroc pork loin with blueberry barbecue sauce and thyme yogurt. The always-popular weekend brunch brings out additional not-your-typical-breakfast choices like braised pork and egg tostada or pizza with ham, truffled potatoes, Gouda, and egg.

English

D3 Gastropub

444 N. LaSalle St. (at Illinois St.)

Phone: 312-222-6200
Web: www.englishchicago.com
Prices: $$

Lunch & dinner Mon – Sat

Merchandise Mart

An art deco façade gives way to a throwback interior of decorative ironwork, old timey photographs, and Victorian felt wallpaper, setting the mood for an evening of eating well and drinking better at this three-story gastropub. The room, with amber wagon wheel light fixtures, serves tasty plates of pub fare, plus artisanal cocktails for office workers and sports fans who appreciate the TVs above the bar.

"Between Bread" options like a fried egg BLT or Angus burger on a pretzel bun are popular, as are the array of sliders featuring Guinness-braised pork belly, Buffalo chicken, or lobster cakes. Substantial English pub fare like shepherd's pie, fish and chips, or bangers and mash are smart options if your initial reason to visit is for the booze.

Epic

D3 Contemporary

112 W. Hubbard St. (bet. Clark & LaSalle Sts.)

Phone: 312-222-4940
Web: www.epicrestaurantchicago.com
Prices: $$$

Lunch Mon – Fri
Dinner Mon – Sat
Grand (Red)

The young, beautiful, and affluent take up nearly every nook in this lofty, seductive space that lives up to its moniker, but there's room for a few hundred more scenesters to sneak in. From the multi-story wall of windows soaring from street level to a sophisticated rooftop lounge for dancing the night away, Epic is dramatic, funky, and verging on too trendy—but also too fun to resist.

Despite staff that sometimes seems like they'd rather be served than serving you, the kitchen acquits itself admirably with a menu as sprawling as the space. Rich Parmesan gnocchi bathed in butter or virtuous white miso-marinated salmon? Oysters from the raw bar or a nostalgic chocolate peanut butter cup? There's a dish to nosh on and a drink to suck down for any mood.

Fleming's

E3

25 E. Ohio St. (bet. State St. & Wabash Ave.)

Phone: 312-329-9463
Web: www.flemingssteakhouse.com
Prices: $$$

Dinner nightly

Grand (Red)

In many ways Chicago is still a meat and potatoes town, and the famous Fleming's chain is as good a place as any to find these faves. A classic steakhouse, Fleming's lounge is painted a rich burgundy and shows off redwood-stained furnishings. The crowd may be a confusing blend of corporates, pre-theater touristas, and gaggles celebrating a special occasion, but they all flock here for staples like an iceberg wedge served with gooey blue cheese dressing and crowned with cherry tomatoes; and potatoes, sliced paper-thin and served gratinée, with layers of cheese and jalapeños. A simply seasoned USDA Prime filet is served tender and enriched with spicy peppercorn sauce. More than 100 wines by the glass make it easy to sip the right vintage with your meal.

Friends Sushi

F2

710 N. Rush St. (bet. Huron & Superior Sts.)

Phone: 312-787-8998
Web: www.friendssushi.com
Prices: $$

Lunch & dinner daily

Chicago (Red)

Pass through an unassuming façade to find this surprisingly mod *sushi-ya* furnished with low stools, bean-shaped tables, and white leather seating that seems to conjure a retro-70s lounge. Yet form and function meld well here, as the friendly and efficient staff tends to the undeniably fun space.

While there is a good selection of cooked dishes on offer, the real focus here is the quality fish served as sushi, sashimi, and maki (further divided into raw and cooked rolls). Dishes are presented with the air of an abstract artist, as brilliantly colored sauces decorate oversized plates of neatly prepared maki. Expect creative, crowd-pleasing combinations as in the salsa maki with white tuna, cilantro, jalapeño, lime, and *masago* topped with tempura crumb.

Frontera Grill

Mexican ✗✗

D3

445 N. Clark St. (bet. Hubbard & Illinois Sts.)

Phone: 312-661-1434   Lunch & dinner Tue – Sat
Web: www.fronterakitchens.com
Prices: $$ Grand (Red)

Loud, fun, and excellent, Frontera Grill is the more casual Chicago home of Chef Rick Bayless—perhaps America's best-known Mexican food enthusiast. While his commercial empire has burgeoned to include TV shows, books, and more restaurants, quality ingredients prepared with signature style remain the focus here.

Tortilla soup is the stuff of legend, and not to be missed by any first-timer. The menu goes on to offer the likes of Mexico City-style deep-fried quesadillas stuffed with locally crafted cheese, or the refined and comforting *posole rojo*, served with traditional garnishes.

Whether here for lunch, brunch, or dinner, know that this lively Mexican spot will be packed. Consider staking a claim at the bar and keeping a keen eye on the nearby tables.

Fulton's on the River

Seafood ✗✗

D4

315 N. LaSalle St. (at the Chicago River)

Phone: 312-822-0100   Lunch Mon – Sat
Web: www.fultonsontheriver.com   Dinner nightly
Prices: $$$ Merchandise Mart

Of all Chicago's many charms, its skyline–built from one iconic skyscraper after the other–is among the best. What better way to appreciate this treasure than to dine on a terrace in the shadow of these architectural wonders? Arrive at this large restaurant in a rehabbed brick warehouse for tables on the terrace of the Chicago River, where you'll also find the most spectacular view.

From here enjoy a homemade lemonade or glass of Champagne and settle in for a full meal. Lunch is popular, thanks to the value-oriented spectrum of soups, salads, fish and chips, burgers, and sandwiches. At night Fulton's becomes a classic steakhouse with seafood and steaks to the max, plus oysters, crab cakes, and all the usual trimmings.

Gene & Georgetti

C3

500 N. Franklin St. (at Illinois St.)

Phone: 312-527-3718　　　　　　Lunch & dinner Mon – Sat
Web: www.geneandgeorgetti.com
Prices: **$$$$**　　　　　　　　🚇 Merchandise Mart

With such wonderful consistency for decades (and surely, for decades to come), dining here is akin to stepping into a time machine. Outside, cab drivers deliver women with hairdos that are still "set" at the beauty parlor. Inside, find crowds of suit-clad regulars who still believe in the three-martini lunch. Upstairs is a quieter, more subdued place to dine near a wintry wood-burning fireplace. Nonetheless, everyone is welcome here, from Chi-town politicos to the average Joe.

The menu offers a hybrid of Italian-American classics and standard steakhouse fare. The steaks are huge (get ready for that doggie bag) and sides equally so. The veal Parmesan is decadent and delicious. Cocktails trump the wine list, sticking with the feeling of the era.

Gilt Bar 😊

C4

230 W. Kinzie St. (at Franklin St.)

Phone: 312-464-9544　　　　　　　　Dinner Tue – Sat
Web: www.giltbarchicago.com
Prices: **$$**　　　　　　　　　🚇 Merchandise Mart

Put in your earplugs before stepping inside this sexy, modern gastropub. Even on a weeknight, Gilt Bar is jammed with a young, spirited crowd looking for a drink, a bite, and high-volume chatter under low-lit filament bulbs and whimsical chandeliers.

The menu begs for sharing: worthy standouts include toasted country bread spread with foie gras, or even pastas like orecchiette floating in a spicy sausage ragù. The hot spot vibe continues late into the night, making it an engaging stop for desserts including a sticky date cake crowned with a butter-brown sugar crumble drizzled with caramel sauce and flecked with coffee ice cream. The bar boasts an impressive beer list and a notable selection of whiskey, bourbon, and Scotch.

Gino's East

Pizza

633 N. Wells St. (at Ontario St.)

Phone: 312-943-1124   Lunch & dinner daily
Web: www.ginoseast.com
Prices: Grand (Red)

When sated diners cover the walls of this massive, dark, and dizzyingly loud Chicago deep-dish pizza parlor with scratchy graffiti–a Gino's East tradition–they tell the story, add to the legends, and speak to their longstanding loyalty for this divey yet venerable institution.

Be prepared for a wait, as families, tourists, couples, and regulars linger side-by-side for the famous deep-dish and thin-crust pizzas, all made to order. Both versions start with a round of sturdy golden dough before piling on tomato sauce, then layers of toppings, and finishing with copious handfuls of cheese. Though pepperoni and sausage are requisite offerings, a cheese and spinach pie isn't just a halfhearted concession to health but a true regional specialty.

Giordano's

Pizza

730 N. Rush St. (at Superior St.)

Phone: 312-951-0747   Lunch & dinner daily
Web: www.giordanos.com
Prices: Chicago (Red)

Value, friendly service, and delicious deep-dish pizza make Giordano's a crowd sweetheart. With several locations dotting the city and suburbs, this restaurant has been gratifying locals with comforting Italian-American fare for years. Come during the week–service picks up especially at dinner–to avoid the cacophony.

Giordano's menu includes your typical salads, pastas, et al., but you'd do well to save room for the real star: the deep-dish. Bring backup because this pie could feed a small country. The spinach pie arrives on a buttery pastry crust, filled with spreads of sautéed (or steamed) spinach and tomato sauce, and topped with mozzarella and Parmesan cheese. For those cold, windy nights, opt for delivery—their website sketches a detailed menu.

Chicago ▶ River North

207

graham elliot

Contemporary

217 W. Huron St. (bet. Franklin & Wells Sts.)

Phone: 312-624-9975   Dinner nightly
Web: www.grahamelliot.com
Prices: $$$ Chicago (Brown)

Jim Colombo

In lieu of bread, a basket of popcorn dusted with truffle oil, chive powder, and Parmesan hints that another talented Chicago chef is about to turn fine dining preconceptions upside down. Graham Elliot Bowles refers to his food as "bistronomic"—a fusion of casual, hearty bistro dishes and the wow-'em pyrotechnics of modernist cuisine. Though it sounds space age, there's nothing to fear.

Instead of a hushed temple where murmuring servers deliver preciously plated food, graham elliot's guests kick back in a handsome, industrial room with exposed ventilation ducts and worn brick. Over a pumping soundtrack, baby-faced and casually styled crowds peruse a pared-down menu featuring three menu items in each of five categories: Cold, Hot, Sea, Land, and Sweet. Build a meal Lego-style or take the pressure off with five- or ten-course prix-fixe menus.

Highlights of the uniformly tempting menu may include an homage to Wisconsin in the form of caramelized pheasant bratwurst over sharp cheddar risotto, apple *brunoise*, and beads of wheat beer gelée; or heritage Jidori chicken breast with wilted Tuscan kale, toasted gingerbread crumbs, and a trio of supple cranberries—dried, pickled, and sweet.

GT Fish & Oyster

Seafood 𝖷𝖷

C3

531 N. Wells St. (at Grand Ave.)

Phone: 312-929-3501
Web: www.gtfishandoyster.wordpress.com
Prices: $$

Lunch Mon – Fir
Dinner nightly

Coastal transplants pining for fish shack flair can thank Chef Giuseppe Tentori of Boka for flexing his fins at this sexy seafood-centric spot. The décor is subtle and leans towards a maritime theme without getting too crabby-chic and kitschy. A dominating mural of a skeletal marlin and communal seating around a boomerang-shaped surfboard makes it easy to slurp down a martini and a dozen Blue Points.

Along with the requisite lobster rolls, oysters, and king crab legs, unexpected pairings please. Shrimp and foie gras terrine keeps its richness with orange apricot chutney and a pickled pearl onion salad. Tuna *poke* with sesame oil gets slight sweetness from mango purée. Seafood-phobes, take note: a few "not fish" options like strip loin will fill your belly.

Harry Caray's

Steakhouse 𝖷𝖷

E4

33 W. Kinzie St. (at Dearborn St.)

Phone: 312-828-0966
Web: www.harrycarays.com
Prices: $$$

Lunch & dinner daily

🚇 Grand (Red)

The gone-but-never-forgotten Chicago sportscaster Harry Caray was known for his trademark "Holy Cow!" Guests might feel the need to utter it as they see the famous broadcaster's bronze bust complete with giant glasses. As Harry Caray is iconic to the Windy City, so, too, are steakhouses, so it makes sense that the restaurant that sports his name is a classic steakhouse specializing in USDA Prime corn-fed beef.

Make sure you show up hungry here: the 18oz dry-aged, bone-in ribeye or 23oz Porterhouse are on the hefty side of what is an ample selection on this massive, meat-centric menu. Like most steakhouses, all the sides–classics including garlic mashed potatoes, creamed spinach, and sautéed mushrooms–are served à la carte.

Hubbard Inn

International

110 W. Hubbard St. (bet. Clark & LaSalle Sts.)

Phone: 312-222-1331	Lunch Mon – Fri
Web: www.hubbardinn.com	Dinner Mon – Sat
Prices: $$	Grand (Red)

River North already teems with over-the-top dining options, but Hubbard Inn backs up its theatrical panache with serious culinary talent. Wide, wood-planked tables and cozy leather chairs warmly lit by frosted globes evoke a modern English country tavern with intriguing Mediterranean accents—like tiles adorning the walls of the two-story space.

An oversized chalkboard behind the bar lists the Inn's craft beer selection: order a draught before digging into a cocotte of vegetables including Moroccan kale, almonds, and cauliflower in fiery *harissa* broth. Exquisitely finished seafood standouts include grilled jumbo prawns with buttery mushrooms or seared golden trout with Manila clams, spring onions, *guanciale*, and a gorgeous jumble of ribboned chilies.

Hub51

International

51 W. Hubbard St. (at Dearborn St.)

Phone: 312-828-0051	Lunch & dinner daily
Web: www.hub51chicago.com	
Prices: $$	Grand (Red)

Hub51 got a ton of buzz when it opened in 2008 because of the boys backing the bar. The twenty-something sons of legendary Chicago restaurateur Rich Melman are behind this large, crowded bar-slash-eatery and were determined to make it appeal to a hip, downtown crowd. Having a nightclub, SUB 51, right downstairs doesn't hurt.

The menu appeals to the under-40 set with a hybrid offering of Tex-Mex, sushi, sandwiches, salads, and other things folks order when they get off of work. Fish tacos are well-conceived; the popular *shakishaki* tuna is crunchy and tangy; and the carrot cake super decadent with extra scoops of whipped cream and cream cheese icing. Drunker appetites can choose a green chile cheeseburger or the Dude, an aged 18oz ribeye with the works.

Japonais

A1

Fusion XXX

600 W. Chicago Ave. (bet. Larrabee St. & the Chicago River)

Phone: 312-822-9600
Web: www.japonaischicago.com
Prices: $$$

Lunch Mon – Fri
Dinner nightly
Chicago (Blue)

For nearly a decade, Japonais has remained sleek and sexy while attracting the see-and-be-seen contingent in droves. Sultry scenesters relax on oversized ottomans or take in romantic river views in the windowed lounge, while efficient servers nimbly take care of large parties and navigate the crowds.

The Asian fusion menu continues to impress from start to finish: a refreshing seaweed salad spiked with citrus and pickled cucumber; and The Rock, a signature preparation of tender New York strip steak cooked tableside on a sizzling-hot rock, are standouts. Finish on a high note with desserts that put exotic touches on all-American staples, like the *kabocha* squash cheesecake with five-spices, frothy pineapple mousse, and a dense almond cookie crust.

Joe's

F3

American XXX

60 E. Grand Ave. (at Rush St.)

Phone: 312-379-5637
Web: www.joes.net
Prices: $$$$

Lunch Mon – Fri
Dinner nightly
Grand (Red)

An outpost of the Miami landmark, this Joe's may not be a Chicago original, but it certainly feels like one. It seems like it's been here forever, due in large part to the clubby ambience and the crew of golf shirt-wearing regulars. It's always jumping, especially with the business boys at lunch.

File it under the "when in Rome" rule, so yes, you should start with the stone crabs. But there's a flood more to this menu with steakhouse faves like oysters Rockefeller; ribeyes aside creamed spinach; some Southern-flecked dishes (fried chicken); as well as odes to Florida (did you guess grouper?). Desserts like coconut cream and peanut butter cream pie are American through and through, but for the classic Joe's finish, get the key lime pie.

Keefer's

E4

Steakhouse ✗✗✗

20 W. Kinzie St. (bet. Dearborn & State Sts.)

Phone: 312-467-9525
Web: www.keefersrestaurant.com
Prices: $$$$

Lunch Mon – Fri
Dinner Mon – Sat
📋 Grand (Red)

From the warm welcome and efficient service to the contemporary menu, everything Keefer's does, it does well. While Chicago has no shortage of steakhouses, this one distinguishes itself with a friendly bar area showing bistro-style booths and menu, and a vibe that is updated and upscale in the main dining room—this is a modern classic whose menu follows suit.

Find all the anticipated cuts of meat, sauces, and sides to feast on in an à la carte style. But also try the chef's signature items for something a little different: sides like the potato croquettes (imagine deep-fried mashed potatoes with all the toppings inside); braised endive in sauce Mornay; and broccoli salad combining florets, fennel, apple, and cheese with a lemon vinaigrette.

La Madia

D3

Italian ✗✗

59 W. Grand Ave. (bet. Clark & Dearborn Sts.)

Phone: 312-329-0400
Web: www.dinelamadia.com
Prices: $$

Lunch & dinner daily
📋 Grand (Red)

This contemporary take on the pizzeria, where subway tiles mix with marble at the pizza station, bustles with activity while remaining a comfortable spot for couples or crowds. Booths throughout the high-ceilinged space, barstools at the open kitchen, and sleek bar give ample room for *mangiare*. Peruse the extensive wine list, with options by the bottle or by the glass in four- and seven-ounce pours, and exquisite stemware to match.

The well-edited menu features modern riffs on Italian fare such as Sardinian flatbread filled with herbed chicken, almonds, and currants; or thin-crust pizzas with quality toppings like sweet Italian sausage, fresh mozzarella, and caramelized onions. Split the dense chocolate *tortino* with your tablemates for dessert.

Mastro's

Steakhouse 🍴🍴🍴

E3

520 N. Dearborn St. (at Grand Ave.)

Phone: 312-521-5100

Web: www.mastrosrestaurants.com

Prices: $$$$

Dinner nightly

🚇 Grand (Red)

Big spenders and power brokers bring swagger to the latest steakhouse chainlet hoping to make its mark on Chicago's meat scene. Clubby, plush décor, a crooning pianist, and generously poured martinis telegraph old-school swank, though servers radiate genuine Midwestern friendliness, and the crowd eats it all up. Reservations are essential, even for this spacious, multi-floored setting with nooks for private dining.

Large and succulent portions of wet-aged prime steak arrive simply broiled on screaming hot plates, with sauces and accompaniments upon request. Show restraint with the list of two dozen traditional sides like garlic mashed potatoes and creamed spinach in favor of a new classic: the rich, smooth, salty, sweet, and revelatory butter cake.

Mercadito

Mexican 🍴🍴

D4

108 W. Kinzie St. (bet. Clark & LaSalle Sts.)

Phone: 312-329-9555

Web: www.mercaditorestaurants.com

Prices: $$

Lunch & dinner daily

🚇 Merchandise Mart

It's Mexican, but if you're thinking mariachi bands and sombrero-donning staff, you've got it all wrong. Mercadito, just steps from the Merchandise Mart in the design-centric River North, is a far cry from the usual haunts. Instead, it's the very definition of urban-chic with its funky light fixtures and specially commissioned art from graffiti artist, Erni Vales. The Sandoval brothers got it right times three in New York; this is their fourth offspring. The menu pinpoints a plethora of small dishes that build a tasty Mexican meal. With six varieties of guac and salsa, three ceviches, luscious *botanas*, and ten differing tacos, something is bound to catch your eye. Steering off the main road are pork tacos with grilled pineapple and goat's milk flan.

Chicago ▶ River North

213

Nacional 27

Latin American 𝔛𝔛𝔛

C2

325 W. Huron St. (at Orleans St.)

Phone: 312-664-2727

Web: www.n27chicago.com

Prices: $$

Dinner Mon – Sat

🖳 Chicago (Brown)

♿

☞♀

Celebrating the 27 recognized Latin American countries through name and cuisine, Nacional 27 serves up sultry pleasures in a wonderfully diverting environment. From the dusky enticements of the central bar, energetic music, and weekly events like complimentary salsa dancing lessons, it's easy to get distracted before you sample the food.

The extensive menu of passionately flavored small plates, ceviches, paellas, and the signature N27 roast suckling pig *Cubano*, show off traditional Latin elements in unexpected combinations. Dishes like the *chimichurri*-crusted filet atop showstopping potato-chorizo hash with a malbec reduction; and the barbecued lamb taco with guava, black beans, sweet agave, and creamy avocado salsa hit all the right notes.

Osteria Via Stato

Italian 𝔛𝔛

E2

620 N. State St. (at Ontario St.)

Phone: 312-642-8450

Web: www.osteriaviastato.com

Prices: $$

Dinner nightly

🖳 Grand (Red)

♿

🍽

🎎

☞♀

⌁

Tucked inside the downtown Embassy Suites is a little taste of Italy. Osteria Via Stato's dark and cozy décor fashions the quintessential charming Italian trattoria. Inside, the space is halved, with a pizzeria in the front and dining room toward the back, though there is minimal difference between these menus.

Come hungry, since the restaurant's portions (and prices) are generous. The à la carte menu has it all, with pastas in half or full portions. The best way to sample the fare is to arrive with friends and order the Italian dinner party. This family-style meal comes with antipasti, two pastas, an entrée, sides, and you can even ask for seconds. Confused about wine? Fuggedaboutit and go with "just bring me wine," at three different price points.

NAHA ⌘

American 🍴🍴🍴

D3

500 N. Clark St. (at Illinois St.)

Phone:	312-321-6242	Lunch Mon – Fri
Web:	www.naha-chicago.com	Dinner Mon – Sat
Prices:	$$$	Grand (Red)

Lara Kastner

Gazing through a wall of windows toward the corner of Clark and Illinois, it's easy to breathe a sigh of contentment watching the urban tableau play out beyond the glass while comfortably ensconced in one of the restaurant's banquettes and surrounded by shades of cream, gray, and deep taupe. A meal at NAHA is an instant soother, a simple luxury that never feels pretentious or stuffy.

If your idea of relaxation starts with pre-dinner drinks, the smattering of wooden tables and sizeable bar in the front lounge are an open invitation to begin. Natural and industrial elements mix freely and harmoniously in the restaurant, as the bar's warm woods segue into lanter boxes filled with grassy reeds throughout the dining room.

The Zen-meets-Mediterranean vibe of the space—equal parts calm and gusto—extends to the plates coming from Chef Carrie Nahabedian's kitchen: dribbles of tangy green apple broth zing with lusty roasted chanterelles and crisp-skinned Arctic char. And no one will lift an eyebrow should you mop up the last drops of velvety roasted squash soup using a griddled goat cheese sandwich. Vanilla bean-infused polenta adds an earthy touch to the delicate custard of a gâteau Basque.

215

Paris Club

D4

French ✗✗

59 W. Hubbard St. (bet. Clark & Dearborn Sts.)

Phone: 312-595-0800   Dinner nightly
Web: www.parisclubchicago.com
Prices: $$ Grand (Red)

Jammed with the top five percent of the city's hippest and most attractive residents, Paris Club might knock you flat with the sound waves ricocheting from the ceiling's iron beams to the subway-tiled walls to the communal wooden tables. A bar spanning the vast front room helps corral the pretty young things, but this lounge-cum-eatery nonetheless runs smoothly with the pampering service expected from the newest Lettuce Entertain You venture.

French gastropub fare that's a tasty step above typical lounge food offers a respite from the burger-centric menus at similar Chicago hot spots. Small plates like jars of pork rillettes, mac and cheese gratinée, or lamb meatballs with *harissa*-spiked tomato sauce are reliable options from the extensive menu.

Phil Stefani's 437 Rush

F3

Italian ✗✗

437 N. Rush St. (bet. Hubbard & Illinois Sts.)

Phone: 312-222-0101   Lunch Mon – Sat
Web: www.stefanirestaurants.com   Dinner nightly
Prices: $$$ Grand (Red)

Phil Stefani's 437 Rush offers an Italian-themed menu, bolstered by steakhouse fare. This lone structure brings a bar (dressed with a painted mural) up front, where diners can relax when they first enter. Then, let the cordial waitstaff lead you to one of two dining rooms, each with a similar décor—wood accents, paneled-and-tile floors, and warm walls.

White-clothed tables carry a foray of food, presented in fine white china. Italian-born Federico Comacchio brings his native's sensibility to a tandem of treats including pappardelle with house-made sausage ragout and goat milk ricotta; or risotto with organic buttercup pumpkin, Swiss chard, and robiola. Less theatrical, but as tasty, are the Caesar salad, steaks, seafood, and sweets.

Pizzeria Uno

E3

Pizza ✗

29 E. Ohio St. (at Wabash Ave.)

Phone: 312-321-1000
Web: www.unos.com
Prices: 💶

Lunch & dinner daily

🔲 Grand (Red)

Since 1943, this establishment has been laying claim to the (somewhat disputed) title of creating the original Chicago-style pizza. Its tiny booths and wood tables wear their years of graffiti etchings like a badge of honor. Nonetheless, an intricate pressed-tin ceiling reflects the cheery atmosphere as everyone counts down the 40 or so minutes it takes for these deep-dish pies to bake.

Of course, the main attraction here is, was, and always will be the flaky, buttery crust generously layered with mozzarella, other toppings, and tangy tomato sauce that comprise this belly-busting pizza. The menu also includes a selection of good basic bar food like Buffalo wings and a simple salad, but most just save the room for an extra slice.

Pops for Champagne

E3

Contemporary 🍽

601 N. State St. (at Ohio St.)

Phone: 312-266-7677
Web: www.popsforchampagne.com
Prices: $$

Dinner nightly

🔲 Grand (Red)

25 years? Now that's something to celebrate! Pops for Champagne has long been a Windy City fixture. Crowds eager to toast everything from the end of a work week to a new marriage come for a bit of the bubbly (or perhaps the Quebecois—apple ice wine and brut Champagne) and stay for the bites. There is a fine listing of cheeses and charcuterie, but nibble instead on tastily prepared plates like lamb pâté with pickled cherries and violet mustard; or even charred baby octopus with curry roasted cauliflower and *agrodolce* raisins.

The dining room is attractively donned with crackled green glass-topped tables, large windows, and an onyx-amber bar filled with choices. There's even live music some nights to further lighten your effervescent mood.

Prosecco

Italian XX

C2

710 N. Wells St. (bet. Huron & Superior Sts.)

Phone: 312-951-9500
Web: www.prosecco.us.com
Prices: $$

Lunch Mon – Fri
Dinner Mon – Sat
Chicago (Brown)

Champagne hues and vintage, Venice-inspired style create an atmosphere of casual elegance here at Prosecco, where bountiful portions of sumptuous Italian satiate adoring locals. Of course, the namesake sparkling beverage is offered in fifty different varieties. But first let the friendly and efficient staff guide you through a luscious *zuppa* seasoned with oregano, basil, rosemary, and finely minced black truffle, drizzled with truffle oil and served with Parmesan-topped bread for sopping. For a bit of spice, the *spaghetti alla diavola* gets things right—al dente pasta and fresh shrimp, tossed in herb-packed tomato sauce kicked up with red pepper flakes.

In the warmer months, enjoy a seat under the black and gold awning of the spacious patio out front.

Quartino

Italian XX

E2

626 N. State St. (at Ontario St.)

Phone: 312-698-5000
Web: www.quartinochicago.com
Prices: ☜☜

Lunch & dinner daily

Grand (Red)

Nobody feels left out in the cold at Quartino, the inviting Italian spot that has group dining down to a science. It earns its accolades catering to crowds with reasonably priced food and lots of it. Colleagues get to know each other better over heaping plates of pasta, while best buddies enjoy sampling small plates of short ribs and roasted sausage.

You can try a little bit of everything here, where even the all-Italian wine list (available in ¼, ½, and full carafes, as well as bottles) is meant to be divvied up. The menu dances across Italy for its inspiration, striving to represent the best of its culinary regions. Find a great selection of Neapolitan thin-crust pizzas, house-made *salumi*, tempting small plates, freshly made pastas, and *risotti*.

RL

American 🍴🍴

F1

115 E. Chicago Ave. (bet. Michigan Ave. & Rush St.)

Phone: 312-475-1100　　　　　　　　　　　Lunch & dinner daily
Web: www.rlrestaurant.com
Prices: $$$　　　　　　　　　　　　　　　🚇 Chicago (Red)

Book a table at RL and you'll instantly feel like a member of the pedigreed elite. This place looks like a stage set for the American dream, so it's no surprise that Ralph Lauren is behind it. The ambience is clubby and posh (think rich mahogany paneled walls, leather banquettes, gleaming crystal) and the crowd is equally attractive. Thanks to the friendly staff, you'll never feel like an outcast. However, if you're lacking the natty uniform, its location inside the Ralph Lauren store is a boon.

A hot spot for brunch, the perennially packed RL echoes the brand's traditional American sensibility with its tried-and-true burgers; popular salads, like the "riff raff"; classic seafood dishes, like crab Louis; and a tasty crème brûlée to finish.

Roy's

Hawaiian 🍴🍴

E2

720 N. State St. (at Superior St.)

Phone: 312-787-7599　　　　　　　　　　　　　　Dinner nightly
Web: www.roysrestaurant.com
Prices: $$　　　　　　　　　　　　　　　　🚇 Chicago (Red)

Roy's may celebrate its Hawaiian roots in its food and background music, but this sophisticated spot with floor-to-ceiling windows and elegant seating does not play to any clichés.

This extremely popular outpost of the nationwide chain has many signature dishes (like macadamia nut-crusted mahi mahi or hibachi grilled salmon), but it also includes selections created specifically by the on-site chef. The Hawaiian fusion cuisine that Roy's is known for focuses heavily on simply prepared, quality seafood such as Hawaiian-style *misoyaki* butterfish with wasabi-ginger-cilantro cream; and crab dynamite-crusted *hebi* with coconut rice and kimchi-lime butter sauce.

Hit the packed bar for the budget-friendly $5 Aloha happy hour (Sunday-Thursday).

Sable

American XX

E3

505 N. State St. (at Illinois St.)

Phone: 312-755-9704   Lunch & dinner daily
Web: www.sablechicago.com
Prices: $$ 🔲 Grand (Red)

Chicago's hotel restaurants have a knack for making a name for themselves and attracting guests and locals alike. Sable, tucked inside the Palomar, is no exception. Inside, it's sleek, cosmopolitan, and contemporary, while the expansive garden patio is a major hit. From an open kitchen, diners are presented with an eclectic American menu that has something for everyone and is designed for sharing.

Dishes may include Wisconsin-fried cheese curds with spicy ketchup; pretzel-crusted fried calamari with bourbon-honey mustard; pork ribs with apple cider-bourbon glaze; or duck confit flatbread with caramelized fennel, dried cherries, and thyme. The brick oven flatbread pizzas are delicious, and the bar's cocktail list is impressive.

Scoozi

Italian XX

B2

410 W. Huron St. (bet. Hudson Ave & Sedgwick St.)

Phone: 312-943-5900   Dinner nightly
Web: www.leye.com
Prices: $$ 🔲 Chicago (Brown)

Dining at Scoozi is like popping in on a neighbor who happens to be a fabulous cook. It is the kind of place filled with families (both literal and metaphorical) settling into oversized leather booths, adding to the fun yet relaxed vibe—its enormous size makes this feat all the more impressive. Reasonable prices have everyone planning to return soon.

On the menu, expect lovely Italian-American classics, perfectly cooked and satisfying, that boast the marks of a very professional kitchen. Linguini *frutti di mare* is spiked with just the right amount of heat, and a tender Italian pot roast with pearl onions, carrots, and fresh rosemary is enrobed in a wonderfully full-bodied sauce. Desserts like deep-fried apple "ravioli" are a sweet twist on tradition.

Shanghai Terrace

F1

Chinese ✗✗

108 E. Superior St. (bet. Michigan Ave. & Rush St.)

Phone: 312-573-6695
Web: www.peninsula.com
Prices: $$$

Lunch & dinner Mon – Sat

🖳 Chicago (Red)

When sporting a chinoiserie design, there is a fine line between setting a theme and looking like a Disneyfied cliché. But, Shanghai Terrace carries off the ethereal Asian look with *mucho* class and distinction. Set inside the posh Peninsula Hotel, this svelte sanctum draws an affluent crowd who come as much for the setting (adorned with Chinese antiques and furnishings, and a staff accoutered sharply in red Mandarin jackets), as they do for the food.

This isn't your average run-of-the-mill shrimp fried rice kinda place, so await a nice medley of Asian-accented entrées like lobster with bamboo shoots, ginger, and spicy black beans; roasted, crispy-skinned Peking duck with hoisin and scallions; and Hong Kong-style beef tenderloin with black pepper sauce.

Shaw's Crab House

E4

Seafood ✗✗

21 E. Hubbard St. (bet. State St. & Wabash Ave.)

Phone: 312-527-2722
Web: www.shawscrabhouse.com
Prices: $$$

Lunch Sun – Fri
Dinner nightly

🖳 Grand (Red)

There aren't that many restaurants that have tuxedoed waiters welcoming guests in jeans, as well as a kid-friendly menu. But that's the story at Shaw's, a mainstay for both locals and visitors. The ambience is old-school with black patent leather booths and big band music.

Crab is always on the menu, though it varies by season: Dungeness, king, stone, soft shell, and blue. The crab cakes are as simple a presentation as imaginable, yet tasty. The single round patty is all large lump Maryland crab with very little filler, served golden brown and kissed with spiced mayonnaise. For a non-crab option, try the horseradish-crusted grouper, prepared simply, but just right. Tuesdays, Thursdays, and Sundays the joint is jumping with live music at the oyster bar.

Smith & Wollensky

Steakhouse

E4

318 N. State St. (at the Chicago River)

Phone: 312-670-9900
Web: www.smithandwollensky.com
Prices: $$$

Lunch & dinner daily

State/Lake

Chicago crawls with mighty steakhouses, but this babe (of the famed national chain) sits gorgeously on the Chicago River bank, and thus, lures all. Inside forever loved Smith & Wollensky, find handsome décor details like dark wood furniture, polished brass, and other accoutrements. The crowds are large (a common sight here), but the staff navigates them with little trouble.

The kitchen churns out steakhouse classics like dry-aged steaks with heaping sides of mashed potatoes and onion rings; and shrimp cocktail—three prawns lying beside three (mustard, tomato, and avocado) sauces. But you're here for the steaks, and they are well charred and perfectly cooked. Don't skip their signature steak sauce—it adds a great kick to the meat.

Sunda

Fusion

D3

110 W. Illinois St. (bet. Clark & Lasalle Sts.)

Phone: 312-644-0500
Web: www.sundachicago.com
Prices: $$

Lunch Sun – Fri
Dinner nightly
Grand (Red)

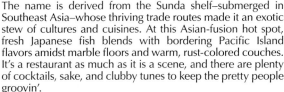

The name is derived from the Sunda shelf–submerged in Southeast Asia–whose thriving trade routes made it an exotic stew of cultures and cuisines. At this Asian-fusion hot spot, fresh Japanese fish blends with bordering Pacific Island flavors amidst marble floors and warm, rust-colored couches. It's a restaurant as much as it is a scene, and there are plenty of cocktails, sake, and clubby tunes to keep the pretty people groovin'.

Hanging box lanterns dim at sundown, perhaps announcing the arrival of such colorful, creative, and tasty dishes as a Brussels sprout salad tossed with shallots, red chilies, ground shrimp, and *nuoc cham*. Pan-fried oxtail potstickers with a wasabi cream and lemongrass lollipops of grilled beef complete the experience.

Topolobampo ⁛

D3

Mexican ✗✗

445 N. Clark St. (bet. Hubbard & Illinois Sts.)

Phone: 312-661-1434
Web: www.rickbayless.com
Prices: $$$

Lunch Tue – Fri
Dinner Tue – Sat
🚇 Grand (Red)

Brendan Lekan

Though it shares a building and entrance with its casual sister spot Frontera Grill (chili-whisperer Rick Bayless' flagship restaurant), Topolobampo delivers a full-throttle dining experience that's a joyful reminder of why it still leads the pack when it comes to high-end Mexican cuisine.

Dramatically and warmly dressed, the dining room blends traditional elements like terra-cotta Saltillo tile floors with modern copper and cobalt blue accents. Vibrant Mexican art and sculptural floral arrangements read as fresh, not dated, always impressive for a restaurant that's been doing its thing since 1989. Well-versed servers make menu decisions less daunting with nuanced explanations.

Textures and flavors do a well-coordinated tango in dishes like *pato en pipian de castaña*, featuring exquisitely crispy yet juicy duck breast with velvety ancho-chestnut *mole*; or a crunchy *patita de puerco* croquette that reveals tender bits of ham hock and trotter once the fork sinks in. Small touches like the balance of spicy chiles, tart tomatillo, bitter chard, and rich *crema* in a bowl of *chilaquiles*; or homemade goat milk caramel atop dessert crêpes spotlight the kitchen's skill with great ingredients.

Union Sushi + Barbeque Bar

C2

230 W. Erie St. (at Franklin St.)

Phone: 312-662-4888
Web: www.eatatunion.com
Prices: $$

Lunch Mon – Fri
Dinner nightly
Chicago (Brown)

It's loud, graffiti-tagged, and mad fun in this über-contemporary, hopping Japanese joint. The bi-level space rocks a colorful, urban design, drawing in a young, hip crowd hungry for the likes of grilled *robata* specialties, noodle dishes, and traditional and creative takes on sushi.

Sample skewers of grilled *kushiyaki* (though alligator can be an acquired taste) then dig your chopsticks into a prosciutto-wrapped scallop topped with wasabi-avocado purée, fried ginger, and sweet plum sauce; or the excellent Bay Street California roll, with crunchy cucumber, spicy chili-mayo, golden brown crab cake, wrapped in nori and rice topped with fresh *masago*. Sate the sweet tooth with Killer Yuzu Pie—a tangy, rich, creamy sensation crowned with whipped cream.

Vermilion

E3

10 W. Hubbard St. (bet. Dearborn & State Sts.)

Phone: 312-527-4060
Web: www.thevermilionrestaurant.com
Prices: $$

Lunch Mon – Fri
Dinner nightly
Grand (Red)

From the stunning oversized photographs shot by India's leading fashion photographer Farrokh Chothia, to the bold, modern styling crafted by architectural firm Searl, Lamaster and Howe, this sleek, sultry, and sexy spot is clearly not your average Indian restaurant.

The surprises continue to the palate, where dishes marrying the marvelous flavors of India and Latin America dazzle and delight. Peruse the menu, and your eye will stop on some seemingly familiar dishes, but expect the unexpected at this bold and inventive scene. Dishes like duck *vindaloo arepa* with brushed pomegranate molasses, curry leaf, and mango, or white chocolate and cauliflower soup are outstanding; while the heady spices of the lamb shank *gassi* are simply intoxicating.

Zealous

Contemporary XXX

419 W. Superior St. (bet. Hudson Ave. & Sedgwick St.)

Phone: 312-475-9112

Web: www.zealousrestaurant.com

Prices: $$$

Dinner Tue – Sat

Chicago (Brown)

Understated in décor but ambitious with its food, Zealous has always marched to its own offbeat tunes. A longtime resident of a loft-like space on a less-traveled block of River North, the room–designed by Chef/owner Michael Taus–feels vaguely Zen, with Asian touches like bamboo, Japanese screens, and quiet murmurs of conversation rippling over the New Age music and bouncing off the 15-foot glass-enclosed wine cellar.

In the kitchen, Taus plays with an eclectic mix of ingredients pulled from cuisines around the globe–Scottish gravlax with *garam masala*-fried Brussels sprouts, for example–piled into intricate towers and platings. Pick à la carte or submit to the chef's whims with tasting menus like the seven-course omakase-style Spontaneous tour.

Look for our symbol Ȣ, spotlighting restaurants with a notable sake list.

225

Streeterville

If you simply had to pick a neighborhood that truly recapitulates Chicago, it would be Streeterville. Home to the Magnificent Mile, the iconic John Hancock Building, and the fun-loving Navy Pier, skyscraping and stirring Streeterville takes the cake.

Absorb the sights and smells of the stunning surroundings, especially upon arrival at Water Tower Place's **foodlife**—a simple food court elevated to an art form, located on the mezzanine floor of the shopping mall. Before going further, know that this isn't your average mall or airport food court. Instead, this United Nations of food courts satiates with 14 different kitchens whipping up everything from Chinese potstickers and deep-dish pizza to fried chicken. **Wow Bao** (also located within the landmark building), doles out

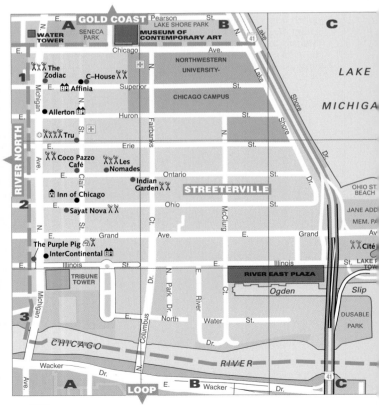

some of the best handheld treats in town (like steamed veggie-and-meat-filled buns), and is so popular, they had to open a second spot in the Loop. The coolest part? Buy a card that gives you access to the many stands.

Food Court Fun

Prefer panini and pastry? Stop by the legendary **Hancock Building**, otherwise known as food lovers paradise. The Italian deli **L'Appetito** is perfect for comforting breakfasts, Italian-and American-style sandwiches, baked goods, and other classic delights. Lucky locals and office types can shop for groceries with sky-high prices to match the staggering view at **Potash Brothers**, a supermarket stunningly set on the 44th floor of the Hancock Building.

Museums and Markets

The Museum of Contemporary Art houses one of the world's leading collections of contemporary art, but it's also the peppers and potatoes that lures gaggles far and wide, to the farmer's market held here on Tuesdays from June through October. Those with fat wallets should hit up posh gourmet supermarket **Fox & Obel** for gorgeous groceries year-round. With a mission to showcase the love and creativity surrounding quality food, this European-style bazaar also houses a delightful café (or market bistro) whose menu struts a spectrum of spectacular treats for all-day dining. Such fine brunch, lunch, and dinner menus combined with boutique wines makes this place a huge higlight (especially among gourmands) in vibrant Streeterville. Carry on this darling adventure at **Teuscher**, **Godiva**, and **Lindt**—they all have boutiques here; but it is Chicago's own **Vosges Haut-Chocolat** that has made a name for itself by rocking taste buds with exotic ingredients—curry and chocolate anyone?

Tasty Treats

Sure, it's crowded and a little bit carnival-like, but that's why we love it. Navy Pier can be tourist central, but it's also a dreamy junk food paradise. Begin with one of 27 different flavors of popcorn available at **The Popcorn Palace &**

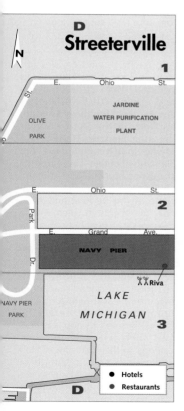

Candy Emporium. With a food philosophy as simple as crafting the finest and most fresh ingredients into delightful treats, this popcorn paradise remains beloved and bustling all year-round. After popcorn prowling, move on to more substantial chow by grabbing an all-natural Chicago-style dog (with mustard, onion, relish, sport peppers, tomato, pickle, and celery salt) from **America's Dog**. This dog heaven showcases a gargantuan repertoire of city-style dogs from Houston, New York, and Philadelphia, to Detroit, Kansas City, and San Francisco. In the mood for some crunch? Venture towards world-famous **Jiminy Chips** for some of the most addictive kettle-cooked, made-to-order potato chips. Also on the menu and prepared with top-notch techniques are sweet potato chips, pita chips, and tortilla chips. The choices are plenty, so make your pick and settle down for a crisp feast.

Streeterville Faithfuls

The **Billy Goat Tavern** is a Streeterville institution. Now known more for its famous "cheezeborger, cheezeborger" Saturday Night Live skit, it's a "buy the tee-shirt" type of place with a spot in Navy Pier, and the original just off Michigan Avenue. The tavern's menu which includes breakfast specials, an array of steaks, and sandwiches galore is sure to please all who may enter its hallowed portals. Jonesing for a juicy burger? Hit up **M Burger** (another outpost thrives in River North), along with the hordes of business lunchers, tourists, and shoppers. It should be renamed "mmm" burger for its tasty, meaty gifts. Bacon, cheese, and secret sauce comprise the signature M burger, but if you're feeling guilty, you can always order the all-veggie Nurse Betty. If you're the sort who craves breakfast for dinner, linger at Michigan Avenue's **West Egg Cafe**. This comfortable coffee corridor may serve lunch and dinner as well, but crowds really flock here for their deliciously decadent omelettes, pancakes, waffles, and other "eggcellent" dishes including "The Swiss Account" featuring eggs, ham, mushrooms, and Swiss cheese baked to perfection, and crowned with black olives, tomatoes, and sour cream.

Sip and Savor

And for those whose tastes run more toward Champagne and cocktails than cheeseburgers and crinkle-cut fries, there's always the **Signature Lounge**, located on the 96th floor of the John Hancock Center. An idyllic spot for nightcaps, the Signature Lounge also presents staggering brunch, lunch, dinner, and dessert menus that employ some of the freshest and most fine ingredients in town. While their creative concoctions are a touch pricey, one glimpse of the sparkling city scape will have you beaming.

And finally, the Northwestern Hospital complex is another esteemed establishment that dominates the Streeterville scene. Besides its top medical and surgical services, also catering to the spectrum of staff and visitors, are a parade of dining gems (cafés, lounges, and ethnic canteens) that loom large over the neighborhood and lake.

C-House

Contemporary ✗✗

A1

166 E. Superior St. (at St. Clair St.)

Phone: 312-523-0923   Lunch & dinner daily
Web: www.c-houserestaurant.com
Prices: $$ Chicago (Red)

Housed in the Affinia Chicago hotel, C-House has a definitive buzz about it (thanks in large part to associations with Chef Marcus Samuelsson). Stylish, yet casual, the striking contemporary space was designed by Brazilian architect Arthur Casas.

Meals begin with freshly-baked Wisconsin cheese curd bread. Oysters on the half shell, house-pickled herring, and smoked trout terrine are among the C-Bar starters that have developed a loyal following (there's even an oyster station). The entrée selections are concise—choose from fish and chips; poached sturgeon; and grilled Running Waters trout with black radish, fennel, and Meyer lemon. The dessert menu offers a whimsical "Candy Bar" selection of chocolate for those with a sweet tooth.

Cité

Contemporary ✗✗

C2

505 N. Lake Shore Dr. (entrance on Grand Ave.)

Phone: 312-644-4050   Dinner nightly
Web: www.citechicago.com
Prices: $$$

Any restaurant with 360-degree views of a magnificent city skyline and the expanse of Lake Michigan has to know that what's outside is likely to detract from what's inside. That's true at this 70th floor establishment atop Lake Point Tower, where the views of Navy Pier and the lake are particularly breathtaking.

In recent years, neither the decor nor the continental menu has been able to compete with the panoramic views, but some recent kitchen shake-ups have made the competition a bit more interesting. Perhaps start with braised morels beside English peas and creamy egg yolk before moving on to a bone marrow-crusted beef tenderloin. For dessert, bananas Foster flambéed tableside will challenge the Navy Pier for your attention.

Coco Pazzo Café

636 N. St. Clair St. (at Ontario St.)

Phone: 312-664-2777
Web: www.cocopazzocafe.com
Prices: $$

Lunch & dinner daily

Grand (Red)

Doctors finding time between rounds at nearby Northwestern Hospital, tourists, and local denizens all take in the cheery atmosphere at Coco Pazzo Café. This restaurant is proof that a nice setting with good service and tasty food does not have to be high-priced or high-minded. The warm, sunny colors of Italy create a relaxing ambience, while the outdoor seating is in demand during warmer months.

This kitchen delivers a crowd-pleasing mix of Italian-American cuisine that re-creates a nostalgic reflection of Tuscany. Their menu of simple preparations and presentations, like chicken Milanese, as well as daily specials appeal to a wide variety of diners. Despite the area's deep-pocketed competitors, Coco Pazzo Café delivers surprisingly good value.

Indian Garden

247 E. Ontario St. (bet. Fairbanks Ct. & St. Clair St.)

Phone: 312-280-4910
Web: www.indiangardenchicago.com
Prices: $$

Lunch & dinner daily

Grand (Red)

A few steps above the Streeterville graduate school bustle is a little oasis by the name of Indian Garden. Packed with those who work, teach, and study in the neighborhood, this popular spot gets more crowded during weekends, and the staff often struggles to keep up.

Yet its demand is thanks to consistently solid, traditional Northern Indian dishes, served at reasonable prices in a fun (if clichéd) atmosphere. Favorites include classics such as the *dahi aloo poori*, served with tamarind chutney and *chat masala*, and the chicken *vindaloo*—spicy, decadent, and rich with ghee, served family style in copper vessels. A full bar and the requisite variety of *lassi* help wash down these classics. Budget-seekers can try the traditional Indian buffet at lunch.

Les Nomades

A2

French XXX

222 E. Ontario St. (bet. Fairbanks Ct. & St. Clair St.)

Phone: 312-649-9010

Web: www.lesnomades.net

Prices: $$$$

Dinner Tue – Sat

 Grand (Red)

Rare moments of excellence can define a meal here, even if the consistency doesn't carry through the other courses. In fact, Les Nomades may even begin the night at its best, serving the perfect martini in a chilled cut-crystal glass from the gorgeous wooden bar. The menu starts with the likes of five assorted house pâtés, presented with modern twists in mustard sauce, wine gelée, and slivered cornichons; or an elegant duck consommé, perfectly clear, with a slice of foie gras mousse. While many offerings are rooted in French classics, the American dishes at Les Nomades does at times lose its way and ambition trumps taste.

Floral sprays, contemporary art, and a *très charmant* little fireplace add to the historic charm and make for a cozy evening.

The Purple Pig

A2

Mediterranean X

500 N. Michigan Ave. (at Illinois St.)

Phone: 312-464-1744

Web: www.thepurplepigchicago.com

Prices: $$

Lunch & dinner daily

 Grand (Red)

Grace under pressure defines the atmosphere at this fantastically busy spot overlooking the Chicago River. Despite the constant hum of action, comfort radiates from every corner of the wide room, where friendly conversations from skillful bartenders and strangers at the next seat all become pleasant dining companions whether seated at the counter or one of the many communal tables.

Once you've pulled up a stool and taken a first sip of wine from the wall-mounted selection, thoughts of devouring the entire menu set in. Try the aromatic charred octopus with green beans, fingerling potatoes, and salsa verde; or dunk some woodsy and earthy *jamón serrano*, oyster and black trumpet mushrooms, and grilled bread into the yolk of an oozing duck egg.

Riva

D2

700 E. Grand Ave. (on Navy Pier)

Phone: 312-644-7482

Web: www.rivanavypier.com

Prices: $$

Lunch & dinner daily

Navy Pier may be loaded with dining choices, but Riva stands out for its seafood-driven menu and unrivaled views of Lake Michigan. Yachts and tall sailing ships serve as an idyllic backdrop for this nautical-themed restaurant run by the ever-expanding Phil Stefani Group. Escape the hustle and bustle in this stylish dining room with soaring windows featuring the cityscape at sunset.

The menu is rich with seafood favorites and brings together the usual classics, such as lobster corn bisque and coconut shrimp on sugarcane skewers. Entrées are creatively enhanced, as in the seared ahi tuna with baby bok choy, king oyster mushrooms, and a Thai demi-glace. Landlubbers need not fear, since prime steaks and meats are showcased as well.

Sayat Nova

A2

157 E. Ohio St. (bet. Michigan Ave. & St. Clair St.)

Phone: 312-644-9159

Web: www.sayatnovachicago.com

Prices: $$

Lunch Mon – Sat
Dinner nightly
🚇 Grand (Red)

Streeterville's business crowd knows a good deal; that's why they flock to Sayat Nova. Here generous portions and reasonable prices are always on the menu. Also adding to its allure is a sidewalk patio, perfect for family feasting on warm days. Inside, find tables tucked intimately along the wall, while intricately designed metal luminaries lend a pleasant exoticism to the space.

The menu is made up of tasty, boldly spiced Armenian and Middle Eastern treats. Perhaps begin with creamy *hommos*, heaped with tahini, garlic, and olive oil and finished with a spike of paprika and parsley. Follow it up with a satisfying entrée: choose from a variety of kebabs, or go for a lesser-known dish like ground lamb *kibbee* served with *jajik*, a refreshing yogurt sauce.

Tru ✿

A1

Contemporary 🍴🍴🍴🍴

676 N. St. Clair St. (bet. Erie & Huron Sts.)

Phone: 312-202-0001

Web: www.trurestaurant.com

Prices: $$$$

Dinner Mon – Sat

Chicago (Red)

Mark Ballogg

Every comfort has been carefully considered at Tru: the greetings are polite; tables are well-spaced; linen napkins coordinate with your clothing; and the serene, modern design flows flawlessly from royal blue banquettes to tufted stools and glossy white walls. This is a perfectly museum-quiet setting for jacketed gentlemen to contemplate the meticulously selected wines from around the globe, including exotic producers from India and Lebanon.

This sense of seriousness extends to the menu of contemporary French cuisine. While the offerings are primarily served as a three-, six-, or nine-course prix-fixe, a few luxurious supplements include sturgeon caviar tastings and Australian Wagyu beef. Dinners here might begin with an amuse-bouche of cucumber gelée topped with cucumber salad, chive blossoms, and a richly flavored Bouchot mussel velouté. The kitchen's masterful range of French techniques is on display in *tournéed* potatoes cooked in saffron broth, with neat quenelles of lobster mousse, plump langoustine, and bouillabaisse.

Gorgeous presentations carry through to desserts like the layered *brunoise* of red and white Port-macerated apples with cider glaze and green apple sorbet.

The Zodiac

American 𝖃𝖃𝖃

 A1

737 N. Michigan Ave. (at Superior St.)

Phone:	312-694-4050	Lunch Mon – Sat
Web:	www.neimanmarcus.com	
Prices:	**$$**	🚇 Chicago (Red)

Nestled inside the Neiman Marcus department store, this fourth-floor restaurant (different than the third-floor quick-service café) offers exactly what you'd expect of a restaurant that bears the Neiman Marcus imprimatur. It is elegant, but refined and not ostentatious, with a contemporary décor.

Each meal starts with a Neiman Marcus signature—a complimentary serving of a demitasse cup of chicken broth and a warm, well-executed popover with strawberry butter. From there, choose from soups, salads, and sandwiches, the kind of light fare you'd want during a break from shopping or sightseeing. The menu items themselves may not be particularly innovative (such as an Asian chicken salad), but everything is presented in the style you'd expect of Neiman's.

Your opinions are important to us. Please write to us at: michelin.guides@ us.michelin.com

West Loop
Greektown · Market District

THE NEW WEST LOOP

What a difference a century (or two) makes—the West Loop was once home to smoke-spewing factories and warehouses, but walk through this natty neighborhood now, and you'll find young professionals instead of struggling immigrants. Transformed into luxurious lofts, cool nightclubs, art galleries, and cutting-edge restaurants, the warehouses and factories are a far cry from their former existence.

Immigrants staked their claim to this neighborhood years ago, and traces of ethnic flavor are still found here. It's not as big as it once was, but Little Italy's Taylor Street still charms with its old-world, slightly kitschy feel. It is delis, groceries, and restaurants galore.

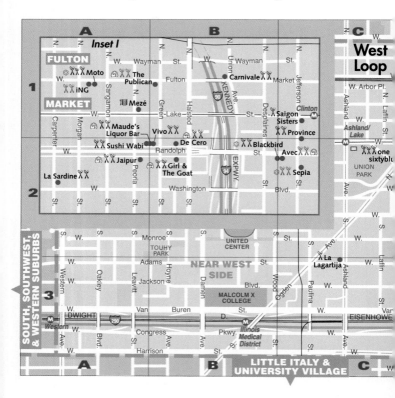

A Taste of Greece

Maintain this Mediterranean vibe by heading over to Greektown, where everybody's Greek, even if just for the day. Shout "oopa" at the Taste of Greece festival, held each August, or stop by the **Parthenon** for gyros and some serious showmanship —they even serve flaming *saganaki* cheese. A deluge of Greek restaurants line these blocks and are perfect for those looking to snack; as well as for groups who wish to linger over large spreads. Speaking of "oopa," Oprah Winfrey's Harpo studios are located here, in a former armory. Although Chicago's other first lady called it quits after 25 years on her legendary talk show in May of 2010, the studios remain open and are now the home of Rosie O'Donnell's talk show among other projects. If Greek and Italian foods don't fit the bill, there's surely something to whet your appetite along Randolph Street, often referred to as "Restaurant Row." From sushi to subs, this street has it all. For those who enjoy binging at breakfast, head on over to **Dodo at Dino's**. This local favorite satiates all and sundry with

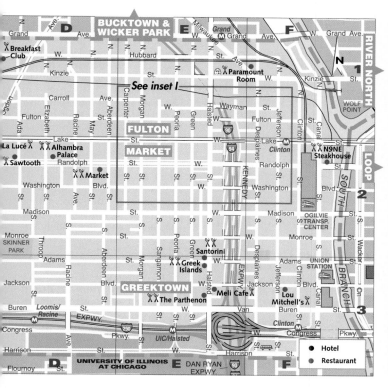

its daily brunch proffering of seasonal frittatas, French toast, and yes, Japanese pancakes!

For a magnificent night about town, you can even round up 1,000 of your closest peeps to dine together at one of the many (and enormous) Moroccan-Mediterranean restaurants showcasing a spectrum of treats from hummus, baba ghanoush, and *lebna*, to more faithful spreads like shrimp *charmoula*, *dolmeh*, and kibbeh. Further west on Randolph, find **The Tasting Room**, a two-level stop for excellent wines accompanied by a good selection of à la carte dishes, artisan cheeses, small plates, and sinful desserts including a rich dark chocolate fondue.

Crafting Culinary Skills

Rather whip it up than wolf it down? Beef up your kitchen skills at the Calphalon Culinary Center, where groups can arrange for private hands-on instruction. Mastered the bœuf Bourguignon? Get in line at **Olympic Meat Packers**. This old-school meatpacking jewel is one of the last holdouts in the area. It's certainly not for the squeamish, but the butchers slice and dice the perfect meat to order. Troll the stalls at the **Chicago French Market** for organic cheeses, roasted nuts, gourmet pickles, flowers, and other specialty items for your next dinner party. Don't have a ramekin or Dutch oven? Northwestern Cutlery Supply stocks everything a chef could need—even the requisite white coat. Treasure hunters mark the spot at the Chicago Antique Market. This massive indoor/outdoor market is held the last Saturday of each month from May through October, and stocks everything from jewelry to furniture.

Beer and the Ballgame

Hoops fans whoop it up at Bulls games at the United Center, which is also home to the Stanley Cup winners—the Blackhawks. Depending on the score, the most exciting part of the night might be post game, especially if over a beer at **Beer Bistro**. You'll need to bring your most decisive friends, since this place has 124 different types of bottled beer (and 21 on tap). To nibble on the side, tried-and-true pub grub such as spinach and artichoke dip, fried calamari, beer-battered chicken fingers, and mac & cheese are sure to satisfy.

Another spot for those who like a little brawl with their beer is **Twisted Spoke**. This proverbial biker bar (serving shrimp Po'Boys, meatloaf sandwiches, barbecue Kobe brisket, and smut & eggs after midnight on Saturdays), is complete with tattoos and 'tudes to match. The music is loud, crowds are big, and drinks are plentiful, but it's all in good testosterone-and-alcohol-fueled fun.

Switching gears, lovely ladies sip Champagne at Chicago's hot and happening **Plush** restaurant and lounge. If you've indulged in one too many slurps of bubbly (or a stellar cocktail), grab a blanket (and some fresh air), and head to Union Park for a much-needed alfresco nap.

Alhambra Palace

D2

Middle Eastern 🍴

1240 W. Randolph St. (bet. Elizabeth St. & Racine Ave.)

Phone: 312-666-9555

Web: www.alhambrapalacerestaurant.com

Prices: $$

Dinner nightly

🚇 Ashland (Green/Pink)

"Palace" aptly describes this mammoth restaurant. With a lounge, dining room, and even its own large sidewalk protected from the elements, everything here is on the larger-than-life scale.

The menu provides a fusion of different Middle Eastern dishes. The cream-free lentil soup, served with freshly made, perfectly charred pita would be enough for a satisfying lunch. But if you stopped there you wouldn't get a chance to order the other standouts. The Mezza combo offers a sampling of well-seasoned baba ghanoush, hummus, falafel, and stuffed grape leaves. The Toshka is a Middle Eastern *panino* of sorts, grilled pita stuffed with ground beef and cheese. For dessert the baklava is well-made, topped with thick honey, crushed pistachio, and almonds.

Avec

C2

American 🍴

615 W. Randolph St. (bet. Desplaines & Jefferson Sts.)

Phone: 312-377-2002

Web: www.avecrestaurant.com

Prices: $$

Dinner nightly

🚇 Clinton (Green/Pink)

After a devastating fire ravaged the restaurant in 2010, citywide favorite Avec is back with its modern-meets-rustic communal tables and stylishly easygoing attitude intact, and half the city lining up for a seat once more. A no-reservations policy means waits can be brutal for primetime dining, but early birds and night owls will benefit from a 3:30 P.M. opening and late night closing.

Share and share alike with simple dishes that showcase blue-ribbon ingredients. House specialty flatbreads are replete with seasonal toppings—Gorgonzola, spinach, crispy prosciutto, apples, and raisins perhaps? Chorizo-stuffed dates are too good to ever take off the menu, and if the crispy-skin pork and chicken terrine with pickled onions is a special, grab it!

239

Blackbird ✿

Contemporary ✗✗

B2

619 W. Randolph St. (bet. Des Plaines & Jefferson Sts.)

Phone: 312-715-0708
Web: www.blackbirdrestaurant.com
Prices: $$$

Lunch Mon – Fri
Dinner nightly
🚇 Clinton (Green/Pink)

Douglas Reid Fogelson Photography

In restaurant years, Blackbird is old enough to be the distinguished elder statesman of Chicago's modern fine dining scene, the Madonna to Lady Gaga. But the sharply angled white façade jutting onto West Randolph, and especially the food inside, are just as fresh and exhilarating as when Chef/owner Paul Kahan first flung open the doors in 1997.

A glossy white bar leads into a bright, sleek space that exudes contemporary chic with a hipster twist—daisies in a flower arrangement, a few tattoos peeking out on a hostess. These hints of a cultured but unstuffy experience are on the mark; an infectiously lively vibe pervades both lunch and dinner service.

Blackbird's one of those places where it's hard to whittle down the choices. Unusual flavor pairings in each dish make you wonder if it's possible to order the whole menu. Cuttlefish "noodles" tossed with lime juice and avocado purée are unexpectedly craveable, with pumpkin seeds and scallion greens for crunch. Smoky sous vide lamb tenderloin is punched up with Vidalia onion jam, cherries, and burnt cinnamon. A simultaneously sweet, savory, and tangy chocolate cake with whipped goat's milk and hibiscus sorbet is a firework finish.

Breakfast Club

A m e r i c a n

1381 W. Hubbard St. (at Noble St.)

Phone: 312-666-2372

Web: www.chicagobreakfastclub.com

Prices:

Lunch daily

 Ashland (Green/Pink)

It may share the name of one of John Hughes' favorite teen flicks, but inside, this "Breakfast Club" is totally "Pretty in Pink." The walls and furniture are dusty rose, and the servers wear hot pink polo shirts. There's even a pink canopy over the outdoor seats open in warm weather.

Those movie references may be dated, but the food here isn't stale. Classic breakfasts start the day off right with hearty choices like a chorizo-filled Mexican skillet; the crispy perfection of pan-fried potato pancakes; stuffed French toast; or biscuits and gravy. Side everything with some ham sliced off the bone. Lunch offers traditional fare, like burgers, club sandwiches, grilled cheese, and meatloaf.

The Breakfast Club has an early curfew—no dinner service here.

Carnivale

Latin American

702 W. Fulton Market (at Union Ave.)

Phone: 312-850-5005

Web: www.carnivalechicago.com

Prices: $$

Lunch Mon – Fri
Dinner nightly

 Clinton (Green/Pink)

The exterior of Jerry Kleiner's hot spot obscures its mammoth size, but the name says it all. This colorful venue features a pan-Latin theme park of the cuisine and culture of the Caribbean, Central, and South America.

Carnivale's menu varies significantly between lunch and dinner, but the fusion style and tasty drink menu stays the same regardless of the time of day. At lunch try the *remolachas*, a tasty beet salad with goat cheese and a sharp sherry vinaigrette; or hit the whitefish tacos accompanied by yuzu-tartar sauce and jicama salad. In the evening, taste the artisan Spanish hams and cheeses, or opt for a cool ceviche, or smoky wood-grilled pork. Forget that diet and end with crispy churros, served with chocolate and caramel sauces.

De Cero 😊

Mexican ✗✗

814 W. Randolph St. (at Halsted St.)

Phone: 312-455-8114
Web: www.decerotaqueria.com
Prices: $$

Lunch Tue – Fri & Dinner Tue – Sun
Clinton (Green/Pink)

The duo behind the super successful Sushi Wabi has done it again. This time, they've applied their creative, edgy formula to Mexico. As expected, it's a bit of a scene, with the loud music and a neat, natty vibe, but the amiable staff and laid-back locale help to keep things in check.

Thankfully, there are no native clichés in sight at this West Randolph gem. The menu may have numerous selections, but remember, this is light and simple Mexican. Come to relish in fine and fragrant fare and homemade tortillas holding 12 types of fresh tacos, so don't expect that food coma. Wash down a few shrimp tacos or the *huitlacoche* quesadilla with a Mexican beer, tequila, or better yet, a limey and lip-smacking margarita.

Girl & The Goat 😊

Contemporary ✗✗

809 W. Randolph St. (bet. Green & Halsted Sts.)

Phone: 312-492-6262
Web: www.girlandthegoat.com
Prices: $$

Dinner nightly
Clinton (Green/Pink)

Chef/owner Stephanie Izard's extraordinary passion project continues to draw avid fans to West Randolph. Though their ardor makes reservations a necessity, it's heartening to see such a mix of couples, business diners, hardcore foodies, and even families with kids sharing plates across communal tables in the rustic, industrial-chic space.

Sharing is the thing to do with the intensely flavorful food, paired in surprising and tasty combinations. Wood-fired dishes from the open kitchen's roaring oven are always popular. Though the menu changes frequently, bold standouts may include tender grilled *sepia* tossed with hazelnuts, smoked cherry tomatoes, and *bonito* flakes; or shaved slices of moist bitter-chocolate cake topped with shiitake ice cream.

Greek Islands

E3

Greek ✗✗

200 S. Halsted St. (at Adams St.)

Phone: 312-782-9855
Web: www.greekislands.net
Prices: ⬢⬢

Lunch & dinner daily

⬛ UIC-Halsted

This restaurant is as much a Chicago experience as a place to eat. For 40 years, Greek Islands has packed a mix of local business folks and tourists into its multiple dining rooms. This place is always buzzing, thanks to the crowds, the guitar-strumming background, and the bar's shouts of "Opa!"

The menu highlights traditional Greek (and Greek-American) fare such as grilled octopus, *skordalia melitzanosalata*, flaming *saganaki* cheese, rotisseries of meat for gyros, and daily specials. Even simple sides are tasty, such as fluffy rice served with rich and thick yogurt. Focus is on the food and not the presentation, but portions are accommodating, with many favorites offered as family-sized entrées for sharing or half-orders for children.

iNG

A1

Contemporary ✗✗

951 W. Fulton Market (bet. Morgan & Sangamon Sts.)

Phone: 855-834-6464
Web: www.ingrestaurant.com
Prices: $$$

Dinner Tue – Sat

⬛ Clinton (Green/Pink)

This latest and characteristically unusual concept from Homaro Cantu argues that this little stretch along Fulton Market may soon have the highest food IQ in the country. Pay by the hour and expect the unexpected with a contemporary Asian-influenced tasting menu, or open that origami paper box at your table, nibble the delight within, and unfold to discover it doubles as the menu.

Let the noodle-maker, visibly stretching and slapping the elastic dough in the front window, whet your appetite for house-made udon with rock shrimp tempura on lemongrass skewers paired with a melting orb of coconut juice. Other international dishes with quirky American twists include the "waffle" of frozen donut mousse with mango sorbet, crème anglaise, and chocolate sauce.

243

Jaipur 😊

A2

847 W. Randolph St. (bet. Green & Peoria Sts.)

Phone: 312-526-3655
Web: www.jaipurchicago.com
Prices: $$

Lunch Mon – Fri
Dinner nightly
🚇 Clinton (Green/Pink)

Conveniently located on the West Randolph restaurant row, Jaipur is popular with the weekday Loop crowd at lunch and the faddy dinner crowd that loves the scene on the weekends. The menu is a collection of hits at this standout among the many Indian restaurants in town. Main courses like *lamb pasanda*; Kerala fish curry fragrant with coconut; or chicken biryani are authentic, boldly flavorful, and quite delicious. Traditional sides like *saag paneer* and *chana masala* are well-executed. Flavor fiends shouldn't miss the *aloo papdi*; and dessert lovers should order the *rasmalai*, a disc of fresh cheese soaked in cardamom-sweetened milk.

Good value combination meals are offered at lunch, a refreshing break from the ubiquitous Indian buffets.

La Lagartija

C3

132 S. Ashland Ave. (bet. Adams & Monroe Sts.)

Phone: 312-733-7772
Web: www.lalagartijataqueria.com
Prices: 💰💰

Lunch & dinner Mon – Sat

🚇 Ashland (Green/Pink)

May we take a moment to talk about the salsas? One, a tangy tomatillo verde with lime juice, cilantro, and green chiles; the other a smoky roasted red chile—both like harbingers of deliciousness. Pop into this jaunty joint, where prismatic walls shout out Spanish food words in funky fonts, and the namesake lizard shows up in artsy renditions about the room. Chef/owners Luis Perea and Laura-Cid Perea captain this operation, making it one of the best taquerias in all of Chi-town. Sink your chops into a juicy taco *al pastor*—pork, spit-roasted with pineapple, shaved, and then topped with onion and cilantro; or the heavenly shrimp taco—three lightly battered prawns, fried and tossed into a fluffy homemade corn tortilla with shredded lettuce and chile-mayo.

La Lucé

D2

Italian 🍴

1393 W. Lake St. (at Ogden Ave.)

Phone: 312-850-1900
Web: www.lalucewestloop.com
Prices: $$

Lunch Mon – Fri
Dinner nightly
Ⓜ Ashland (Green/Pink)

It should come as no surprise that La Lucé looks like it's straight out of a Hollywood set. This restaurant, snuggled inside a Queen Anne Victorian dating back to 1892, is often used as a location for films and TV shows. From the exterior copper work and meat locker with original milk glass panels, to the wood-burning stove, La Lucé is the real deal.

The Italian-American cooking and that quintessential old-time vibe may have you looking over your shoulder for Vito Corleone, but at least your last meal will be a good one. Choose from classics like veal Parmesan, chicken Marsala, stuffed pork chops, spaghetti with meatballs, and homemade cannoli. Meat and cheese ravioli melt in your mouth, and the pizzas, served at lunch, are worth the 20-minute wait.

La Sardine

A2

French 🍴🍴

111 N. Carpenter St. (bet. Randolph St. & Washington Blvd.)

Phone: 312-421-2800
Web: www.lasardine.com
Prices: $$

Lunch Mon – Fri
Dinner Mon – Sat
Ⓜ Clinton (Green/Pink)

A dependable French-style bistro, La Sardine has one of the most American of claims to fame: it is located literally in front of the entrance to Harpo Studios, Oprah Winfrey's media empire. For years, live television tapings fed audience-member diners into this eatery, although it is also popular with locals and staffers who appreciate its solid food and warm ambience.

Many bistro-goers expect French onion soup as a bellwether, and on this point La Sardine's rich, brothy, sweet, and cheesy stew brimming with onions cooked until tender but still recognizable, does not disappoint. Specials like the halibut are simple, well-priced, and made with the freshest ingredients. A nice wine list and excellent espresso finish off the meal with French flair.

Lou Mitchell's

F3

American ✗

565 W. Jackson Blvd. (bet. Clinton & Jefferson Sts.)

Phone: 312-939-3111   Lunch daily
Web: www.loumitchellsrestaurant.com
Prices: 💰💰   🚇 Clinton (Blue)

At the top of Chicago's list of beloved names is Lou Mitchell. This eponymous diner is by no means an elegant affair, but thanks to its fluffy omelets and iconic crowd, it has been on the Windy City's must-eat list since 1923. Don't panic at the length of the lines: they are long but move fast, and free doughnut holes (one of the restaurant's signature baked goods) make the wait go faster.

Back to those omelets: they may be made with mere eggs, like everyone else's, but somehow these are lighter and fluffier, almost like a soufflé, stuffed with feta, spinach, onions, or any other ingredients of your choice. They arrive in skillets with an Idaho-sized helping of potatoes. Save room, because everyone gets a swirl of soft-serve at the meal's end.

Market

D2

American ✗✗

1113 W. Randolph St. (bet. Aberdeen & May Sts.)

Phone: 312-929-4787   Lunch & dinner daily
Web: www.marketbarchicago.com
Prices: $$ 🚇 Ashland (Green/Pink)

It's a bar for people who think sports jackets are sports apparel, so don't show up in a Derrick Rose jersey. While there are TVs blaring the game, Market wears a lofty air that may not suit your typical sports enthusiast. But, the rooftop views are something to behold—get there before the multitudes.

Bring on those truffled fries; Market's menu dodges from sandwiches to burgers with quirky names like The South-Side Slugger with angry onions, smoked ham, and a fried egg. The mac and Gouda muffins aren't really muffins, but become "almighty" when paired with a cool beer. Bench warmers (lamb lollipops with a spiced Moroccan glaze); the Big Buff (grilled chicken sandwich); and mustard- and apple-glazed salmon will leave even game fiends smitten.

Maude's Liquor Bar

B2

French ✗✗

840 W. Randolph St. (bet. Green & Peoria Sts.)

Phone: 312-243-9712   Dinner Tue – Sat
Web: www.maudesliquorbar.com
Prices: $$ Clinton (Green/Pink)

Ooh la la! Mismatched crystal chandeliers, antique curio cabinets, and vintage chairs create a luxurious atmosphere straight outta 19th century Paris—but what else would you expect from the team that sexed up the gastropub over at River North neighbor Gilt Bar? Embrace the moment with a flute of bubbly or a period-appropriate cocktail like the smokey violet smash.

Food and drink are straight-up French bistro favorites. Grab oysters and frites at the dark, cozy upstairs bar or hold court at a farmhouse table for tiered seafood towers and French onion fondue. The masterpiece roast half chicken that's crispy outside and juicy inside needs no embellishment. For a grand finale, crack into the sugared veneer of a perfectly ironed crème brûlée.

Meli Cafe

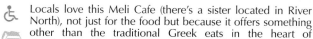

E3

American ✗

301 S. Halsted St. (bet. Jackson Blvd. & Van Buren St.)

Phone: 312-454-0748   Lunch daily
Web: www.melicafe.com
Prices: 😊😊   UIC-Halsted

Locals love this Meli Cafe (there's a sister located in River North), not just for the food but because it offers something other than the traditional Greek eats in the heart of Greektown. The proximity to UIC and the Loop packs folks into this yellow dining room decorated with rows of marmalades. Pick homemade apricot and grape or another favorite for your toast.

Meli is open through lunch, but breakfast is where it's at. The kitchen specializes in organic egg dishes such as omelettes, frittatas, and Benedicts. The sun-dried tomato and basil frittata, for example, is mighty wholesome and chock-full of ingredients. Waffles, French toast, and fancy sweet and savory pancakes and crêpes are alternatives for those who don't feel eggy.

Mezé

A1

International

205 N. Peoria St. (at Lake St.)

Phone: 312-666-6625

Web: www.mezechicago.com

Prices:

Dinner Tue – Sat

 Clinton (Green/Pink)

Mezé (named for the Middle Eastern-style small plates relative) is a see-and-be-seen-type of joint, one that gets louder as the night goes on. While there are plenty of folks enjoying an adult beverage or two, the global menu doesn't play second fiddle to the high energy and luxurious ambience of the lounge.

The rich flavors from the Americas, Asia, the Mediterranean, and the Caribbean are mingled in the dishes here. Seared tuna is served upon wonton chips with a pungent wasabi cream, creating a nice spicy-sweet snack. The chicken quesadilla is toasted just enough to melt the cheese and is served with a zippy chipotle dipping sauce. Happy hour is a bargain with discounted tapas and bottles of wine to go with that goat cheese and tomato tart.

N9NE Steakhouse

F2

Steakhouse 𝖷𝖷

440 W. Randolph St. (at Canal St.)

Phone: 312-575-9900

Web: www.n9ne.com

Prices: $$$

Lunch Mon – Fri

Dinner Mon – Sat

 Clinton (Green/Pink)

"New" is typically the watchword that determines whether or not a night spot is trendy. But even after a decade N9NE Steakhouse still attracts the city's beautiful people for mingling, ogling, and, and, eating. The restaurant's name comes from the age the owners were when they first met. Those owners include Michael Morton, of Morton's steakhouse fame.

So, it stands to reason that N9NE can serve a good steak. The food is taken seriously, and the menu is simple, but not staid. Also fitting the nightlife vibe are the surf and turf specials, prepared like sliders, with beef tenderloin on one tiny sandwich and Maine lobster on the other. The shrimp cocktail is a little pricey but worth it simply for the kick of the horseradish-tomato cocktail sauce.

Moto ✿

Contemporary XXX

A1

945 W. Fulton Market (bet. Morgan & Sangamon Sts.)

Phone:	312-491-0058
Web:	www.motorestaurant.com
Prices:	$$$$

Dinner Tue – Sat

🚇 Clinton (Green/Pink)

Michael Ruggirello

Located in a working, breathing meatpacking district, designed with modern lines and a façade that can be easily overlooked, populated by chic diners anticipating adventure, and helmed by a talented kitchen about to take them on a surprising ride—Moto's every ounce of being and purpose is rooted in the vanguard. Be sure to mute your phone upon entering, but this menu encourages tweeting (literally).

On Chef/owner Homaro Cantu's bill of fare, curious elements collide in spectacularly delicious ways. While other modernist kitchens have failed with discordant combinations, Moto succeeds in nudging familiar flavors in radical new directions. This is evident in dishes like fresh and sweet king crab that arrives in a "cake" of butter wonderfully infused with tastes of the sea, set upon a swirl of fennel-frond purée. Whimsical and completely unexpected combinations may arrive as delicate nobs of quail with a cherry-paper crackerjack box, candied peanuts, crackerjack powder, and cocoa bits reduction, finished with the intoxicating scent of crushed basil.

"Tea time" desserts are lovely and harmonious, as in Earl Grey mousse with chocolate, blood orange nibs, and a smear of raspberry coulis.

one sixtyblue

C2

Contemporary XXX

1400 W. Randolph St. (at Ogden Ave.)

Phone: 312-850-0303
Web: www.onesixtyblue.com
Prices: **$$**

Dinner Mon – Sat

Ashland (Green/Pink)

This West Loop winner, part of Michael Jordan's restaurant group, is a lay up with its creative Mediterranean-influenced food. Chef Michael McDonald whips up some serious artistry here. Unexpected combinations and preparations keep you on your toes in this retro place, where you can also peek in on the action of the open kitchen or jam to the beats of the vibey soundtrack.

Chef McDonald's riffs on the classics are all over the place. The blue bar burger (offered at the bar) on a pretzel bun with a fried pickle and triple cream Brie; or goat meatballs over saffron pappardelle with *guanciale* and spicy tomato sauce (served at the dining room) keep things down to earth. For a cheat sheet version, come weeknights for the three- and seven-course prix-fixes.

Paramount Room

F1

Gastropub X

415 N. Milwaukee Ave. (bet. Hubbard & Kinzie Sts.)

Phone: 312-829-6300
Web: www.paramountroom.com
Prices: **$$**

Lunch Thu – Sun
Dinner nightly
Grand (Blue)

In some ways, this popular gastropub merits multiple listings, because each of its levels has a different vibe, depending on your mood. Housed in a former speakeasy, Paramount Room offers the friendly American Tavern plus the resurrected Prohibition-era basement lounge.

Check out the beer list when thirsty. It includes Belgian, craft-brewed, domestic, and imported beers, such as the Obamagang, brewed in honor of President Barack Obama's inauguration. The menu fits the nosh-style kind of eating that takes place at a tavern, such as ale-steamed mussels, onion soup, sandwiches, and decadent desserts that are all several steps above typical bar fare. The website lists daily specials, such as all-you-can-eat fish and chips and discounted Kobe beef burgers.

The Parthenon

E3

Greek ✗✗

314 S. Halsted St. (bet. Jackson Blvd. & Van Buren St.)

Phone: 312-726-2407

Web: www.theparthenon.com

Prices: 💲💲

Lunch & dinner daily

🔲 UIC-Halsted

"Opaa!" From the signature shout, to the crowds, to the decor, to the size of the room, to the well-connected clientele, to the spits with gyros meat roasting in the front windows, this Greek mainstay is stereotypical Greektown. It is loud, bustling, and fun—the kind of place you'd go with a group of co-workers, not for a romantic tête-à-tête.

The menu is large and classic; all the traditional Greek favorites are here. Order the dolmades, tender grape leaves filled with a mixture of onion-scented ground beef and rice, and you'll have enough to share with friends or to munch on for lunch the next day. End the meal with the baklava, which has a lovely infusion of cinnamon in the filling, complemented by the well-browned flaky dough.

Province

American ✗✗

C1

161 N. Jefferson St. (bet. Lake & Randolph Sts.)

Phone: 312-669-9900

Web: www.provincerestaurant.com

Prices: $$

Lunch Mon – Fri

Dinner Mon – Sat

🔲 Clinton (Green/Pink)

Take a glance at the menu, playfully divided into categories like "bites" and "bigger," and you might think it relies on gimmicks, but a few tastes prove that a pro is running this show. Fuschia accented walls and tree branches suspended from the ceiling fashion a modern and cool space that looks and feels like a breath of fresh air.

Equally cool, the American cuisine has a unique Spanish/Latin bent and showcases artisanal ingredients from sources like Anson Mills and Gunthorp Farms. Fashion your own feast, building from "small" plates of goat cheese fondue to "big" portions of rabbit confit or even "bigger" entrées like the ten-hour barbecued lamb. Or enjoy the range by sticking to lots of little "bites" like squash and spring onion *taquitos*.

251

The Publican

B1

837 W. Fulton Market (at Green St.)

Phone: 312-733-9555
Web: www.thepublicanrestaurant.com
Prices: $$

Lunch Sun
Dinner nightly
💻 Clinton (Green/Pink)

This hot spot from the Blackbird and Avec team remains a see-and-be-seen foodie favorite. From the line outside, to the long bar, to the communal restroom sink, to the Scandinavian-design that is both stylish and very Viking, no detail of the visual experience has been overlooked. Happily, equal attention is paid to the culinary experience.

With a beer sommelier, the global and eclectic list offers 100 varieties of ales, ciders, and beers. The menu is heavy on pork dishes, such as pork rinds and aged ham, but also features a well-prepared chef's selection of terrific freshly shucked oysters, local vegetables with house-made aïoli, and Monterey Bay sardines. The provenance of the ingredients is all-important and duly emphasized on the menu.

Saigon Sisters

C1

567 W. Lake St. (bet. Clinton & Jefferson Sts.)

Phone: 312-496-0090
Web: www.saigonsisters.com
Prices: 💰💰

Lunch Mon – Fri
Dinner Mon – Sat
💻 Clinton (Green/Pink)

Saigon Sisters is two restaurants in one: during lunch hours, Fulton River District workers line up for lively grab-and-go casual counter service; which transforms at dinner into a cozy, low-lit, sit-down restaurant with ambitious, westernized Vietnamese fare.

Stopping by at lunch, it's easy to fill up on the killer *bánh bao*: steamed buns filled with a choice of caramelized chicken, Wagyu beef in coconut milk, or to-die-for hoisin-glazed pork belly, all dressed with pickled carrot, daikon, cilantro, and jalapeño. Or try one of many modern variations on the classic *bánh mì*. Dinner is a more upscale affair, tasting menus and prix fixe options–cleverly displayed on blackboards–offer great value, along with à la carte starters and entrées.

Santorini

E3

Greek ✗✗

800 W. Adams St. (at Halsted St.)

Phone: 312-829-8820
Web: www.santorinichicago.com
Prices: 💰💰

Lunch & dinner daily

🖥 UIC-Halsted

Named for the idyllic Greek island, Chicago's Santorini honors its home country by serving some of the best Greek food this city has to offer. Its charming taverna-style dining room, amiable service, and authentic ambience likewise deserve accolades for being among the most pleasant to be found in Greektown. Whitewashed walls, copper pots, and wood-beamed ceilings define the look, while upbeat Greek music sets a lively tone. Everyone feels like family here—note the groups arriving in droves.

All of the usual classics are on the well-rounded menu, but pay attention to rotating specials, like the hearty lamb *stamnas*, roasted until tender, and tucked with sautéed vegetables inside fluffy crêpes, then blanketed in melted Greek cheeses.

Sawtooth

D2

Vietnamese ✗✗

1350 W. Randolph St. (at Alda St.)

Phone: 312-526-3320
Web: www.sawtoothrestaurant.com
Prices: $$

Dinner nightly

🖥 Ashland (Green/Pink)

Hang with the cool kids at Sawtooth. This glassy, ultramodern restaurant opened in late 2010, and has already attracted a loyal following of trendy types who come as much for the scene as they do for the Vietnamese fare. With a space this sexy, it's certainly no wonder. Bright and airy, yet wearing an unmistakable lounge feel (with the requisite beats et al), Sawtooth is comfortably cutting edge.

The contemporary Vietnamese cuisine covers all of the bases. Begin with an appetizer such as sugar cane shrimp, charcuterie, or crispy, spicy Sawtooth wings before tucking into specialties like shaking beef, mushroom-stuffed roasted quail, grilled pork chop, and clay pot catfish. A nice selection of cocktails completes the swanky experience.

Sepia ✵

Contemporary ✕✕

C2

123 N. Jefferson (bet. Randolph St. & Washington Blvd.)

Phone: 312-441-1920
Web: www.sepiachicago.com
Prices: $$

Lunch Mon – Fri
Dinner nightly
🚇 Clinton (Green/Pink)

Doug Snower

Sepia deftly balances all the traits that one might readily attribute to an idyllic urban getaway. The brick façade is inviting, the design is a gorgeous interplay of modern and rustic, the welcoming staff is warm enough to melt away mid-winter's harshest chill, and if that isn't enough, then a cocktail or three from the expertly prepared list in the intimate bar should do the trick.

Despite its many charms and graces, the real reason why the sophisticated crowd seems so jovial is the cooking. Meals here are a pleasure from start to finish, thanks to the contemporary style, mastery of technique, and creativity of Chef Andrew Zimmerman. Delicate flavors and a sense of elegance are clear in perfectly cooked pastas such as pheasant agnolotti served with an enticing mass of black trumpet mushrooms with *albufera* sauce. Seasonality is not merely considered with ingredients but also in the style of each dish, as in the cold-weather hearty duck breast, seared and accompanied by house-made duck sausage, braised red cabbage, and duck-fat roasted fingerling potatoes.

Modern sensibilities come to mind with excellent sweets such as the coffee-cardamom custard tart with a chocolate-Frangelico sauce.

Sushi Wabi

A2

Japanese ✗✗

842 W. Randolph St. (bet. Green & Peoria Sts.)

Phone: 312-563-1224
Web: www.sushiwabi.com
Prices: $$$

Lunch Mon – Fri
Dinner nightly
🚇 Clinton (Green/Pink)

It may be cramped, crowded, and not particularly comfortable, but Sushi Wabi remains a great option for creative maki along the West Loop's golden mile of restaurants.

The space (and staff) fashion an industrial-chic look, with poured cement floors, loft ceilings, and music that seems to bounce from every surface, including the massive menu of raw and cooked dishes. Most everyone–from the lunchtime business folk to weekend trendsters who remembered to reserve in advance–comes here for the unique maki presented with minimalist Japanese style. Expect rolls that highlight a range of fillings rather than the very fresh fish, as in the Godzilla, combining tempura shrimp, avocado, and tobiko with cream cheese, *sriracha*, eel sauce, *masago* and wasabi mayo.

Vivo

B2

Italian ✗✗

838 W. Randolph St. (bet. Green & Peoria Sts.)

Phone: 312-733-3379
Web: www.vivo-chicago.com
Prices: $$

Lunch Mon – Fri
Dinner nightly
🚇 Clinton (Green/Pink)

Life is cheery at the congenial Vivo, resting on Randolph Street's restaurant row. This Italian idol's casual vibe is palpable both outdoors on the patio, and inside the pleasant dining room capped with exposed ductwork and brick walls. Those in the know angle for the most desired table in the house—perched in the converted elevator shaft with fantastic views. Expect well-prepared, rustic Italian cooking here, brought to you by informal yet attentive waiters.

Appetizers like *caprese* salad and bruschetta signal the kitchen's dedication to the classics; and entrées like penne with spicy chicken sausage, broccoli rabe, and sun-dried tomatoes; and the fish of the day (ask for it) round out a traditional menu. It's nothing new, but tasty all the same.

North &
Northwestern
Suburbs

North & Northwestern Suburbs

Evanston is the suburb that even city-dwellers love. As is the case in any metropolis, sometimes the suburbs fall victim to urban one-upmanship, but Chicago's first stop over the northern border lures city folk with its lakefront charms and foodie finds. Additionally, Evanston is home to Northwestern University and the Woman's Christian Temperance Union, resulting in an incongruous mash-up of college-town hangouts and odd liquor laws.

Hotbed for Goodies

Evanston's Central Street is a swath of quaint boutiques and cafés. Serious gourmands stock up at the famed **Spice House**, reputed for their incredible spectrum of high-quality and unique spices, seasonings, rubs, and mixes. All these flavors will certainly inspire and nurture your inner Grant Achatz. It's also a solid choice for housewarming gifts. Nearby on Central Street is **Rose's Wheatfree Bakery and Café**. A rare and relevant establishment, they've garnered a giant following, all of whom come routinely for a treasure trove of gluten-free goodies including breads, cookies, cakes, cupcakes, and muffins to take home. Also sought after is the café menu of pizzas, salads, and sandwiches. Moreover, they carry the beloved Tennessee-style Grampa Boo's Basting and Barbecue Sauce for some thrilling at-home

grilling. Evanston and the tony North Shore are also known for **Belgian Chocolatier Piron**—this decadent den features a variety of handmade chocolates and gift items; and also brings some of the finest (and richest) Belgian chocolates to Evanston.

Dog Day Delights

On the other side of the spectrum and shunning all things gluten-free and highbrow is **Wiener and Still Champion**, a hot dog stop where National Corn Dog Day is celebrated with the works (*sans* ketchup). When ordering, remember that the Chicago dog is a specific thing: A steamed, all-beef hot dog with yellow mustard, Day-Glo relish, chopped onion, tomato wedges, pickle spear, sport peppers, and celery salt on a poppy seed bun. That neon relish is made with sweet pickles and dyed a bright green (sort of like the Chicago River on St. Patrick's Day). Dunk their deep-fried pickles into sauces that reach as high as "truffle-mushroom" or as low as "bacon-bacon."

Other delights on the menu include chargrilled burgers, chicken, fish, dippin' dogs, and meatless options all of which may (and should!) be accompanied with a side of their crunchy and "Somewhat Famous Fries." Another inordinately famous and faithful hot dog and burger base is **Poochie's** in Skokie. For a more retro-experience, approach the iconic **Superdawg**, with its dancing hot dogs dressed in spotted gear. This family-owned and operated drive-in will make you feel as if you've just entered the set of *American Graffiti*. With its super-menu of super-dogs (made with pure beef), burgers, sandwiches, beverages, and soda fountain specialties including floating scoops of ice cream in bubbling root beer, this is as much a family tradition as it is a landmark since 1948.

True fast foodies pay homage to the golden arches at the McDonald's Museum in Des Plaines. The building is a re-creation of the original store, with massive displays of fresh potatoes being peeled and root beer drawn from a barrel by a uniformed crew of mannequins, fashioning a diorama that is as visually authentic as it is weird. It is no surprise that Chicago has its fair share of highway fast food stops. After all, the concept was virtually invented here when the Fred Harvey company (which Hollywood immortalized in Judy Garland's *Harvey Girls* film), went from catering to railway passengers to motorists. It partnered to build the visually imposing series of mid-century "oases" stretching over the Illinois Tollway now catering to modern-day travelers.

Ethnic Enclaves

In such a diverse urban center, it is no wonder that other ethnic enclaves are also thriving. Along Devon, you will find one of the country's larger South Asian communities. This corridor of South Asia showcases authentic restaurants, *desi* diners, shops, and grocery stores serving a mainly Indian and Pakistani clientele. Come for *tandoori* and leave with a sari!

Presenting everything Japanese under one roof is **Mitsuwa Marketplace** in Arlington Heights. This enormous supermarket carries everything from top-notch beef, sushi, and sashimi to Japanese baked goods, books, and cosmetics. Journeying from South Asia to the Middle East and closer to Park Ridge, Des Plaines, and Niles, find an array of ethnic supermarkets filled with Greek and Middle Eastern specialty items. The influence of a massive Mexican population is found here as well within deliciously authentic tacos, tortas, and other foods at the many taquerias and casual restaurants dotting these sprawling suburbs.

There is a new generation of casual eateries and fast food concepts booming in this area. For instance, **bopNgrill** is frequented for its fantastic, messy, huge burgers and Korean fusion fast food; **Buffalo Joe's** is *the* go-to spot for chicken wings on Clark St.; **Rollin' To Go** is a favorite among Northwestern students; and **Al's Deli** is a neighborhood fixture. With fast food forgotten, end a day here at **Amitabul**. This fusion Korean restaurant prepares delicious, healthy, and "simply vegan" items. Imagine a host of tasty dishes and refreshing drinks and you will start to get the picture. Also offered are Buddhist delicacies with organic vegetables, nuts, and spicy sauces for a vegan-friendly meal that, somehow, couldn't be more American. It is truly a gem that transcends traditional tastes.

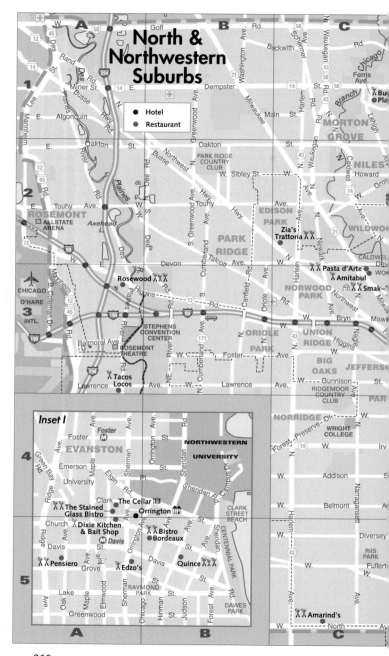

North & Northwestern Suburbs

- ● Hotel
- ● Restaurant

A
B
C

1
2
3

Inset I

EVANSTON

NORTHWESTERN UNIVERSITY

4
5

Labels and points:

Golf
Rand Rd.
Des Plaines
Miner St. E.
Algonquin
Oakton St.
Oakton St.
Busse
Northwest Hwy
Touhy Ave.
Touhy Hwy
EDISON PARK
Zia's Trattoria
PARK RIDGE
PARK RIDGE COUNTRY CLUB
W. Sibley St.
Devon Ave.
Rosewood
Higgins Rd.
Pasta d'Arte
Amitabul
NORWOOD PARK
Smak
CHICAGO O'HARE INTL.
Coleman Dr.
STEPHENS CONVENTION CENTER
ROSEMONT THEATRE
Balmoral Ave.
ORIOLE PARK
UNION RIDGE
Bryn
Higgins
Nagle
BIG OAKS
JEFFERSON
Tacos Locos
Foster Ave.
Lawrence Ave.
Gunnison
RIDGEMOOR COUNTRY CLUB
PARK
NORRIDGE
WRIGHT COLLEGE
Forest Preserve Dr.
Irving
Addison
Belmont
Diversey
RIIS PARK
Fullerton
ALLSTATE ARENA
ROSEMONT
Axehead L.
MORTON GROVE
NILES
Howard
WILDWOOD
CALDWELL
WOODS

Foster
Green Bay Rd.
Emerson
University
Clark
The Cellar
The Stained Glass Bistro
Orrington
Church
Dixie Kitchen & Bait Shop
Davis
Bistro Bordeaux
Pensiero
Grove
Edzo's
Quince
RAYMOND PARK
Lake
Greenwood
CLARK STREET BEACH
CENTENNIAL PARK
DAWES PARK
Amarind's
North Ave.

260

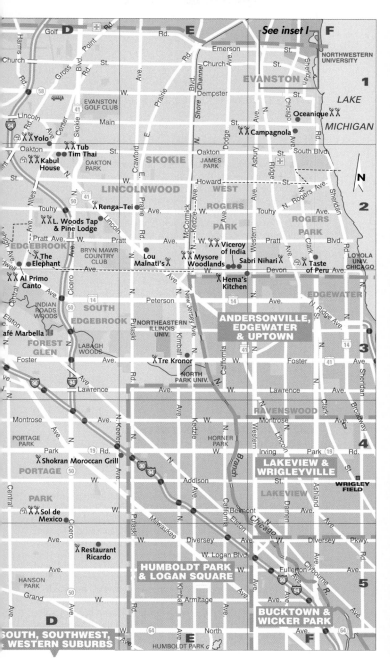

Al Primo Canto

Brazilian ☓☓

5414 W. Devon Ave. (bet. Central & Lehigh Aves.)

Phone:	773-631-0100	Dinner Tue – Sun
Web:	www.alprimocanto.com	
Prices:	**$$**	

Vaulted ceilings, exposed brick and wood, and a striking wall of windows set the stage for elegant rotisserie cooking inspired by Brazilian galeterias. Al Primo Canto's popular all-you-can-eat menu is equally gaucho- and Italian-inspired: after covering the table with an assortment of huge pasta bowls, the kitchen sends out platters of roasted meats, vegetables, and potato sides for a family-style feast.

Whether choosing the all-you-can-eat option or ordering à la carte, don't ignore the restaurant's signature rotisserie chicken, infused with white wine, sage, garlic, and the smoky scents of the wood-burning fire. A minty caipirinha with tropical fruit purée and gratis Brazilian cheese bread (*pão de Queijo*) for the table complete the experience.

Amarind's

Thai ☓☓

6822 W. North Ave. (at Newcastle Ave.)

Phone:	773-889-9999	Lunch Mon – Sat
Web:	www.amarinds.com	Dinner nightly
Prices:		

Amarind's corner location and turret-like entrance is a favorite of Oak Parkers and others looking for affordable, solid Thai food in a family-friendly environment. Weekday specials and accommodations for kids keep tables filled day and night. A bright and pleasant décor dotted with Thai artifacts, tapestries, and artwork set the scene.

Start with deliciously filled chive dumplings served with a dipping sauce of soy, chili, and black vinegar. Follow with spicy grilled pork loin coated in a savory marinade of lemongrass, shallot, garlic, scallion, mint, lime juice, and chili paste (note that if you like things spicy, ask your server to alert the kitchen). Accompany tasty dishes like these with a cold glass of sweet and creamy Thai iced tea.

Amitabul

Korean

6207 N. Milwaukee Ave. (bet. Huntington & Raven Sts.)

Phone: 773-774-0276   Lunch & dinner Tue – Sun
Web: www.amitabulvegan.com
Prices: 💰💰

With its Korean-inspired menu of "Healing Buddhist Spiritual Vegan Cuisine," Amitabul strives to heal all that ails you (and even if it doesn't, the food is still really tasty here).

Get those immunities humming again with dishes like "Green and Greener Nirvana," or perhaps the ultimate panacea, "Dr. K's Cure All Noodle Soup." Munch on steamed *mandoo* vegan dumplings, with flavors that come alive in a duo of salty red-chili and sweet soy dipping sauces. Spice lovers tuck into the "Yin and Yan," coin-sized slices of chewy brown rice cakes stir-fried in a spicy red chili sauce with a host of perfectly fresh and crunchy vegetables. Libations are limited to energizing juices and cozy teas, which may not be enough to brighten the lack of ambience here.

Bistro Bordeaux

 French

618 Church St. (bet. Chicago & Orrington Aves.), Evanston

Phone: 847-424-1483   Lunch Sun
Web: www.lebistrobordeaux.com   Dinner nightly
Prices: $$ Davis

Bistro Bourdeaux hits that American ideal of the classic "French" bistro right on *le nez*. The old-world ambience is created thanks to details such as smoky mirrors, ancient pots and pans hanging on hooks, pressed-tin ceilings, and the list goes on. The service is well timed, and the prices just right for a night out.

Just as the décor meets the "Frenchified" brasserie expectations, so, too, does the food. The onion soup is classically done in an American style, with caramelized onions and a blend of rich melted cheeses. Choose from roasted skate wing, chicken liver pâté, or escargots for classic French flavor. Desserts meet expectations, too. You won't find a berry coulis bathing your *île flottante* in Lyon, but in Evanston, it's just fine.

Burt's Place

P i z z a

8541 Ferris Ave. (bet Capulina & Lincoln Aves.), Morton Grove

Phone: 847-965-7997 Dinner Wed – Sun
Web: N/A
Prices:

If you're dedicated to deep-dish pizza, follow these three rules to guarantee a memorable meal at Burt's Place: make a reservation and place your order a few days in advance, call as soon as or just before the restaurant opens to reliably reach a staffer, and arrive on time to ensure a still-hot and bubbling pizza. Why go to all this trouble for a pizza? Quite simply, because Burt's, a neighborhood favorite that looks the part with its tchotchke-covered, wood-paneled dining room, makes great deep-dish and that's it.

With limited oven space, timing is paramount. But when a generous slice with a thick, caramelized crust, tangy tomato sauce, piles of toppings, and the perfect balance of cheese hits your table, you'll know why you made the effort.

Café Marbella

S p a n i s h

5527 N. Milwaukee Ave. (bet. Bryn Mawr & Catalpa Aves.)

Phone: 773-853-0128 Dinner Tue – Sun
Web: www.cafemarbella.com
Prices: **$$**

The unassuming location of this tapas spot is perfect for large groups who want to pass around plates, tasting a little bit of everything. The décor is understated, with red clay tile floors, brick archways, and simple booths, all the better to allow diners to focus on the authentic food.

The restaurant's talented team of chefs have cooked in some of the city's most favored Spanish-style kitchens; and the reason this is so clearly apparent is because the tapas are prepared quite well here. Look for classics like gazpacho *Andaluz*, *gambas al ajillo*, and *piquillos con atún*. Tortilla *Española* is cooked as if the kitchen were in Spain, not on the northwest side, while sautéed Rioja-style chorizo lounges among large, buttery, tender white beans.

Campagnola

Italian ✗✗

F1

815 Chicago Ave. (at Washington St.), Evanston

Phone:	847-475-6100
Web:	www.campagnolarestaurant.com
Prices:	$$

Dinner Tue – Sun

🖥 Main

Who says you have to head downtown for a fabulous night out on the town? Campagnola is proof that the suburbs can sizzle. From its sultry, soft lighting to its exposed brick walls and comfy banquette seating, Campagnola seems to be designed with a tète-à-tète in mind.

The subdued sophistication of the dining room is echoed in the kitchen, where the chef ensures that the best designs are indeed simple. You won't find a high-falutin carte filled with adjectives describing fancy ingredients or fussy cooking techniques. Instead, this menu, where dishes like chicken *al mattone* and linguini dancing with spicy shrimp headline, is purely about simplicity. From start to finish, Campagnola satisfies with every beautiful bite.

The Cellar

International 🍽

A4

820 Clark St. (bet. Benson & Sherman Aves.), Evanston

Phone:	847-425-5112
Web:	www.thecellarevanston.com
Prices:	🍪

Dinner nightly

🖥 Davis

The Cellar bombasts (and rightly so) an international small plates nosh-fest, where a killer list of brews and a cozy-hip vibe make it a beloved destination among locals and Northwestern University faculty. Sister to The Stained Glass Bistro 'round the corner, this is the more casual sibling—though it's every bit as cosmopolitan.

Tasty bites fall under three categories: "European," "American," and "Worldwide"; jumping from juicy micro-burgers, smothered in blue cheese on a brioche bun; and lobster coconut curry; to crispy fish tacos with spiced *crema*. Ales hail from around the country and globe spotlighting local breweries like Metropolitan Brewing Co.; and traversing the U.S. (Three Floyds, Dogfish Head) and Europe (St. Bernardus Tripel Ale, Belgium).

Dixie Kitchen & Bait Shop

Southern ✗

A5

825 Church St. (bet. Benson & Sherman Aves.), Evanston

Phone: 847-733-9030
Web: www.dixiekitchenchicago.com
Prices: ⬤⬤

Lunch & dinner daily

🚉 Davis

Kitsch and college campus combine at this paean to Southern food. The inexpensive prices and considerable portions have made it a favorite of budget-driven students, so be prepared to wait for a table.

Meals start with a cornmeal griddle cake and progress to plates of flavorful fare like fried chicken, jerk catfish, crayfish étouffé, Dixie ribs, jambalaya, and other classics from south of the Mason-Dixon line. The catfish Po'boy is perfectly fried without a touch of oiliness, layered on a French roll with lettuce, tomato, and remoulade. The rich gumbo is deliciously swimming with shrimp, chicken, and andouille sausage.

Desserts like peach cobbler or pecan pie sweeten the deal and their breakfast makes for an over-the-top start to any day.

Edzo's

American ✗

A5

1571 Sherman Ave. (bet. Davis & Grove Sts.), Evanston

Phone: 847-864-3396
Web: www.edzos.com
Prices: ⬤⬤

Lunch Tue – Sun

🚉 Davis

Burger shop plus nearby college campus usually equals one thing, but Edzo's somehow takes the formula and gets a different answer. Yes, this close to the Northwestern University campus Edzo's attracts a lot of students and faculty. And, yes, the menu is burgers, fries, and shakes. But this isn't just a shack—there's plenty of room for dine-in eating.

And perhaps a burger is a burger is a burger. But these are some burgers. Order yours as a single, double, or triple, then pick your cheese and toppings—how about pepperjack and hot *giardiniera*? Or there's always the crowd-pleaser: the patty melt. Side your burger with some heavy-duty fries; buffalo, truffle or loaded fries top the list. A spicy Mexican chocolate milkshake rounds out the decadence.

The Elephant

D2

Thai 🍴

5348 W. Devon Ave. (bet. Central & Minnehaha Aves.)

Phone: 773-467-1168   Lunch & dinner Mon – Sat
Web: www.theelephantthai.com
Prices: 💰

Mood-lifting hues and brightly painted pachyderms perk up the walls of this small, cheery neighborhood favorite, where fragrant classics loaded with fresh ingredients make it the go-to spot for local families dining in and taking out. Notes of lemongrass, Thai basil, galangal, and Kaffir lime leaves wafting through the air remind everyone of the deeply infused flavors that are soon to come in traditional dishes like Panang curry or basil roasted duck.

Warm the belly with a bowl of *tom kha kai*—a silky yet tangy broth of coconut milk, lime, and herbs with sliced chicken breast. Heat-seekers should tackle the spicy chicken, sautéed with bamboo shoots, bell peppers, and carrots, tossed in an intensely flavored red curry sauce with steamed jasmine rice.

Hema's Kitchen

E3

Indian 🍴

2439 W. Devon Ave. (bet. Artesian & Campbell Aves.)

Phone: 773-338-1627   Lunch & dinner daily
Web: www.hemaskitchen.com
Prices: $$

Bustling Devon Avenue is the go-to neighborhood for Indian and Pakistani vittles, music, movies, clothing, and other delights. And Hema's Kitchen is one of the stalwarts of the area, a favorite of locals (so much so, a second location opened in Lincoln Park), despite the fact that there is no shortage of restaurants from which to choose.

The menu, by Hyderabad native chef Hema Potla, includes some old favorites and twists on the classics. The chicken roll is basically an Indo-wrap, with a kebab rolled in butter-brushed *paratha*, along with verdant green chutney. Lamb *rogan josh* is a mouthwatering curry; sweet, nutty, spicy, and tart, seasoned with cardamom, cloves, and other spices. And pistachio *kulfi* is a creamy, sweet ending to a spicy meal.

Kabul House

D2

Afghan ✗✗

4949 Oakton St. (at Niles Ave.), Skokie

Phone: 847-674-3830
Web: www.kabulhouse.com
Prices: $$

Lunch Tue – Sat
Dinner Tue – Sun

Relocated to a bright and airy corner location in the heart of Skokie, Kabul House is fast becoming a beloved local spot. Its mix of contemporary cream-and-wood décor interspersed with Afghan art and tapestries lends a visual complement to the menu's authentically spiced dishes.

Two kinds of tender steamed dumplings–*aushak* with leeks and scallions, or *mantoo* with ground beef and onion–burst with flavor when drizzled with spicy tomato-meat sauce and minted yogurt; while each of the meats in a three-kabob combo of chicken, lamb, and beef are moist, smoky, and perfectly seasoned. Finish with a bowl of *firnee*, the traditional Afghan pudding infused with cardamom and topped with pistachios, or relax with a sweet cup of black tea with bergamot oil.

Lou Malnati's

E2

Pizza ✗

6649 N. Lincoln Ave. (bet. Avers & Springfield Aves.), Lincolnwood

Phone: 847-673-0800
Web: www.loumalnatis.com
Prices:

Lunch & dinner daily

Lou Malnati got his start in Chicago's very first deep-dish pizzeria. In 1971, he opened his own, and it's been golden ever since. With 30 locations around Chicago (the original is a bit of a time warp), Lou's remains family-owned and operated with great food and devoted service.

Check their website for a vast menu of pizzas, pastas, and other Italian classics. Portions are colossal: begin with stuffed spinach bread–that great Chi-style garlic, spinach, and cheese combo with tomatoes stuffed into bread–and you'll struggle to stay upright. Try the "Lou" pizza—buttery pastry-like crust crowned with spinach, mushrooms, and sliced tomatoes then doused in sauce and slathered with cheese.

Bonus: you can ship Lou's anywhere in the U.S. through their website.

L. Woods Tap & Pine Lodge

D2

American ✗✗

7110 N. Lincoln Ave. (at Kostner Ave.), Lincolnwood

Phone: 847-677-3350   Lunch & dinner daily
Web: www.lwoodsrestaurant.com
Prices: $$

Under light-decked antlers and exposed wood beams, families crowd warmly into the leather booths at this popular Lincolnwood lodge for American comfort cuisine. Large portions mean you'll likely be taking half your meal home, so don't be afraid to ask for a doggie bag.

Try nostalgic favorites like baked meatloaf, chicken pot pie, and baby-back ribs, or lighter options like the L. Woods chopped salad, house-made veggie burger, and pesto-topped flatbreads. The messy but tasty pulled-barbecue chicken sandwich piles crunchy coleslaw and crispy fried onion straws onto a heap of tender, slow-cooked meat. A wedge of tangy, creamy key lime pie is a bracing refresher after a bowl of outstanding turkey and vegetable chili that is hearty enough for a full meal.

Mysore Woodlands

E2

Indian ✗✗

2548 W. Devon Ave. (bet. Maplewood Ave. & Rockwell St.)

Phone: 773-338-8160   Lunch & dinner daily
Web: www.mysorewoodlandschicago.com
Prices: ⬮⬮

Mysore Woodlands rises above this competitive strip of south Asian eateries thanks to its unique focus on South Indian delights, vegetarian style. It may feel like a banquet hall and the service is quick, but the flavors here are bold, intense, and uniquely delicious across the vast menu of authentic stews, curries, and specialties. It is the local favorite for *dosas* and *uthappam*, each with a variety of fillings.

Those who are unsure of what to choose have an advantage here with the tasty *thali*—a large, traditional platter of assorted metal bowls boasting their spectrum of spices and tastes. These may include *sambar* (tamarind broth with vegetables); *poriyal* (fried okra, carrot, onion, potato, and zucchini), and creamy rice pudding for dessert.

外

Oceanique

Seafood XX

F1

505 Main St. (bet. Chicago & Hinman Aves.), Evanston

Phone: 847-864-3435   Dinner Mon – Sat
Web: www.oceanique.com
Prices: $$$$ Main

If you have to ask what kind of food one can expect at Oceanique, you may need to get your head checked, or at least your eyes. After all, the name pretty much says it all—straightforward French-influenced seafood. Located not far from Evanston's Ridge historic district, Oceanique opens its arms to a steady stream of shoppers and residents. It's all in the family as well, since Chef/owner Mark Grosz shares the reins with his son (who manages the acclaimed wine collection).

The chef gussies up his seafood and meat dishes with sauces and spices. Try the grilled calamari and shrimp with sake essence for a powerful punch. Can't decide? Go for the seven-course chef's tasting menu, offered with or without wine pairing.

Pasta d'Arte

Italian XX

C3

6311 N. Milwaukee Ave. (bet. Highland & Mobile Aves.)

Phone: 773-763-1181   Lunch Tue – Fri
Web: www.pastadarte.com   Dinner nightly
Prices: $$

If there were such a contest, Pasta d'Arte could easily be a frontrunner for friendliest restaurant in Chicago. The chef-owned, family-run trattoria is a local favorite, owing in part to its staff, which combines personal warmth with professional knowledge. Guests can view the same level of skill reflected in the semi-open kitchen, as they settle into the intimate dining room or make their way to the heated courtyard patio. Hearty and traditional Italian dishes comprise the bill of fare, perhaps including tender veal saltimbocca in a silky butter-white wine sauce, or a warming bowl of vegetable-barley soup that is the perfect antidote to a blustery Chicago evening. Lunches are lighter yet still satisfy with several types of pizzas and panini.

Pensiero

A5   Italian ✕✕

1566 Oak Ave. (bet. Davis & Grove Sts.), Evanston

Phone: 847-475-7779   Dinner Tue – Sun
Web: www.pensieroitalian.com
Prices: $$$

🅿 Davis

Va Pensiero got a makeover and now the lower level of the Margarita European Inn houses Pensiero. This is one Evanston eatery that doesn't get overrun with Northwestern students. Rather an adult crowd dines here, appreciating the upscale setting and perceived refined service.

Pensiero isn't particularly inventive, but serves solid and flavorsome Italian fare that's generally crowd-pleasing. A mint-scented pea flan with Maryland crab salad tossing peppery arugula and carrot vinaigrette is a colorful way to begin your feast. Pastas are pretty straightforward, but meat and seafood delights like the grilled red snapper with potatoes, crispy prosciutto, and a roasted red pepper vinaigrette are memorable to say the least.

Quince

B5   Contemporary ✕✕✕

1625 Hinman Ave. (bet. Church & Davis Sts.), Evanston

Phone: 847-570-8400   Dinner Tue – Sun
Web: www.quincerestaurant.net
Prices: $$$

Quaint and charming Quince, discreetly tucked away in Evanston's The Homestead, is the perfect setting for a romantic tête-à-tête or elegant family repast. The dining room mimics the ambience of the inn which draws on Southern colonial style for its décor inspiration. Mauve and wood-paneled walls along with cream furnishings dress the intimate space embellished with a bookshelf-framed fireplace.

The polished staff brings forth a bevy of Chef Andy Motto's preparations and may unveil keen creations such as squash blossoms stuffed with ground chicken and dressed with artichoke purée and pistachio foam; or pan-seared halibut sauced with basil-shellfish emulsion and teamed with garlic-dressed romaine chiffonade, poached quail egg, and white anchovy.

271

Renga-Tei

Japanese ✗

 E2

3956 W. Touhy Ave. (at Prairie Rd.), Lincolnwood

Phone:	847-675-5177	Lunch Mon & Wed – Fri
Web:	N/A	Dinner Wed – Mon
Prices:	**$$**	

Striking bamboo-paned, paper-covered windows jazz up a clean, brick façade; the building stands out amidst its bland, strip mall neighbors. Inside, expect waves of smiles and attentiveness from the mature staff in stylish 60s updos, and a spacious, clean space flecked with showy Japanese kitsch. Snag a seat at the sushi bar, where fresh fish–still kissed with the spray of the sea–gets handled with expert care. Slices of gorgeous abalone or Santa Barbara sea urchin make for excellent sashimi; and dishes like *tonkatsu* (tender, panko-crusted pork cutlets) keep things traditional.

A refreshing twist on the spicy tuna roll is a welcome change—hand chopped tuna tossed with spicy chilies, then rolled with rice and nori and topped with a touch of sauce.

Restaurant Ricardo

Mexican ✗

 D5

4429 W. Diversey Ave. (bet. Kilbourn & Kostner Aves.)

Phone:	773-292-0400	Lunch & dinner daily
Web:	N/A	
Prices:	💰	

Though it's often referred to as Taqueria Ricardo, this authentic Mexican restaurant adjoining the Latin-American market Carniceria Ricardo is so much more than a quick stop for tacos. In a small, cheerful room festooned with Mexican artwork, quick and friendly servers crisscross the tiled floor to grab plates from the mosaic-lined kitchen, where a wood fire permeates the food with smoky goodness.

Those in the know plan their shopping trips to leave time for the moist *pollo a la leña* straight from the rotisserie, grilled skirt steak with scallions and peppers, and incomparable tacos *al pastor* with roasted pork, pineapple, and fresh cilantro on white corn tortillas. Wash it all down with a glass of perfectly sweet and cinnamon-spiced *horchata*.

Rosewood

Steakhouse

A3

9421 W. Higgins Rd. (at Willow Creek Dr.), Rosemont

Phone: 847-696-9494
Web: www.rosewoodrestaurant.com
Prices: $$$

Lunch Mon – Fri
Dinner nightly

The Windy City loves its steakhouses, and nowhere is it more apparent than at this independent restaurant that has been thriving for more than two decades amid the popular chains near O'Hare. Inside the serene space, coffee-colored leather chairs and wood paneling create a classic Rat Pack vibe.
Succulent USDA Prime steaks get top billing here, such as the 16 oz. Kansas City strip, cooked perfectly to order. Spend the extra dollars on a peppercorn, Cajun, blue cheese, or horseradish crust on any steak for an added indulgence. French onion soup, smoked salmon on flatbread, shrimp cocktail, mashed potatoes, and baked apples round out the menu. Fresh seafood, like the horseradish-crusted ahi tuna, is a good option for those who want something different.

Sabri Nihari

Indian

E2

2502 W. Devon Ave. (bet. Campbell & Maplewood Aves.)

Phone: 773-465-3272
Web: www.sabrinihari.com
Prices: ⊜⊜

Dinner nightly

On a stretch of Devon Avenue filled with halal meat stores, fabric shops, and Indo-Pak groceries, find this bright restaurant with an air of formality and satisfying Pakistani-focused cuisine. Whether eating somewhere that serves only *zabiha* meat (slaughtered in strict accordance with the Islamic faith), is of importance to you or not, this spot is well worth a visit (easiest to arrive by car or bus).
The signature beef *nihari* dish is de-boned and braised in a thickened brown sauce, served with slivers of jalapeño peppers and ginger root. A *biryani* may feature caramelized onions and chicken cooked until tender, topping tasty basmati rice. Classics like *dal, haleem*, kebabs, freshly made naan, and other Pakistani favorites round out the affordable menu.

Shokran Moroccan Grill

Moroccan

E4

4027 W. Irving Park Rd. (bet. Keystone Ave. & Pulaski Rd.)

Phone: 773-427-9130
Web: www.shokranchicago.com
Prices: 😊😊

Dinner nightly

🚇 Irving Park (Blue)

Judging by the ordinary façade, commercial surroundings, and hovering highway, you may be tempted to pass right by. But, oh, the delights that would be missed! Arabic for "thank you," Shokran is a scrumptious spot for homemade Moroccan, where rich silk fabrics billow from the ceiling; framed mother-of-pearl artifacts hang on burnt sienna walls; and hookah pipes and copper chargers bedeck the room.

Brace yourself for the couscous royale—melt-in-your mouth braised lamb; juicy merguez (spicy sausage stuffed with ground lamb and beef); tender zucchini, rutabaga, carrots, and chickpeas snuggled into fluffy couscous. Satiate the sweet tooth with handmade cookies—from almond pastries to *fekkas*, each morsel is fresh and irresistible. Thank you, Shokran.

Smak-Tak 😊

Polish 🍴🍴

C3

5961 N. Elston Ave. (bet. Markham & Peterson Aves.)

Phone: 773-763-1123
Web: www.smaktak.com
Prices: 😊😊

Lunch & dinner daily

Knotty pine paneling, wood chairs, and a small fireplace transform the tiny Smak-Tak into a ski cabin-like getaway. This kitchen cooks up some of the city's best Polish food, which is saying a lot given the plethora of Polish eats in the area.

Portions are huge, and while the staff happily packs up leftovers, diners should plan their ordering so they can try a little of everything. Do not skip the amazing *pierogi*. Versions include cheese and potato, sauerkraut and mushrooms, blueberry, plum, cherry, sweet cheese, or strawberry; and all are tossed in melted butter with sour cream on the side. Potato pancakes served with applesauce; meat-stuffed cabbage; hearty hunter stew; and grilled, old Polish-style kielbasa are other stomach-busters.

Sol de Mexico

D4

Mexican

3018 N. Cicero Ave. (bet. Wellington Ave. & Nelson St.)

Phone: 773-282-4119
Lunch & dinner Wed – Mon
Web: www.soldemexicochicago.com
Prices: **$$**

Mama Mexicana leads the *mole*-making magic here at Sol de Mexico, firing up dishes with awe-inspiring authenticity. Creative, moan-worthy, and true-blue delights weaves their way across the menu: Alaskan sablefish with *hoja santa*, *chile güero*, and sweet plantains; New Zealand rack of lamb in a classic Oaxacan black *mole*. Belly buzzing in anticipation? Get to it with *ayamole*, creamy roasted pumpkin soup kissed with *guajillo* chiles; heavenly *chuleta de puerco en mole verde*, wood-grilled pork chops laid across a *mole* served with a stack of smoky tamales and crunchy chayote; and bliss out with *natillas*, a cinnamon rice pudding drizzled with mango purée.

Take the edge off with one of several tequilas from their extensive selection.

The Stained Glass Bistro

A4

American

1735 Benson Ave. (bet. Church & Clark Sts.), Evanston

Phone: 847-864-8600
Dinner nightly
Web: www.thestainedglass.com
Prices: **$$**

Sharing a kitchen with The Cellar (its sister restaurant around the corner), this is the more upscale, globe-trotting elder. The sexy urban space (think exposed ductwork and beams; wood floors) is a perfect setting for the spruced up modern American cooking with international inflections.

Roasted free-range Amish chicken cozies up next to sweet corn tamale, red *mole*, and roasted chayote squash; and baby octopus rests alongside oil-cured olives, soft polenta and oven-dried tomatoes. Old-fashioned crab cakes get a sweet corn *arepa* and chive oil.

In the mood for just a little sip of wine? You're in luck—over thirty wines by the glass are offered, changing on a daily basis. Try the "Wine Sampler," three different half glasses, for a dash of variety.

Tacos Locos

Mexican

A3

4732 N. River Rd. (at Lawrence Ave.), Schiller Park

Phone: 847-928-2197 Lunch & dinner daily
Web: www.tacoslocosllc.com
Prices:

There are no missteps at this table-service taqueria, a happy corner in the Chicagoland suburbs. Despite the fact that it is tucked into a small strip mall in Schiller Park, Tacos Locos is a cozy, family-run spot that pairs friendly service with high quality Mexican food prepared with care at a superb value.

The solid menu is loaded with tried-and-true tacos, tortas, and other classics, but it's the little details that stand out. Cooks quickly grill each massive burrito for an extra-crispy exterior, and addictive *choriqueso* blends Chihuahua cheese with chorizo, roasted poblanos, and mushrooms for a decadent take on *queso fundido*. Locals know to stop by on weekends when tamales, menudo, and other specialties are available on a limited basis.

Taste of Peru

Peruvian

F2

6545 N. Clark St. (bet. Albion & Arthur Aves.)

Phone: 773-381-4540 Lunch & dinner daily
Web: www.tasteofperu.com
Prices: **$$**

Yes, it's a cliché, but don't judge a book by its cover. Sure, it is located in a generic strip mall and is flanked by a Laundromat and nail salon, but look past Taste of Peru's lackluster location and less-than-appealing exterior, and you'll certainly be rightly rewarded.

Inside, it's kitschy Peru, but you're not here for the aura. You're here for the fiery and funky food that draws everyone from gourmands to Guy Fieri. Chat up the passionate owner–who will give you a quick education in Peruvian cuisine–as you inhale generous portions of ethnic comfort food like *papa rellena* (mashed potatoes stuffed with tender steak), and *cau cau* (honeycomb tripe stew). The owner keeps his cooking secrets close to the chest, but that's ok, since you'll be back again soon.

Tre Kronor

E3 _Scandinavian_

3258 W. Foster Ave. (at Spaulding Ave.)

Phone: 773-267-9888
Web: www.trekronorrestaurant.com
Prices:

Lunch daily
Dinner Mon – Sat

If you had a Swedish grandmother, this is the food she would pile in front of you for breakfast: thick waffles laden with bananas, berries, and whipped cream; light and buttery pancakes soaking up warm and tart lingonberries; or a Stockholm omelet filled with Havarti and *falukorv* sausage. Should your palate prefer savory dishes, Tre Kronor has also got you covered with a *Reubenssen* of slices of tender corned beef, oozing *Jarlsberg* cheese, and tangy sauerkraut on toasted rye bread; or Swedish meatballs with pickled cucumbers and lingonberry sauce.

After satisfying your cravings amid adorably Nordic wood furnishings and wall murals, burn a few calories by walking across the street to the Sweden Shop to outfit your home in Swedish imports.

Tub Tim Thai

D2 _Thai_

4927 Oakton St. (bet. Niles Ave. & Skokie Blvd.), Skokie

Phone: 847-675-8424
Web: www.tubtimthai.com
Prices:

Lunch & dinner Mon – Sat

A casual stop in suburban Skokie, this Thai find is as accommodating as they come. The setting is pleasant, with dark wood furnishings and pastel walls showcasing a revolving display of artwork typically for sale.

The affordable menu is equally accommodating and the kitchen delights with tasty recipes and quality ingredients. Diners can request the level of spice desired; but if it's not hot enough, there are pickled chilies, chili paste, and chili powder on the table. Choices run the gamut of the traditional Thai options such as shrimp dumplings; spicy basil chicken; pad Thai; and sweet coconut rice with mango for dessert. Tub Tim Thai is never a splurge, but lunch is a particular bargain with an appetizer, salad, and main course for under $10.

Viceroy of India

E2

2520 W. Devon Ave. (bet. Campbell & Maplewood Aves.)

Phone: 773-743-4100
Web: www.viceroyofindia.com
Prices: 💰

Lunch & dinner daily

A walk down Devon Avenue is like a daycation to India. Each storefront is packed with saris, Bollywood videos, snack shops, restaurants, and other retail businesses offering up a taste of home to Chicago's enormous Indian population. Streets are packed (and, as a result, parking sometimes a challenge) most nights, making for great people-watching.
Viceroy of India is a favorite among the many options on Devon both because of its small café, for sweets and take-out, and its upscale dining room, which accommodates large parties. A reasonably priced lunch buffet; a particularly good *dosa* served with coconut-based chutney; and fragrant lamb *saag* are a few of the draws. The tamarind rice, with its nuts and herbs, has a perfect sour, yet fragrant, note.

Yolo 😊

D1

5111 Brown St. (bet. Floral & Lincoln Aves.), Skokie

Phone: 847-674-0987
Web: www.yolomexicaneatery.com
Prices: $$

Dinner Tue – Sat

For some of the best salsas and sauces in the Chicagoland area, drive just beyond city limits to Skokie, where a crowd of loyal regulars constantly fills the small but charming dining room at Yolo. The welcoming space, punctuated by Mexican art and white linen-topped tables, is a neighborhood destination for traditional Mexican food.
Authentic dishes prepared with top-quality ingredients showcase the restaurant's skill with complex flavors and spices. *Camarones Ixtapa* marinate in a *guajillo* and *morita* pepper sauce; achiote salsa bathes tender strips of steak in tacos *cuño xtiqui*; and pork tenderloin pairs with creamy poblano purée. Even the typical dessert staple of flan is elevated by the woodsy taste of cinnamon rather than cloying sweetness.

Zia's Trattoria

C2

Italian

6699 N. Northwest Hwy. (at Oliphant Ave.)

Phone: 773-775-0808
Web: www.ziaschicago.com
Prices: $$

Lunch Tue – Fri
Dinner nightly

This venerable neighborhood standby welcomes a steady flow of business lunches that turns into a dinner parade of locals, all coming for the relaxed atmosphere and approachable, rustic Italian fare. Exposed brick walls and wrought-iron lantern sconces approximate the feel of an authentic trattoria, and the white linen tablecloths belie the affordably mid-priced meals.

Pastas are as rich with flavors as they are generous, and Italian classics like *vitello saltimbocca* and *pollo al limone* are offered along with more contemporary main courses like *gamberi Calabrese*, balancing fiery Calabrian peppers with cooling mint. Soups and specials change daily—try the velvety cream of potato with rich undertones of caramelized garlic when it's on the menu.

Park your car without a problem when you see ⌐☞ for valet parking.

South, Southwest & Western Suburbs

South, Southwest & Western Suburbs

With perhaps a few high-profile exceptions (here's lookin' at you, President Obama's Hyde Park), the neighborhoods of the city's west and south sides and the west and south suburbs rarely make the pages of traditional visitors' guides. Instead, they're saved for residents who work and live in these city environs.

Feeding Families

While it's true that these neighborhoods may not have the museums, hotels, or 24-7 service of those more centrally located, they are a foodie's dream, with lesser-known groceries, takeout joints, and ethnic eateries. Back in the day, some of these neighborhoods, including Back of the Yards, once home to the famous Chicago Stockyards, changed the food industry.

Today the Marquette Park neighborhood where, in 1966, Martin Luther King, Jr. brought his civil rights marchers, may seem questionable after dark. But it is worth a ride for no reason other than the mighty mother-in-law. No, not visiting a relative. That's the name of **Fat Johnnie's Famous Red Hots'** best dish: A tamale, a kosher hot dog, chili, and (processed) cheese on a bun, handed through a window. This may be a shabby and shaky trailer, but Fat Johnnie's hot dogs (a mainstay for over 30 years now) have a reputation of their own and have been luring hungry hot dog lovers from near and far. The rest of Marquette Park (near 63rd St.)

features predominantly Mexican storefronts, taquerias, and other food vendors.

Film buffs love the fact that Marquette Park (the 600-acre actual green space, not the neighborhood) was featured in the iconic movie *The Blues Brothers.*

Eastern European Eats

Closer to Midway International Airport, near Archer Heights, is a concentration of Eastern European shops mixed among classic Chicago-style brick bungalows. One favorite is **Bobak's Sausage Company**, with its 100-foot-long meat counter. This meat lover's nirvana is a Chicago-based organization that caters mainly to food entities, grocery stores, and delis. Shopping here is entertainment in and of itself. Purchase a hot lunch to eat on the spot or buy a range of delicious sausages (Polish-style) and other deli meats to take home. For a bigger and better taste of Chicago, you can also choose to buy from their bulk-pack items, retail-pack items, and imported specialties. Want to try this at home? They also proffer a list of recipes. For a more Polish and Lithuanian take on deli dishes, try Evergreen Park's **AJ's Meats**.

Ireland in Chicagoland

Nearby Beverly is the hub of the city's Irish bar scene, something many people first discover during the raucous South Side Irish St. Patrick's Day parade. But all year long bars serve corned beef, cabbage, and plenty of cold beers. Beverly's Pantry sells cookware and teaches locals how to use it in a series of ongoing classes. Non-food attractions in Beverly include a number of Frank Lloyd Wright houses and other significant architectural monuments (not to mention a real castle).

Farther north and closer to Lake Michigan, cerebral hub Hyde Park attracts Obama fans, academics, students, and more architecture buffs. Professors and students at the University of Chicago crowd the surrounding cafés, restaurants, and bars geared towards the smarter set.

Summer Snacking

During baseball season, don't miss the White Sox at the U.S. Cellular Field. A lick of a five-flavor ice cream cone from the **Original Rainbow Cone**, a Chicagoland staple since 1926, is an equally thrilling experience. Housed in a pretty pink building, the original menu may also unveil a range of splits, shakes, and sundaes; as well as a decadent carte of ice cream flavors such as black walnut, New York vanilla, and bubble gum-banana.

Chicago's Beloved Bites

Those without any heart or cholesterol problems ought to try the beloved breaded steaks (with a mélange of toppings) from **Ricobene's**, which has several locations on both the south side and in the south suburbs. Ricobene's also caters to the beefy best in everyone by serving up those Chicago classic pan, deep-dish, or thin crust pizza pies alongside other delectable dishes like their mouthwatering

barbecue specialties (a full slab dinner?); Italian-esque sandwiches (imagine the Sloppy Joe and Vesuvio Italian classic sandwich); Chicago-style hot dogs; and char-broiled burgers. Suburban Oak Park may be more famous for past residents like Ernest Hemingway and Frank Lloyd Wright, but nonetheless, foodies care more about vinegar-maker Jim Vitalo. His amazing, subtle herb-infused **Herbally Yours** vinegars are sold at the **Oak Park Farmer's Market** on Saturdays in the summer.

Grazing Through the Middle East

Suburban Bridgeview, home to Toyota Park, where the Chicago Fire soccer team plays, is one of the region's best stops for authentic and fine Middle Eastern fare. Throughout this area, you'll find restaurants outfitted with grills and bakeries galore. Visit a myriad of centrally-located stores, and be sure to take home snacks like pita, hummus, and baba ghanoush; as well as fresh groceries for a night of magnificent Middle Eastern cooking. It would be blasphemous to end your meal without a taste of sweet, so after you've consumed your fill of falafel and the like, move on to sweeter respites in this Middle Eastern Corridor, namely **Elshafei Pastries** for some flaky baklava and other pistachio-pocked delights.

For more saccharine satisfaction, sojourn at **Albasha Sweets** and **Nablus Sweets**. One bite of these syrupy, luscious (and creamy) sweets and pastries will leave you smiling for the rest of the evening. Can there be any other way to end such fresh, fun, and fine fare?

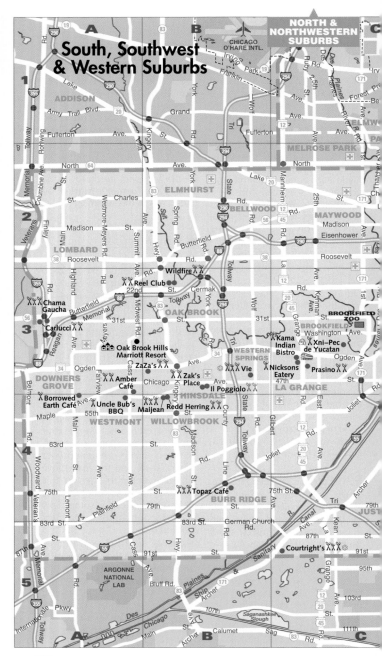

South, Southwest & Western Suburbs

NORTH & NORTHWESTERN SUBURBS

284

Al Bawadi Grill

D5

7216 W. 87th St. (bet. Harlem & Oketo Aves.), Bridgeview

Phone: 708-599-1999
Web: www.albawadigrill.com
Prices: $$

Lunch & dinner daily

Housed in a former fast food joint on busy 87th Street, Al Bawadi Grill doesn't exactly shout "peaceful oasis," but the owners have done a lot with what they've got. Water fountains, faux palm trees, and etched glass set the scene for the kind, hospitable service. A colorful pile of pickled vegetables as well as a smoky eggplant salad are brought to the table for diners to enjoy while they peruse the grill-centric menu.

Hummus is velvety and artfully presented, dotted with olive oil, chilies, and sumac accompanied by warm pita. The Al Bawadi mixed grill includes three kinds of kebabs– shish, *kefta*, and chicken kebab–accompanied by grilled onion, tomato, and two styles of rice. Wash it all down with a freshly squeezed juice or smoothie.

Amber Café

A3

13 N. Cass Ave. (at Burlington Ave.), Westmont

Phone: 630-515-8080
Web: www.ambercafe.net
Prices: $$

Dinner Tue – Sat

Set on the main drag of tiny Westmont, Amber Café has been serving a touch of elegance since 2004. The dining room exudes calm with walls cloaked in seafoam green and exposed brick. Paved with rosy, polished wood floors, tall windows replete with steel-hued sheer drapes, and tables boasting white linen and fresh flowers, Amber Café is *très* romantic.

Stroll past the pebbled-glass wine cabinet to the cozy micro-tiled bar. Catch dinner here from a menu based on American ideals with Mediterranean sensibilities. Grilled octopus gets flavor and pep from charred tomatoes and pickled chilies; pan-roasted Alaskan king salmon is pristinely plated over a bed of vegetables; and a sweet corn panna cotta is cleverly laced with fresh caramel corn and blueberries.

Amelia's

F3

Mexican

4559 S. Halsted St. (at 46th St.)

Phone: 773-538-8200
Web: www.ameliaschicago.com
Prices:

Lunch & dinner daily

 This neighborhood bright light offers Mexican cuisine with a creative slant. The well-maintained space is generously sized, great for families, and is attractively done—brick walls are hung with colorful paintings of mountainside scenes and baskets of flowers, tall slender windows are dressed with crinkly orange drapes, and gently swirling ceiling fans lend a chill vibe.

Lunch serves tortas, fajitas, and enchiladas, while dinner offers starters such as the *tamal nejo*, revealing a toothsome cornmeal filling topped with shredded white meat chicken and a complex and richly satisfying red *mole* made from a family recipe. Globally-flecked entrées include the likes of grilled pork tenderloin with a ginger rice cake, hominy, andouille sausage, and tomatillos.

Autre Monde

D2

Mediterranean

6727 W. Roosevelt Rd. (bet. Euclid & Oak Park Aves.), Berwyn

Phone: 708-775-8122
Web: www.autremondecafe.net
Prices: $$

Dinner Tue – Sun

Oak Park (Blue)

 A far cry from the major chains dominating Berwyn's culinary landscape, Autre Monde brings the sophisticated seasonality of a typical Gold Coast hot spot to the suburbs without losing any flair. Foreign films represented in blow-up poster form and as muted background television visuals give the room a Euro-cool feel, though the restrained bare wood works as an amplifier for happy families filling up the restaurant.

The kitchen paints with a Mediterranean palette, turning out plates like cured fresh sardines; gremolata-drizzled *burrata*; or cracker-thin flatbreads with an array of toppings like wild mushrooms, roasted peppers, and *za'atar*. And local's not just a buzzword here: a greenhouse out back is responsible for as much produce as it can grow.

Borrowed Earth Café

Vegetarian ✗

A4

970 Warren Ave. (bet. Highland Ave. & Main St.), Downers Grove

Phone: 630-795-1729
Web: www.borrowedearthcafe.com
Prices: $$

Lunch & dinner Tue – Sat

This suburban stalwart is as earnest as they come. The environmentally friendly dining room cleverly encourages diners to learn to appreciate a raw food way of life. The aesthetic is more Woodstock than Gwyneth Paltrow, but the food is good enough for any health-conscious Hollywood celeb.

Enjoy a guiltless lasagna made with thin sheets of zucchini, juicy tomatoes, grated carrots, loads of creamy pesto, and fluffy cashew "ricotta." It arrives with a side of kale-licious salad: kale, hemp seed, and cabbage tossed with the house dressing. For even more of the leafy power green, try the addictive and delicious kale chips. The out-of-this-world cheesecake is a revelation and easily surpasses run-of-the-mill dairy cheesecakes, minus the guilt.

Carlucci

Italian ✗✗

A3

1891 Butterfield Rd. (off I-355), Downers Grove

Phone: 630-512-0990
Web: www.carluccirestaurant.com
Prices: $$

Lunch Mon – Fri
Dinner nightly

Live in the suburbs long enough and you will end up celebrating a promotion with co-workers, niece's high school graduation, or another milestone at Carlucci's. The suburban office park setting doesn't help raise expectations from the outside; but inside, the space is warm and welcoming, and the service attentive and professional.

The food is equally surprising. The *petto di pollo ripieno*, a breaded chicken breast stuffed with ricotta, prosciutto, and peas, is so tasty you may need to refill your bread basket so you don't miss a drop of its lemon butter sauce. Ingredients in the tasty *insalata Genovese*–romaine, black olives, cherry tomatoes, and tuna–are individually seasoned before being tossed together. For dessert, treat yourself to bread pudding.

Chama Gaucha

Steakhouse ✗✗✗

3008 Finley Rd. (at Butterfield Rd.), Downers Grove

Phone: 630-324-6002
Web: www.chamagaucha.com
Prices: $$

Lunch Mon – Fri
Dinner nightly

Chama Gaucha is a sort of carnivorous carnival that will have you crying uncle after devouring pounds of delicious skewered meats grilled over the open-fire *churrascaria*. Meals begin at the bountiful salad bar, but save plenty of room for the piping hot and juice-dripping meats. Chicken, pork, sausage, bacon-wrapped filet, lamb—it's all here and ready for the taking. The wine list focuses on reds for a good reason, but go Brazilian and order a caipirinha.

The mood feels theatrical, with passadores or gauchos flaunting machismo in slicing spit-roasted meats from long metal skewers, Zorro-style right at the table. Just be sure to have your red and green signs at the ready, so servers know when to stop. It's glorious gluttony at its best.

Cucina Paradiso

Italian ✗✗

814 North Blvd. (bet. Kenilworth & Oak Park Aves.), Oak Park

Phone: 708-848-3434
Web: www.cucinaoakpark.com
Prices: $$

Dinner nightly

🚇 Oak Park (Green)

Set within the charming boutique-lined confines of Oak Park, Cucina Paradiso draws an arty neighborhood crowd. Brothers Nick and Anthony Gambino grew up in the food business (Dad was the owner of Nancy's Stuffed Pizza), so they know their way around a kitchen. From the awning-covered sidewalk to the vintage posters, this place has comfortably quaint all wrapped up.

On Mondays, half-price wines pack 'em into the bar, and throughout the week this is a solid choice in the neighborhood. Service is spotty but the food tastefully prepared. It is standard Italian-American grub—dishes like veal Marsala and desserts like tiramisu reign. As expected, there's plenty of pasta (they even offer whole wheat and gluten-free varieties).

South, Southwest & Western Suburbs

289

Courtright's ❀

French 🗴🗴🗴

C5

8989 Archer Ave. (bet Cemetery & Willow Springs Rds.), Willow Springs

Dinner Tue – Sun

Phone: 708-839-8000
Web: www.courtrights.com
Prices: $$$

Elizabeth Boundos

Travel over the river and through the woods–literally, as Courtright's sits between the Chicago River and the Cook County Forest Preserve–to a genteel brick cottage with a comfy country club feel. Woodland creatures might stroll through the landscaped garden prominently framed in the dining room window, while arts and crafts-influenced accents like stylized blooms on the patterned carpet, a carved wood fireplace, and leafy metal sconces echo nature's decor outside.

Family-owned for more than 50 years, Courtright's has likely seen the same families celebrate graduations to anniversaries over the decades. These multigenerational appreciators of such old-school hospitality are also likely returning for exceptional values on Chef Jerome Bacle's seasonal five-course menu or diner's choice of a three- or four-course prix-fixe.

A soupçon of French influence finds its way into nearly every dish, mixing classic techniques with inventive touches. Cucumber "raita" with goat cheese and scallions enriches a delicate but velvety asparagus soup, while a supple rabbit saddle sits on a creamy mix of bacon, barley, and peanuts along with an earthy carrot purée and a subtle cumin-infused reduction.

Han 202 😋

Chinese 𝔛𝔛

605 W. 31st St. (bet. Lowe Ave. & Wallace St.)

Phone: 312-949-1314   Dinner Tue – Sun
Web: www.han202.com
Prices: 🍪

Visit Han 202 and be pleasantly surprised by its sparkling clean, chic-minimalist décor. The dining room is replete with red-stained wood tables, each topped with a lotus blossom votive; and the partially open kitchen offers a peek at an orderly staff churning out creatively prepared Chinese cuisine.

Han 202 only offers a prix-fixe menu which is uniquely ambitious at a very reasonable price. Perhaps begin with blue crab wonton soup, whose plump, silky dumplings are both delicate and chock-full of crab; and incredibly tender filets of Mongolian beef in a sweet-salty brown sauce showcase fine product, expertly prepared. Meals end on a refreshingly light note and may include a selection of sorbets for dessert.

Il Poggiolo

Italian 𝔛𝔛

8 E. 1st St. (bet. Garfield Ave. & Washington St.), Hinsdale

Phone: 630-734-9400   Lunch Mon – Sat
Web: www.ilpoggiolohinsdale.com   Dinner nightly
Prices: $$

A charming turn-of-the-century building in downtown Hinsdale gets a new lease on life with Il Poggiolo. The balcony, or *il poggiolo*, of this former silent movie theater now gives mezzanine diners a bird's eye view of the handsome bar framed in dark wood and the burgundy tufted banquettes below—as well as the massive fringed red lampshades dangling from the ceiling.

Beyond a fire engine-red meat slicer, the showcase kitchen turns out modern versions of regional Italian cuisine like melt-in-your-mouth meatballs bobbing on fresh marinara sauce in an iron skillet; or handmade ravioli filled with goat cheese, resting on a pea purée and creamy herb-speckled tomato sauce. Airy chocolate mousse surprises those who indulge with its slow-building spiciness.

Kama Indian Bistro

C3 Indian

8 W. Burlington Ave. (bet. Ashland Ave & La Grange Rd.), La Grange

Phone: 708-352-3300
Web: www.kamabistro.com
Prices: $$

Lunch Fri – Sun
Dinner nightly

Across from the Metra, find this petite, inviting Indian storefront. Per Hinduism, Kama (or desire) is one of four goals in life, and as a nod to tradition, this bistro entices via aubergine walls hugging a portrait of the amorous Kamadeva (God of love) himself. Purple is a running theme throughout the slender space; while fresh lavender roses and beaded tea candles add an elegant touch to the tables.

Jeweled throw pillows lay across banquettes and hypnotic sitar music wafts through the room. But seducing one's appetite is the chef's playful intent with unlikely ingredients like shrimp *koliwara* bathed in onion, chili, ginger; and *achari masala*, chicken massaged with an exotic blend of 18 spices. The PB & J naan leaves tiny tots with big smiles.

La Petite Folie

F4 French

1504 E. 55th St. (at Harper Ave.)

Phone: 773-493-1394
Web: www.lapetitefolie.com
Prices: $$

Lunch Tue – Fri
Dinner Tue – Sun

Consistently considered one of the area's best restaurants, La Petite Folie is tucked into a tree-lined courtyard of the Hyde Park Shopping center. Inside, find an unpretentious décor accented by a curved wood bar and cordial service.

The surroundings improve even more as the kitchen cooks up classic French fare made with the best seasonal, local ingredients available. Bargains can be found at lunch, perhaps featuring a three-egg omelet filled with duck sausage and onion confit; or the chopped shrimp in light tomato-cream sauce folded into handmade crêpes. Dinner can be a bargain, too, during the $32 three-course prix-fixe, available from 5:00-6:30 P.M. daily. Classic salads and flaky dessert tarts are sure to please even the most ardent Francophiles.

Maijean

B4   French   XXX

30 S. Prospect Ave. (at Railroad Ave.), Clarendon Hills

Phone: 630-794-8900
Web: www.maijean.com
Prices: $$

Dinner Tue – Sun

In an art nouveau jewelbox where curves straight from a Paris Métro entrance sign undulate from the windowpanes of the entry doors across persimmon-toned ochre walls to an elaborately carved bar, Maijean–named for Chef/owner Nadia Tilkian's late grandmother–celebrates the sensuous pleasures of the palate with elegance. Closely-spaced seating might be too friendly for some, but a sidewalk patio offers breathing room in fair weather.

Tilkian specializes in French comfort cuisine with a global flair, and often brings a dish or two to the table personally. Dinner may include spice-rubbed duck breast drizzled with smoked shallot sauce; salmon tartare popping with bright red roe and tart lemon vinaigrette; or escargots in a sprightly champagne sauce.

Maya del Sol

D2   Latin American   XX

144 S. Oak Park Ave. (bet. South Blvd. & Pleasant St.), Oak Park

Phone: 708-358-9800
Web: www.mayadelsol.com
Prices: $$

Lunch Fri – Sun
Dinner nightly
Oak Park

Holiday lights may twinkle in the window, but this Latin jewel's inventive and tasty plates lure food lovers year-round. The divided den features an ample bar, tables, and TVs on one side; on the other, exposed brick and sunflower-stenciled lamps surround snug booths. Dusky ochre hues set a calming vibe for a family-friendly feast.

Aloof teens and jubilant toddlers share tables with adults who are here for such *delicioso* dishes as champagne gazpacho finished with *cajeta* cheese and crispy tortilla strips; *calabaza rellena* smothered in a sweet corn-butter sauce; and *crepas de cajeta*, lacy crêpes folded over caramelized goat milk syrup, pecans, and plantains.

The fiery stretch limo parked out front is a thrill, but it's truly the food that steals the show.

Nana

F3

American ✗✗

3267 S. Halsted St. (at 33rd St.)

Phone: 312-929-2486
Web: www.nanaorganic.com
Prices: **$$**

Lunch & dinner daily

A precious find on an unassuming street, Nana is a modern magnet for diners who live by fresh, local, and organic eats, but who don't wish to spend an arm and a leg for the pleasure. Bridgeport locals and others gather for Nana's sincere, clean, and Latin-inspired preparations, and to check out the art (dotting the white walls) and jewelry on sale.

The spicy *chilaquiles*–served with a side of eggs, any style– are elevated beyond their usual "leftover tortilla" status thanks to a zingy tomatillo cream salsa. The owner's *mamá*, also the pastry chef at north side favorite, Café 28, makes the delicious desserts. Her cherry and peach cobbler, for example, is topped with a brown sugar-cinnamon crumb dome, spiced up with jalapeño, and packs a surprising punch.

Nicksons Eatery

C3

American ✗

30 S. La Grange Rd. (bet. Calendar & Harris Aves.), La Grange

Phone: 708-354-4995
Web: www.nicksonseatery.com
Prices: **$$**

Lunch & dinner Mon – Sat

Make sure you're starving (and have rescheduled your appointment with the cardiologist) before heading to Nicksons Eatery, as this charming spot in downtown La Grange celebrates country American cooking. Tin ceilings, homely wood floors, and a cowhide-covered banquette lend a barn-like aura to the dining room.

The Baca family, which includes husband and wife Nick and Carson (thus the name), and brother Rick, run the show with finger-lickin' good food. Tasty Texan brisket tacos, pan-seared pork chops, pork ribs, and soft shell crab Po'boys— this is country cooking with a gourmet slant. Those crispy sweet potato fries will hook you! In the sweet vein, key lime pie, double chocolate pecan fudge, and old-fashioned root beer floats offer a slice of Americana.

Noodles Etc.

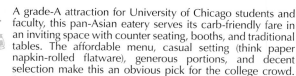

F4

Asian ✗

1333 E. 57th St. (bet. Kenwood & Kimbark Aves.)

Phone: 773-684-2801   Lunch & dinner daily
Web: www.noodlesetc.com
Prices: 〰

A grade-A attraction for University of Chicago students and faculty, this pan-Asian eatery serves its carb-friendly fare in an inviting space with counter seating, booths, and traditional tables. The affordable menu, casual setting (think paper napkin-rolled flatware), generous portions, and decent selection make this an obvious pick for the college crowd. Service is prompt, even when tables are packed.

As is expected from its name, the menu includes a wide variety of noodles including udon, ramen, *pho, pancit*, lo mein, *tom yum*, and plenty of other Asian versions of the dish. There's also a sizeable offering of starters in portions best suited to sharing.

Sure, it's not authentic, but everything here is tasty, well-made, and a very good value.

Prasino

C3

American ✗✗

93 S. La Grange Rd. (bet. Cossitt & Harris Aves.), La Grange

Phone: 708-469-7058   Lunch & dinner daily
Web: www.eatgreenlivewell.com
Prices: $$

The fact that Prasino has a "smoothie sommelier" should be a clue that this is not your run-of-the-mill suburban restaurant. True to its name, Prasino (from the Greek word for "green") is all about being eco-friendly. Light fixtures are made from recycled wine boxes and information about the reclaimed wood furniture is available to interested diners.

Ingredients are organic, sustainably grown, and locally sourced whenever possible. The thick, buttery banana bread topped with pistachio ice cream is a clear winner, as is the roasted cauliflower gratin with sharp cheddar and béchamel sauce. Breakfast is a big deal and pancakes are made to order with your choice of batter (vegan and gluten-free for diehards; or buttermilk and multigrain for others).

Redd Herring

American

B4

31 S. Prospect Ave. (at Park Ave.), Clarendon Hills

Phone: 630-908-7295
Web: www.redd-herring.com
Prices: $$

Lunch & dinner daily

Everyone loves a place where desserts typically outnumber salads (think 2:1). This sums up the fun-loving, neighborhood spirit of Redd Herring, the closer-to-home spot of Chef Roger Herring (of Wrigleyville's Socca). Set in the quaint downtown of Clarendon Hills, this cozy newcomer draws the locals who come in to catch the game, as well as families who want a yummy meal that doesn't come with a toy.

Arrive hungry to this hearty American spot, where popular menu items include fresh and tender halibut fritters, applewood-smoked pork chop with mustard-laced potatoes, and Devil's food cake. The caramelized onion- and cheddar-topped burger on a pretzel roll is a Redd Herring signature, as is the "market price" cotton candy for a little sugary fun.

Reel Club

Seafood

B3

272 Oakbrook Center (off Rte. 83), Oak Brook

Phone: 630-368-9400
Web: www.reel-club.com
Prices: $$

Lunch & dinner daily

Shopping in the behemoth Oakbrook Center could work up an appetite for almost anyone. Reel Club, a Lettuce Entertain You offering at the mall, gives weary shoppers and locals a great alternative to the staid food court.

The menu is focused on seafood, including Sunday's seafood buffet; but there are plenty of American standards such as salads and surf-and-turf. The ahi tuna burger is fresh and tasty, slathered in a lemon-ginger aïoli and served on a toasted brioche with fantastic hand-cut fries. The seafood gumbo is so savory and satisfying it could make a meal on its own; but finish with a Mounds Bar, paying homage to the classic candy bar—it is as decadent as it sounds. A pre-selected flight of five wines offers a well-priced sampling with entrées.

Sen

D2   J a p a n e s e   ✗

814 S. Oak Park Ave. (bet. Harrison & Van Buren Sts.), Oak Park

Phone: 708-848-4400   Lunch & dinner Tue – Sun
Web: www.sensushibar.com
Prices: $$

 Oak Park

It may be a subunit of currency, but it is no coincidence that Sen rhymes with Zen. From river stones pressed into a concrete entryway to a serene poplar-paneled room, minimalism and natural textures form the main strain in this sushi temple. New-age spa music drifts over the warm scene outfitted with benches and stools.

Bento lunches are all the rage here, yet witness a bit of artistry in such stunning creations as crab and pineapple wontons that take the Rangoon to a new level. Inventive maki like the *goka* stuffed with hamachi, avocado, and crowned with seared *otoro*; as well as red dragon with spicy tuna, *tai*, and red *tobiko* show off the *itamae's* shining skill. Tempura-fried ice cream kissed with raspberry sauce beautifully blends bright and sweet.

Shokolad

E2   E a s t e r n   E u r o p e a n   ✗✗

2524 W. Chicago Ave. (bet. Campbell Ave. & Rockwell St.)

Phone: 773-276-6402   Lunch Tue – Sun
Web: N/A
Prices:

Ukrainian, Russian, and Eastern European dishes are comfort food to much of Chicago's population, and diners come to Humboldt Park's Shokolad to indulge their cravings in a bright, casual setting. Must-tries include the potato and cheese *varenyky*, the Ukranian answer to the Polish *pierogi*, and the *pelmeni*, tender, spiced ground pork dumplings.

Sure, cheesecake lollipops aren't authentic Eastern European treats, but these dark or white chocolate-covered cheesecake rounds are favorites of regulars. In fact, they may be responsible for introducing many people to Shokolad. Highlighting the prowess of the pastry department, there's a bakery showcase with sweets to take away.

Regulars tout the Sunday brunch, by far one of the best around.

Topaz Café

B4

780 Village Center Dr. (at Blue Ridge Pkwy.), Burr Ridge

Phone:	630-654-1616	Lunch Mon – Sat
Web:	www.topazcafe.com	Dinner nightly
Prices:	**$$$**	

Dining at the tony outdoor Burr Ridge Village Center might be as sexy as mall eats can get, and Topaz Café stands out as the epitome of suburban chic. At lunch, the columned space fills with power shoppers toting bags, then hits a sultry note as the lighting dims softly to amber for dinner. Get intimate with nightly specials at the bar, but be forewarned that your date might get distracted by the sporting event du jour on one of the multiple TVs.

Steaks, seafood, pastas, and salads dominate the pleasantly contemporary American menu. Standouts include dense and hearty homemade potato gnocchi, or roasted Amish chicken set atop creamy polenta and drizzled with rich jus. Dark chocolate crêpes with Grand Marnier cream are an appropriately refined finish.

Uncle Bub's BBQ

A4

132 S. Cass Ave. (at Dallas St.), Westmont

Phone:	630-493-9000	Lunch & dinner daily
Web:	www.unclebubs.com	
Prices:		

Suburban Westmont is known for just three things: being the former home to Blues legend Muddy Waters, being the current home to Beanie Baby-maker Ty, Inc., and Uncle Bub's BBQ.

This large roadhouse serves hundreds of barbecue fans every day. They order at the counter (next to the big ol' bucket o' hot peppers.) Their favorite is the chicken, served smoked and grilled with an extra zigzag of Bub's secret sauce on top. The rub makes the chicken moist and smoky, and it pairs well with the classic corn bread (shaped into a mini loaf) and green beans. All Bub's meats (pork, chicken, and beef) are slow-cooked at temps no more than 210 degrees. Meaty homemade chili hits the spot, as does the luscious chocolate cake with buttercream frosting.

Vie

B3

4471 Lawn Ave. (bet. Burlington Ave. & Elm St.), Western Springs

Phone: 708-246-2082
Web: www.vierestaurant.com
Prices: $$$

Dinner Mon – Sat

South, Southwest & Western Suburbs

Linda Bergonia

Vie may be steps from the clanging railroad tracks, but once inside, find absolute tranquility. Poised up front is a dapper bar soothingly surrounded by walls washed in grey-blue shades. Take a moment to appreciate such striking details as black-and-white abstract photographs of the immediate outdoors, steel-blue banquettes clinging to walls, and brushed aluminum chairs. Pristinely clothed tables studded with exquisitely unembellished flatware and stemware serve as a sign of what is to come—heartwarming American food infused with a solid dose of skill.

Before the lights turn low, study Chef Paul Virant's American menu, perhaps with the aid of a pebbled glass votive.

To the hum of soft pop, nimble servers offer you plates that may feature country-fried quail with *giardiniera* and rich garlic aïoli. The delightfully rustic cream of local potato soup poured around lightly smoked halibut cheeks, wood-grilled baby leeks, and pickled snow peas shows the kitchen's understanding of balanced flavors. Watch surrounding tables exclaim in delight over prosciutto-wrapped sturgeon set across a wave of polenta, or a crispy waffle potent with brandied peaches, crème fraîche, and candied almonds.

Vito & Nick's Pizzeria

E4

Italian

8433 S. Pulaski Rd. (bet. 84th & 85th Sts.)

Phone: 773-735-2050   Lunch & dinner daily
Web: www.vitoandnick.com
Prices:

 When in Rome, do as the Romans do. When in Chicago, eat pizza. Since 1949, Chicagoans have been eating Vito & Nick's pizzas, made from a recipe that remains a family secret. Pies are available in two sizes (12" or 14"), with toppings like cheese, sausage, pepperoni, anchovies, shrimp, sliced beef, and *giardiniera*. Sausage is the way to go, and you can add an egg on Fridays. Sick of pizza? Hearty plates of spaghetti, ravioli, and *mostaccioli*, with or without meatballs or sausage, round out the menu and you can start with a crisp salad or one of the fried appetizers. Like many Great Lakes locales, on Fridays there is an all-you-can-eat fried smelt special.

Want this taste at home? Order a partially cooked pie to finish in your own oven.

Wildfire

Steakhouse

232 Oakbrook Center (off Rte. 83), Oak Brook

Phone: 630-586-9000   Lunch & dinner daily
Web: www.wildfirerestaurant.com
Prices: $$$

This 1940's-inspired steakhouse has a cozy vibe, despite the location looking out at the mall parking lot, and the crowds who pack these tables. The music playing in the background and the low lighting contribute to the attractive ambience.

A chain-owned shopping mall restaurant might not have been high on the "must eat" list, but like its partner company Lettuce Entertain You is inclined to do, Wildfire exceeds expectations. The menu bulges with sandwiches, salads, and pizzas at lunch; with steaks and seafood added at dinner. Each entrée, like the filet mignon, is cooked tender and to order. High-quality, lean meats add to the pleasurable experience. The classic steakhouse creamed spinach is heavy on the cream and seasoned with butter and nutmeg.

Xni-Pec de Yucatan

 C3

Mexican

3755 Grand Blvd. (at Prairie Ave.), Brookfield

Phone: 708-387-0691
Web: www.xnipec.us
Prices: $$

Lunch Fri – Sun
Dinner nightly

The red walls, Mayan posters, and charming wooden menu seem rather simple here, as if to belie the fact that much of the food is spectacular.

This is immediately apparent when the supremely friendly staff presents their freshly made tortilla chips, clearly tasting of corn, perfect for scooping up the tart red onion salsa or carefully dipping into a tiny ramekin of wicked habanero sauce (guaranteed to leave a mark). Allow the knowledgeable staff to guide you through the very serious menu of Mexican specialties, but consider stopping at the *mole*. A string of adjectives, from enchanting and perplexing to chocolatey and semi-sweet, could be used to describe this rich and balanced sauce of ground chiles and spices, but suffice it to say this: order it.

Zak's Place

 B3

American

112 S. Washington St. (bet. 1st & 2nd Sts.), Hinsdale

Phone: 630-323-9257
Web: www.zaksplace.com
Prices: $$

Lunch Mon – Fri
Dinner Mon – Sat

You could go home after work, fire up the stove, and make yourself a meal, but why bother when you could just pull up a seat at Zak's Place? Any restaurant named after a gone, but not forgotten, beloved pet is sure to comfort and charm. It is American bistro-style to a tee with delicious dark woods, exposed brick walls, pressed-tin ceilings, and a dash of ductwork thrown in for good measure.

Like the décor, which mixes a little old and new, the menu presents a wide array of inventive choices. Sesame-seared ahi tuna with citrus red ink quinoa and soy vinaigrette; chocolate-braised short ribs with white truffle orzo; and seared foie gras with peach bread pudding prove that having a good meal doesn't always have to mean schlepping to the city.

Zaytune

F3

3129 S. Morgan St. (at 31st Pl.)

Phone:	773-254-6300	Lunch & dinner daily
Web:	www.zaytunegrill.com	
Prices:		🚇 Halsted

Don't dismiss this tiny, value-oriented Middle Eastern lair as just another passable Bridgeport eatery. Zaytune, marked by a black awning and brick façade, is a well-kempt place putting out seriously good eats. Owner Daniel Sarkiss is a graduate of Kendall College's culinary program; his love for and flair with fresh ingredients and bold seasonings keeps Zaytune ahead.

Order at the counter and await carefully composed classics like tabbouleh, hummus, baba ghanoush, and fava bean stew that have more than just the local vegans swooning. The grilled flatbread is something you'll want to wrap yourself in on a cold day. Golden brown falafels and chicken shawarma wraps are a sight to behold; while pistachio *kinafa* and walnut *baklava* are a teeny splurge.

ZaZa's

B3

441 W. Ogden Ave. (bet. Richmond & Woodstock Aves.), Clarendon Hills

Phone:	630-920-0500	Lunch Mon – Fri
Web:	www.zazasclarendonhills.com	Dinner nightly
Prices:	$$	

Despite its location among a bevy of car dealerships, this neighborhood favorite carves out a relaxing enclave for itself on a heavily trafficked stretch of road. A hedged patio framed by tiki torches is a pleasant summer perch, and warm mustard walls and cherry wood blinds temper the not-so-*bella* views from the dining room.

The oft-changing menu always has something to please. Carnivores may not be able to resist the one-two punch of pancetta and homemade Italian sausage in *penne Abruzzese*, while those looking for lighter flavors might veer to the plump, crab-filled gnocchi in a creamy vodka-style sauce. Pasta dishes are big enough to satisfy, but the kitchen also churns out hearty and fresh entrées like salmon *acqua pazza* or *vitello limone*.

Where to **Stay**

Blackstone

636 S. Michigan Ave. (at Balbo Ave.)

Phone: 312-447-0955 or 800-468-3571
Web: www.marriott.com
Prices: $$$

 Harrison

328 Rooms

4 Suites

The Renaissance Blackstone Chicago Hotel

It might be owned and managed by Marriott, but there's nothing cookie-cutter about this significant property. First, the location is noteworthy. Walk to Grant Park, Shedd Aquarium, Soldier Field, or the Art Institute, but it's not just the "steps-away" status that gives this hotel its pedigree. Since 1910, the Blackstone has been the beloved choice of celebrities and chief executives, hosting every president since William Taft.

While it may be historical, it is certainly not creaky—this thanks to a spot-on face-lift that took the hotel into the new millennium. The Beaux-Arts exterior makes a stunning first impression, but the sizzle resides solely indoors. There is a bit of wit and whimsy in the public spaces: from gilded leather tufted couches, to the 1,400 pieces of original art, the Blackstone puts a fresh spin on classic details. Rooms and suites are truly modern and wear earthy tones; while bathrooms are boldly decked with white-and-black palettes. Staggering views of the lake are a draw.

Mercat a la Planxa is celebrity chef Jose Garces' temple to Catalonian cooking. Sip sangria and taste some tapas while soaking up the scene at this white-hot Michigan Avenue spot.

Blake

500 S. Dearborn St. (bet. Congress Pkwy. & Harrison St.)

Phone: 312-986-1234
Web: www.hotelblake.com
Prices: $$

 LaSalle

158
Rooms

4
Suites

Ralph De Caro/Panomedia Productions

Spacious rooms, reasonable rates, and a top-notch restaurant prove that Hotel Blake is indeed worth its salt. Housed within the historic Morton Building (the former home of the Morton Salt Company), this hotel effortlessly blends past and present with its modern style and amenities.

Espresso-hued wood-paneled walls with red accents set a handsome tone in the appealing lobby. The attractive minimalist décor is striking, yet the ambience has a relaxed ease. In-room spa services enable *mucho* rest and relaxation, while a glass-walled business center with a separate conference room caters to your work needs.

The rich chocolate and soft beige color scheme is continued in the 162 guestrooms. The accommodations are large and comfortable. Many amenities, like the large desks with ergonomic leather chairs, have business travelers in mind, but it's not all work and no play at the Hotel Blake. Fine linens dress the beds, pleasing artwork adorns the walls, and iHome iPod docking stations replace alarm clocks, but for a further taste of home, bring along Fido (as long as he is under 20 pounds).

Room service is far from your standard fare here, courtesy of the lobby-located Custom House Tavern.

Chicago ▶ Chinatown & South Loop

The Drake

E4

140 E. Walton St. (at Michigan Ave.)

Phone: 312-787-2200 or 800-553-7253
Web: www.thedrakehotel.com
Prices: $$

 Chicago (Red)

461 Rooms

74 Suites

The Drake Hotel

It doesn't get more old-time Chicago than The Drake and this esteemed hotel retains its status as one of the finest in the city. Opened in 1920, The Drake oozes with history. The rich and royal all flocked here in its heyday and while today's guests are more likely to be here for business meetings, not state meetings, the hotel maintains its regal presence.

The grand architecture and impressive lobby are a sign of what's to come. Expect old-world elegance in the rooms and suites. Standard rooms are quite small, but all accommodations are well appointed with a traditional design (think antique furnishings, gilded mirrors, and ornate lighting fixtures).

The walls may not be able to talk in this historic hotel, but the Cape Cod Room's bar can show off a bit—Joe DiMaggio and Marilyn Monroe are among the many who have carved their initials in it. Today's guests will do better to save their knives for buttering the scones at the properly elegant afternoon tea at the Palm Court. From its delicate finger sandwiches to its fine bone china, this rite of passage is a tea to make the Queen proud (in fact, Queen Elizabeth did have tea here, along with other royals throughout the years).

Chicago ▶ Gold Coast

Elysian

11 E. Walton St. (bet. Rush & State Sts.)

Phone: 312-646-1300 or 800-500-8511
Web: www.elysianhotels.com
Prices: $$$$

Chicago (Red)

38 Rooms

150 Suites

Elysian Hotel

You'll think you've died and gone to haute heaven at the super-luxe Elysian. Walk through the cobblestoned motor court that resembles a French château, and step into the striking lobby. This seductive space is the very picture of contemporary minimalism. Its striking chandelier and gleaming marble floors are sure to make a lasting first impression.

The glorious good looks extend to the rooms and suites, where champagne and platinum color schemes and tailored furnishings give off a current British sensibility. It is all very glamorous, and the Carrara marble bathrooms (showers come with leg rests for shaving!) are over-the-top gorgeous.

The service is A-plus. Within this palatial establishment, the uniformed staff delivers polished, gracious, and intuitive service, making guests feel like ladies and lords of the manor. It doesn't end there. Dining is a first-rate affair at two impressive restaurants (Ria and Balsan), while the tucked-away Bernard's Bar has that wood-paneled elegance down pat. Even exercise is elevated to an art form at the spa and health club, where you can unwind with a homeopathic facial or succumb to a lava shell massage after hoofing it on the treadmill.

Chicago ▶ Gold Coast

Four Seasons Chicago

120 E. Delaware Pl. (bet. Michigan Ave. & Rush St.)

Phone:	312-280-8800 or 800-819-5053
Web:	www.fourseasons.com
Prices:	**$$$$**

 Chicago (Red)

176
Rooms

167
Suites

Four Seasons

Four Seasons knows how to pour it on. This elegant hotel has it all—white-glove service, impressive facilities, elegant accommodations, fine dining, and a prime location just blocks from Lake Michigan and within a stiletto's throw of some of the world's best shopping.

The guest rooms and suites are outfitted with a fresh, contemporary decor and are crammed with creature comforts. The beds, dressed with dreamy linens and soft colors, are exceedingly inviting; and the marble bathrooms make a grand and glamorous statement. There are plenty of places to put your feet up and relax, but the window seat is arguably the best. Is there anything better than soaking up the scene in a fluffy bathrobe? From the doormen and front desk to the dining and spa staff, the service is seamless and spot on. Dining choices include the elegant signature Seasons Restaurant, serving French and American cuisine, and the more relaxed Seasons Lounge, where buffets, brunch, and afternoon tea are held. There is always the upper-crusty ambience of Seasons Bar, perfect for cocktails and conversation.

Stress fractures from all of the shopping? Head straight to the spa for some seriously sophisticated therapy.

Indigo

1244 N. Dearborn Pkwy. (bet. Division & Goethe Sts.)

Phone: 312-787-4980 or 800-972-2494
Web: www.hotelindigo.com
Prices: $$

Clark/Division

163 Rooms

2 Suites

InterContinental Hotels Group

There is nothing pretentious about Hotel Indigo. This boutique hotel chain, part of the InterContinental Hotels worldwide chain, is proof that budget doesn't have to be boring. Located on a quiet residential street in the Gold Coast, Hotel Indigo is a breath of fresh air with its summer's dream décor. It is all very beach house on the Scandinavian coast with its white-painted patio-style wood furnishings, white beadboard, gleaming blonde wood floors, and indigo blue and lime green colors.

This hotel has the cottage look down pat, and the upbeat personality extends to the guestrooms. Banish the wintry blues in these mood-elevating, beach shack-style accommodations, where wood floors add a particularly homey aura and walls covered in floral murals bring the outside in.

The luscious colors and inviting ambience are surefire mood boosters. Niceties, such as Aveda bath products, flat screen televisions, and coffee makers add a final touch. Though small, the fitness center has the necessary cardio machines and free weights to fit in a workout amidst shopping and sightseeing. Room service is available in the mornings, and the lobby bar/restaurant features light fare throughout the day.

Chicago ▶ Gold Coast

Park Hyatt

800 N. Michigan Ave. (at Chicago Ave.)

Phone: 312-335-1234 or 877-875-4658
Web: www.parkchicago.hyatt.com
Prices: $$$$

Chicago (Red)

185
Rooms

13
Suites

Park Hyatt Chicago

The Park Hyatt is the place to stay when you want to sneak a peek at how the other half lives. Situated catercorner to the historic Water Tower on the Magnificent Mile, this luxurious getaway occupies the first 18 floors of a sky-reaching tower, home to some of the city's most exclusive private residences.

Park Hyatt is the A student in the Hyatt hotels chain, and this particular Chicago sibling is no exception. It is understated sophistication at its best, offering luxury and comfort to its privileged guests. The contemporary-styled guestrooms don't skimp on size or style, and they offer plenty of conveniences and goodies like high thread cotton bedding, butler service, large safes big enough to hold and charge laptops, and video checkout. The sleek marble and granite bathrooms are equally spacious (oversized tubs, separate walk-in showers) and stocked with deluxe bath salts, Blaise Mautin products, and candles.

From valet parking and turndown to a weekly sommelier-guided wine and spirit tasting, courteous and efficient service is a staple.

The seventh-floor NoMI Kitchen and lounge, which recently underwent a major renovation, continues to boast commanding city views.

Chicago ▶ Gold Coast

Raffaello

201 E. Delaware Pl. (at Seneca St.)

Phone: 312-943-5000 or 800-898-7198
Web: www.chicagoraffaello.com
Prices: $$$

 Chicago (Red)

97
Rooms

73
Suites

Raffaello Hotel

Craving Champagne but on a beer (imported, of course) budget? The Raffaello might just be your biggest and best boon ever. This stylish boutique hotel gives you a swanky Gold Coast address without the pomp–and price–of its fussy competitors.

Located next door to the John Hancock Tower, Raffaello is also just steps from Water Tower Place and the shops of the Magnificent Mile. So it goes without saying that this treasure has a prime location, and the hits just keep on coming at this contemporary spot. The soaring ceilings capped off with an oversized chandelier, and the sparkling marble floors of the lobby are a sure sign of good things to come. Rooms are on the smaller side, so upgrades are worth the extra bucks; but the soothing spirit will leave you smitten. Creams, beiges, and dark woods define the current look, and amenities like high-quality bath products and high-tech extras like iHome players maintain the modern theme. Do business in style in one of the elegant conference rooms, or hit the fully equipped fitness center with spa services.

Never quite made it into the cool clique? Book a table at the hotel's restaurant Pelago and you'll feel like part of the in crowd, instantly.

Chicago ▶ **Gold Coast**

The Ritz-Carlton Chicago

160 E. Pearson St. (bet. Michigan Ave. & Seneca St.)

Phone: 312-266-1000 or 800-621-6906
Web: www.fourseasons.com/chicagorc
Prices: $$$$

Chicago (Red)

344 Rooms

91 Suites

Ritz-Carlton Hotel Chicago

It just does not get any better than this. The Ritz-Carlton Chicago, managed by esteemed Four Seasons, has one of the city's most coveted locations. Situated at Water Tower Place, the shopping of Magnificent Mile is practically served up on a silver platter for guests of the Ritz-Carlton (and there is also direct access to the indoor shops at Water Tower Place).

Valets graciously welcome patrons and then whisk them away to the classically elegant world of the 12th floor lobby. The gentle trickle of the central fountain alludes to the serenity found here. While the lobby shows off a traditional aesthetic, the recently renovated guestrooms and suites are done up with a definitively modern take. Thick, plush, geometric-patterned carpets set the tone for the well-appointed (lavish furnishings, deluxe amenities) and well-planned (plentiful storage, spacious dressing areas, large desks) rooms, ideal for both business and leisure travelers.

From access to the refined Carlton Club, a spa/indoor pool/fitness facility with a seasonal sundeck, to the glass-enclosed Greenhouse with breathtaking Lake Michigan and city views, there are plenty of perks as a guest of this exclusive hotel.

Chicago ▶ Gold Coast

314

Sofitel

20 E. Chestnut St. (at Wabash Ave.)

Phone: 312-324-4000 or 800-763-4835
Web: www.sofitel.com
Prices: $$$

 Chicago (Red)

382 Rooms

33 Suites

Sofitel Chicago Water Tower

Some of architecture's greatest minds built their masterpieces in Chicago, and the Sofitel continues the city's long-held tradition of innovative design. Imagined by French architect Jean-Paul Viguier, this fantastic structure is comprised of a 32-floor prism of white glass and steel. The result? A new landmark in a city synonymous with stand-out buildings.

Of course, the location just a short walk from the Magnificent Mile and Museum of Contemporary Art doesn't hurt either. Neither does great service, and chic designer guestrooms with plentiful amenities and services.

The hip vibe is immediately felt upon entering the lobby, where towering ceilings and sleek décor set a stylish tone. The guestrooms continue the cool theme with modern furnishings, marble bathrooms, and abounding creature comforts (Frette robes, complimentary movie channels). From corporate (staffed and self-service business centers) to personal (concierge), needs are met with grace and know-how by an intuitive staff. Grab a book from the charming library and bone up on architecture while enjoying a drink in the lounge/bar or over a delightful contemporary French meal at Café des Architectes.

Chicago ▶ Gold Coast

Sutton Place

21 E. Bellevue Pl. (at Rush St.)

Phone: 312-266-2100 or 866-378-8866
Web: www.chicago.suttonplace.com
Prices: $$$

 Clark/Division

204
Rooms

42
Suites

Mike Dragovijo/The Sutton Place Hotel

Sure, some of the interiors are a little dated and it could benefit from a little nip and tuck, but the Sutton Place hotel's location–a few steps from the lake and Michigan Avenue–along with its fine concierge service make it worth stomaching the slightly outdated style. The hotel appeals to mature travelers who appreciate the complimentary downtown sedan service and other easily accessible transportation options just outside the doors, as well as the great value for money.

This beloved retreat puts you in the heart of it without the heart attack-worthy price point. The rooms and suites are spacious and feel tranquil. Large double windows look out over the city and many rooms allow for glimpses of the shimmering lake. From large desks to lounge chairs set by the windows, the rooms are comfortable and welcoming.

Business travelers never miss a beat while staying at the Sutton Place hotel. The fourth floor business center and well-equipped conference facilities keep everything humming along. Feeling a little homesick for Mom's country cooking? Head to The Whiskey Bar & Grill. This restaurant has been dishing out yummy comfort foods (burgers, mac and cheese) for over a decade now.

Chicago ▶ Gold Coast

Talbott

20 E. Delaware Pl. (bet. Rush & State Sts.)

Phone:	312-944-4970 or 800-825-2688
Web:	www.talbotthotel.com
Prices:	$$

 Chicago (Red)

120 Rooms

29 Suites

The Talbott

Want to feel like a resident of the swanky Gold Coast? Check right in to the boutique Talbott, a member of the Small Luxury Hotels of the World. This hotel feels like a private residence, and with a location just two blocks from the Magnificent Mile, you can hit the shops and still have energy to walk home.

Inside, the Talbott feels like a classic English estate; dark wood-paneled walls lined with hunting scenes and a roaring fireplace feel straight out of the princely countryside. Far from fuddy-duddy, the hotel displays its sense of humor with a lady bug-dressed cow sculpture scaling the façade. Designed by artist Brian Calvin for the 1999 Chicago Cow Parade installation, the cow adds a serious touch of whimsy to this otherwise traditional hotel.

The accommodations offer a respite from the city pace with their quiet elegance and high-quality amenities (Frette linens, Aveda toiletries). While it has been awarded a Green Seal certification for its eco-sensitive choices, guests' comfort is never compromised.

Bice Ristorante echoes the hotel's relaxed elegance in its attractive dining room and sidewalk café. A great spot for people watching, Bice also delivers room service to hotel guests.

Chicago ▶ Gold Coast

Whitehall

D5

105 E. Delaware Pl. (bet. Michigan Ave. & Rush St.)

Phone:	312-944-6300 or 866-753-4081
Web:	www.thewhitehallhotel.com
Prices:	**$$**

Chicago (Red)

214 Rooms

8 Suites

Gerilyn Frey

Smack dab in the middle of it all sits the Whitehall Hotel. This independent boutique hotel is right in the thick of it, nestled among the shops, restaurants, theaters, and entertainment of the Magnificent Mile and the nightlife of Rush Street. Many of Chicago's major attractions (Millennium Park, Navy Pier) are also just down the road.

This elegant red brick building was once home to full-time residents who occupied apartments, but today's temporary residents are treated to a glorious old-world European style. The lobby is a love letter to the past, with sparkling chandeliers, tufted leather chairs, and elegant wood paneling, and many of the furnishings have been restored to their former grandeur.

The guestrooms and suites have the feel of another era, appointed with four-poster beds, wrought-iron headboards, leather-topped mahogany desks, and hand-painted armoires, but the amenities (luxurious Egyptian cotton sheets) are definitely 21st century. The fitness center and fee-based business center are on the smaller side, but offer the basics, while the second floor meeting rooms are quite large given the hotel's size.

Fornetto Mei brings together the foods and flavors of Asia and Italy.

Chicago ▶ Gold Coast

Majestic

528 W. Brompton Ave. (bet. Lake Shore Dr. & Pine Grove Ave.)

Phone: 773-404-3499 or 800-727-5108
Web: www.majestic-chicago.com
Prices: $

 Addison (Red)

48
Rooms

4
Suites

Majestic Hotel

Need to find yourself a temporary den while hitting up a Cubs game? Opt for the Majestic. This boutique hotel with just 52 rooms is the closest hotel to Wrigley Field, so you can have your fill of beer and dogs and even stay for extra innings without worrying about a long trip home. Just because it's near the ball park doesn't mean this hotel doesn't know how to pour on the sophistication—the intimate space is reminiscent of old-world Europe.

Once ensconced inside one of their guestrooms or suites, you'd never know that you're in bustling Lakeview. Instead, it's peace and quiet in an elegant setting. From the mahogany furnishings and landscape paintings that are riffs on Monet to the gold-toned fabrics, the accommodations are clearly inspired by an English country estate. Try to upgrade to a suite since the standard rooms are on the small side.

Guests are treated to complimentary breakfasts and afternoon cookies. Don't worry about parking headaches, especially on game day, since the hotel does offer a garage. The amenities are limited, so you'll need to dine in an area restaurant and work out in a local gym. But with a price point and location this good, who cares?

Chicago ▶ Lakeview & Wrigleyville

Willows

555 W. Surf St. (bet. Broadway & Cambridge Ave.)

Phone: 773-528-8400 or 800-787-3108
Web: www.willowshotelchicago.com
Prices: $

🚇 Wellington

51
Rooms

4
Suites

Broughton Hotels of Chicago

Maybe it's the quaint tree-lined street in the heart of a residential neighborhood. Maybe it's the designation as a historic landmark (the building dates to 1926). Or, maybe it's just the charming country inn ambience, but the Willows rightfully boasts a distinctive experience in Chicago.

Just a mile from Wrigley Field and a short walk to notable Lincoln Park and lovely Lake Michigan, Willows invites guests to unwind in gracious European-style comfort. French reproduction furnishings and French-influenced wall coverings add sophistication, while honey, green, and brown color schemes lend an inviting, slightly homey, touch.

The Willows is definitely not for those high maintenance, testy travelers who seek hotels brimming with modern services. There is no business center or exercise facility (though they do provide access to a nearby gym), and a simple breakfast is served in the lobby. If you want manicures and martinis, go elsewhere. But if you are the type who wants to live like a local while stretching out in a comfortable, chichi, and copius guestroom, the Willows hotel is a sure bet. Besides, who can resist a place that has an afternoon social with freshly baked cookies?

Villa D'Citta

2230 N. Halsted St. (bet. Belden & Webster Aves.)

Phone: 312-771-0696 or 800-228-6070
Web: www.villadcitta.com   🔲 Fullerton
Prices: **$$**

6
Suites

Chuck Gullett

What's that? The genteel townhouse you were crossing your fingers for was willed to another family member? Forget about it. Just book a room at the unique Villa D'Citta, and you'll get the same feel, without the pesky property taxes. It was originally built in 1887, and this B&B was a private residence until 2009. Stately, sophisticated, and just steps from Lincoln Park's main strip, Villa D'Citta is a luxurious and quiet alternative to the anonymity prevalent in larger hotels.

The residential ambience and bed-and-breakfast style lures couples, discerning travelers, and adventurous types who want to really feel at home in the Windy City. And feel at home they do, where guests have the run of the place. Totter around the gourmet kitchen, grill on the outdoor deck, or hop into the Jacuzzi—it's all part of the experience. There are just a handful of rooms and suites, all decorated with a modern, slightly masculine appeal. Or, empty out the piggy bank and rent the whole kit and caboodle.

Ralph, the host, and his tiny dog Whiskey, will make you feel welcome from the instant you walk in. From restaurant recommendations to sightseeing, Ralph has you covered.

Chicago ▶ Lincoln Park & Old Town

Allegro

171 W. Randolph St. (at Wells St.)

Phone:	312-236-0123 or 800-643-1500
Web:	www.allegrochicago.com
Prices:	**$$**

 Clark/Lake

452 Rooms

31 Suites

David Phelps/Kimpton Hotels

Not on the A list? Check in to the vibrant Allegro and you'll certainly feel like a very important person! Adorned in a slick Hollywood Regency manner, the vibe here is relaxed, fun, and young. Part of the Kimpton hotel chain, the Allegro has that cool boutique-esque ambience, yet it offers the top-notch amenities of a hotel chain.

Brush up on your geometry before heading to the rooms and suites at the Allegro, since geometric patterns are everywhere. From the silver and white wallpaper to the royal blue carpets to the decorative pillows, it is pattern play throughout. The accommodations have a stylish blend of old Hollywood glamour and contemporary dazzle.

Kimpton is known for its many amenities, so expect extras like evening wine receptions, complimentary morning coffee, and no fee/no restrictions pet policies. From KimptonKids programming and in-room spa services to well-equipped fitness facilities, state-of-the-art conference and meeting rooms, and eco-friendly practices, the Allegro lives up to its promises. Relive the days of the three-martini lunch at the Encore Lunch Club & Liquid Lounge or settle in to a comfy booth for some yummy Italian food at 312 Chicago.

Chicago ▶ Loop

Burnham

C3

1 W. Washington St. (at State St.)

Phone: 312-782-1111 or 866-690-1986
Web: www.burnhamhotel.com
Prices: $$

Washington

103 Rooms

19 Suites

David Phelps/Kimpton Hotels

Hotel Burnham has pedigree and panache. A historic landmark built in 1895 as one of the first skyscrapers, the building has been reworked, revamped, and reinvigorated with a dramatic décor. Housed in Daniel Burnham's Reliance Building, Hotel Burnham is part of the Kimpton chain, but this property has a fiercely independent spirit and delivers a well-rounded, unique, and first-class experience.

From caged elevators and mosaic-tiled floors to mailbox slots on the guestroom doors (there's no delivery—they're sealed shut), traces of the building's past add a distinct charm and unique flavor. There's nothing sedate about these accommodations, where regal guestrooms pop with sensational bursts of color and patterns. It's all very fancy, with gilded furnishings and tasseled silk canopy beds, but it's good to be king. Even the closet has a few surprises with leopard- and zebra-patterned bathrobes.

The customary amenities (fitness center, business center, concierge staff) are here, but the unusual touches are most memorable (try parenting a goldfish during your stay). There is also 24-hour room service, but the enjoyable atmosphere at Atwood Café is worth leaving your room.

Chicago ▶ Loop

323

Fairmont

D2

200 N. Columbus Dr. (bet. Lake & Water Sts.)

Phone: 312-565-8000 or 800-526-2008
Web: www.fairmont.com/chicago
Prices: **$$**

 State/Lake

622
Rooms

65
Suites

The Fairmont Chicago, Millennium Park

The Fairmont has always enjoyed a fantastic location convenient to Michigan Avenue and Millennium Park, but now, with its fashionable lobby decked in sleek lines, natural hues, and handsome woods, this hotel sizzles with a fresh style. The look is very mod and the lobby could double as the latest "it" spot, but there is substance behind this style with Fairmont's superior comfort and plush amenities.

The rooms and suites are a study in upscale modern design, where earth tones set a soothing slate, interesting patterns (zebra-striped carpets, bamboo leaf-inspired pillows) inject an upbeat flavor, and artist Warwick Orme's floral artwork captures the eye. Comforts abound, and the Fairmont even offers allergy friendly rooms (PURE) and a dedicated floor for corporate travelers (GOLD).

Aria is the hotel's all-day dining spot and is known for its Asian fare, but the Fairmont really has guests at "hello" with its impressive lobby capped off by an outpost of ENO, where 500 varietals of wine (60 types by the glass!), 35 different types of cheese, and artisanal chocolates await gourmands. Overdid it on the Camembert? Head straight for the 11,000 square-foot fitness center and spa.

Chicago ▶ Loop

324

Hard Rock

230 N. Michigan Ave. (at Water St.)

Phone: 312-345-1000 or 866-966-5166
Web: www.hardrockhotelchicago.com
Prices: $$

State/Lake

370 Rooms

11 Suites

Hard Rock Hotel Chicago

It is likely that you know the Hard Rock shtick. Like a laid-back Smithsonian for rock and roll memorabilia, the Hard Rock has made its name by sharing the hard-living rock star lifestyle with diners and hotel guests, but the Hard Rock Hotel Chicago strays a bit from the standard and shows off some local pride. Housed within the historic Carbide & Carbon Building, the Hard Rock mixes its expected look with art deco architecture. This fun and upbeat hotel offers reasonable prices for the cool vibe and central location.

The guestrooms take the rocker lifestyle quite seriously. If the celebrity costumes displayed in the hallways doesn't clue you in, the rock star-themed artwork certainly will. Dark colors and low lighting are ideal for late night revelers, though business travelers might have trouble getting work done.

The sleek and modern lobby is home to two popular establishments—the Globe Bar with a clubby vibe to match the hotel's reputation, and China Grill, another popular chain known for its hip quotient and fusion family-style upscale food. In case you don't already have one of the ubiquitous Hard Rock t-shirts, you can pick one up in the lobby's Hard Rock store.

Chicago ▶ Loop

Hotel 71

71 E. Wacker Dr. (at Wabash Ave.)

Phone: 312-346-7100 or 800-621-4005
Web: www.hotel71.com
State/Lake
Prices: $$

321 Rooms

36 Suites

Hotel 71

It's not your age, the year, or even your shoe size; Hotel 71 is named for its E. Wacker Drive address. This modern jewel enjoys a spectacular riverfront setting near the pedestrian riverwalk and directly across from Trump Tower. With a 24-hour fitness center, an entire sixth floor dedicated to business needs, and a convenient business center, this hotel is a natural choice for business travelers.

Here, less is more as far as design goes. The sleek, modern decor is soothing and warm. Tan, brown, and golden hues run throughout, while the guest accommodations add plaid patterns and animal prints as interesting accents. The guestrooms are spacious and equipped with ergonomic chairs, large bathrooms, and complimentary in-room coffee. From mini-stereos to three telephones, electronics are plentiful. Those wishing to take in the sights should be sure to book rooms with river views.

Following a renovation that's freshened up the lobby and updated the restaurant as Hoyt's, Hotel 71 is now more than ever ready for its close-up. Its windowed top floor ballroom was a stand-in for Bruce Wayne's penthouse in *The Dark Knight*, and more recently it was used as a backdrop in *Transformers: Dark of the Moon*.

JW Marriott Chicago

 B4

151 W. Adams St. (bet. LaSalle & Wells Sts.)

Phone: 312-660-8200 or 888-717-8850
Web: www.jwmarriott.com
Prices: $$$

 Quincy

581
Rooms

29
Suites

JW Marriott Chicago

The JW Marriott is a perfect blend of old and new. Housed in the Continental & Commercial National Bank building, which opened in 1914 and was designed by acclaimed Chicago architect David Burnham, the hotel has seriously good bones, but its interiors wow with a fresh, contemporary design.

The rooms and suites are handsomely furnished with a dash of art deco (Lucite light fixtures) and a sprinkle of Choinoiserie (Asian-influenced furnishings and artwork). Even the bathrooms show off a touch of glamour with granite, sparkling marble, and chocolate brown wall coverings, but it's not just about good looks at this luxury hotel. JW Marriott spares no comforts; whether it's plush bedding or cushy leather desk chairs, no detail is overlooked.

With 44,000 square feet of meeting space, it's no surprise that this Loop hotel is a favorite for conferences and pow-wows, but don't worry that it's all work and no play. Spend an hour or more in Valeo Spa with its Clarity Chamber complete with heated stone beds, or take a dip in the brand new pool and wash away the stresses of the day. Even if you have to sit next to your chatty co-worker, a table at The Florentine restaurant is worth it.

Chicago ▲ Loop

Monaco

C2

225 N. Wabash Ave. (bet. Haddock & Wacker Pls.)

Phone: 312-960-8500 or 866-610-0081
Web: www.monaco-chicago.com
Prices: $$$

State/Lake

172 Rooms

20 Suites

David Phelps/Kimpton Hotels

Hats off to the Hotel Monaco Chicago, another one of the shining stars in the Kimpton chain. Housed in a former hat factory near the Chicago River, it is within walking distance of the Loop, Michigan Avenue, shopping, and the theaters, but it doesn't rely on its location alone.

Everything about this property speaks to its gracious style and demeanor. The staff, from the first greeting by the doorman to the efficient and helpful front desk clerks, seems genuinely concerned with guests' comfort. The lobby is tastefully appointed with a romantic modern European style and is elegant without being stuffy.

Stripes and diamond patterns create a pleasing contemporary aura in the guestrooms and suites, but it is truly the river and city views that particularly stand out. Rooms are even furnished with cushioned window nooks, known as meditation stations, for relaxing and day-dreaming with a view. Many of the amenities found at other Kimpton properties, such as in-room spa services and goldfish companions, are offered here as well. Adding to Monaco's appeal, the South Water Kitchen serves three meals a day, while a hosted wine hour at 5:00 P.M. allows guests to enjoy complimentary glasses.

Palmer House

17 E. Monroe St. (at State St.)

Phone:	312-726-7500 or 800-445-8667
Web:	www.palmerhousehiltonhotel.com
Prices:	**$$**

Sammy Todd Dyess

1584
Rooms

55
Suites

It doesn't get any more legendary than the Palmer House. This great-granddaddy of Chicago hotels was built 13 days before the great fire of 1871; it was then rebuilt and reopened in 1873 as the world's first fireproof hotel. Back when a nickel got you a vaudeville show, the lobby was a true spectacle; and despite a massive nip and tuck, it continues to soar as a serious scene.

Palmer embraces the Old World: the ceiling, painted with Greek mythological characters, was restored by the same craftsman who worked on the Sistine Chapel. Italian marble, gilded candelabra, carpeted hallways, and grand staircases—it's like a page was ripped from the grand lobby handbook. Where else can you sleep where Mark Twain, Liberace, and Charles Dickens once laid their weary heads?

If walls could talk—the Palmer House has seen and done it all. Electric lighting and elevator service were all pioneered here. At every turn the hotel honors its history, and yet, guests are never asked to forsake today's comforts. From spacious, attractive, and updated accommodations to fine dining at the lovely Lockwood restaurant, the Palmer House lives as comfortably within the 21st century as it did in the 19th.

Chicago ▶ Loop

The Wit

C2

201 N. State St. (at Lake St.)

Phone: 312-467-0200 or 866-318-1514
Web: www.thewithotel.com
Prices: **$$**

State/Lake

238 Rooms

60 Suites

theWit Hotel Chicago

There's definitely a bit of whimsy at the Wit Hotel. Just listen to the sound piped in to the hallways—it's chirping birds by day, crickets by night, and roosters in the morning. Even the wake-up calls are unusual—when was the last time you were awoken by Harry Caray?

This hotel is definitely not your grandfather's Doubletree, though it is in fact managed by it. Instead, it is ultra-modern in both design and décor. The rooms and suites pack a punch with orange chaise lounges and plentiful high-tech amenities. Widescreen TVs are loaded with movies and music channels, while suites come with complete kitchens.

Boasting a bustling scene, the lobby alone exudes a sophisticated energy. Additionally, dining is definitely not an afterthought at this boutique-inspired hotel: State & Lake heats up the local scene with its American cooking; and ROOF–the 27th floor indoor-outdoor space complete with fire pits and a sweeping view of the city–is *the* place to be. This hot spot with DJs galore draws a young, swank crowd. You may find yourself jostling for space in the elevators with these revelers ready for a big night out, but it's all part of the fun at the Wit.

Chicago ▶ Loop

Conrad

521 N. Rush St. (at Grand Ave.)

Phone: 312-645-1500 or 800-266-7237
Web: www.conradchicago.com
Prices: $$$

 Grand (Red)

283 Rooms

28 Suites

Conrad Chicago

It starts with a great location. The city's business and theater districts are close by, while the parks and shores of the lake are a few minutes east, but what makes the Conrad Chicago stand out is its appeal to label lovers—the hotel is adjacent to Nordstrom and the high-end shops of The Northbridge Shopping Center.

It continues with no expense spared in-room treats. The Conrad spoils its guests with a seemingly endless stream of luxury amenities: Pratesi sheets, Acca Kappa bath products, Bose surround sound, and lavish 42″ Plasma televisions. Services are equally plentiful, and include indulgent options like bath butlers and pillow menus. If your credit card got more of a workout than your stroll down the Magnificent Mile gave you, the hotel's fitness center is available 24 hours a day.

And it doesn't end there. The hotel has three inviting and distinct venues. Rendez-Vous has a casual sophistication perfect for light meals or drinks (try the signature chocolate martini), while the Restaurant at Conrad steps it up with Midwestern-focused cooking. Open during warmer months, The Terrace is a sure bet for cozy outdoor enjoyment—movies are even shown on Sundays.

Chicago ▶ River North

dana hotel and spa

660 N. State St. (at Erie St.)

Phone: 312-202-6000 or 888-301-7952
Web: www.danahotelandspa.com
Prices: $$

 Grand (Red)

194 Rooms

22 Suites

Hedrich Blessing

Get to know dana. This boutique hotel certainly has its number on you, that is if you're a young, discerning traveler with a penchant for fine living and high-priced tech toys. The dana hotel perfectly complements its creative, art gallery-filled neighborhood. It captures the essence of industrial chic with stone, wood, and natural design elements. The calling card of this design philosophy–exposed ductwork and piping–is found throughout the hotel in the lobby and private accommodations.

Rich, hand-hewn Jarrah wood floors make a striking statement in the guestrooms, but it is the floor-to-ceiling windows that are the unmistakable star. Exposed concrete and unfinished support pillars show off the signature style, but oversized showers capped off with rain showerheads and pillow-topped beds ensure that you can be cool and cosseted at the same time. Hipsters will find plenty to add to their gadget wish lists after a stay here—the Zeppelin-Bowers & Wilkins sound systems sync to guests' MP3 players for a state-of-the-art sound.

From the modern and spacious spa and the rooftop Vertigo Sky Lounge to the pan-Asian menu at aja, the facilities are all top-notch.

Felix

111 W. Huron St. (bet. Clark & LaSalle Sts.)

Phone: 312-447-3440 or 877-848-4040
Web: www.hotelfelixchicago.com   Chicago (Red)
Prices: $$

225
Rooms

Hotel Felix

Is this where Al Gore has been hiding? He may not be camping out here, but the Felix would certainly warm his heart. This innovative boutique hotel was the first hotel in Chicago designed to meet the specifications of Silver LEED certification. From design elements (carpets are made from recycled materials; floors are cork and bamboo) to practices (paperless front desk; eco-friendly cleaning products), the Felix takes eco-conscious living very seriously.

The rooms and suites perfectly complement the hotel's relaxed modern sophistication. The soft earth tones and simple furnishings are the very definition of urban living.

Cast your worries aside—this is not a hippie commune by any stretch. It doesn't just do good, but it looks good too at this chic, contemporary hotel. Take a seat in the inviting lobby bar (with a working fireplace) and discuss carbon footprints over cocktails or dine on market-influenced American cuisine at the well-received Elate Restaurant (which also provides room service). The Spa features a comprehensive variety of treatments, all guided by the healing properties of plant and flower extracts.

The best part? It doesn't take a lot of green to stay here.

Chicago ▶ River North

James

55 E. Ontario St. (at Rush St.)

Phone: 312-337-1000 or 877-526-3755
Web: www.jameshotels.com
Prices: $$$

Grand (Red)

191 Rooms

106 Suites

The James Chicago

Chicago ▶ River North

It is not surprising that the James has a loyal following with European travelers and stylish young professionals. A great location in River North coupled with a trendy atmosphere make this hotel the perfect package.

It is chic from top to bottom in that Californian/Scandinavian minimalist way. Blonde woods, simple lines, and contemporary furniture all effortlessly create the understated look. Thankfully, the staff eschews that "too cool for school" philosophy found in other hotels that resemble the James.

Standard rooms outfitted with platform beds and wet bars give a taste of the scene, but the lofts, one-bedroom apartments, and penthouse, with more space and better views, are certainly worth the splurge. The accommodations come with plenty of goodies; bathrooms are stocked with Kiehl's products and wet bars feature full-sized bottles.

The business lounge is a boon for corporate visitors (work spaces are not included in all rooms), while the lower-level fitness center and spa have all of the modern updates. Guests develop a special soft spot for David Burke's buzzed-about Primehouse, since the restaurant sends up freshly baked cookies nightly to all guests.

Palomar

505 N. State St. (at Illinois St.)

Phone: 312-755-9703 or 877-731-0505
Web: www.hotelpalomar-chicago.com
Prices: $$

Grand (Red)

238
Rooms

22
Suites

Cris Molina/Kimpton Hotels

Just like its guiding force, the World's Fair, the shiny new Palomar brings innovation, style, and panache to the Windy City. Situated in the heart of River North, this 17-story hotel is one of the latest Kimpton properties to hit the scene. Enter through the glass doors, glide past the chic living room-style lobby, and let the elevators whisk you away to a cosmopolitan and contemporary world.

Bright couches, deep-colored drapes, and carpets covered in big red blossoms create a dramatic look in the rooms and suites alike. Bathrooms continue the modern chic style with cream marble tiles, dark wood finishes, and stainless steel fixtures. The pièce de résistance at the Palomar is its 17th floor sundeck, pool, and fitness center, where you can sunbathe, swim, or sweat with a skyscraper view.

In-room spa services, complimentary morning coffee, and an evening wine hour are among the niceties this hotel extends to its guests. Don't miss Sable Kitchen & Bar's inventive New American food and glamorous setting evocative of the sexy 1940s. All this and you can bring your biggest four-legged friend too, since the Palomar doesn't discriminate against larger pets.

Chicago ▶ River North

The Peninsula

108 E. Superior St. (bet. Michigan Ave. & Rush St.)

Phone: 312-337-2888 or 866-382-8388
Web: www.peninsula.com
Prices: $$$$

📺 Chicago (Red)

257 Rooms

82 Suites

The Peninsula Chicago

From the elegant lobby to the ultra-luxe guest rooms to the top-notch spa and restaurants, The Peninsula delivers an all-around exceptional experience. No detail is overlooked, and it all looks and feels very plush from oversized marble soaking bathtubs, to bedside electronic panels controlling everything from lighting to temperature.

The ESPA Spa and fitness center offers a temple of serenity in the heart of the Gold Coast. The pool, surrounded by glass and offering jaw-dropping views, is quite simply the best in town, while the fitness center is *the* place to sweat and be seen. The luxury quotient also extends to the hotel's many dining selections and glorious beverage offerings. The Peninsula bar is truly fantastic and exudes a dark, luxurious, and clubby ambience. Hugely raved about and regarded as one the best "scenes" in Chicago, the bar is buzzing and lively on weekends. Ritzy crowds flock here to savor some seriously divine cocktails along with a wonderful selection of light bites.

Whether sipping on afternoon tea in the lofty lobby, noshing on flaky croissants at Pierrot Gourmet, or hitting one of the hotel's other restaurants, it's all very posh here.

SAX

 E4

333 N. Dearborn St. (bet. Kinzie St. & the Chicago River)

Phone: 312-245-0333 or 877-569-3742
Web: www.hotelsaxchicago.com
Prices: $$$

Chicago (Red)

333 Rooms

21 Suites

Andrew Bordwin

Bring your lover and leave your work behind when you check into the SAX. A member of the Thompson Hotel group, this hot lair is located in Marina City, defined by its two iconic Bertrand Goldberg-designed buildings (yes, the ones known as the corn cobs). It is on the north bank of the Chicago River and is surrounded by parks, shops, and restaurants located within this multiplex.

The SAX has you at first glance. The lobby has a classy bordello, hip vampire look (think lots of crystal and 18th century-style red velvet upholstered chairs). The guestrooms are identical in spirit to the lobby and are decorated with the same romantic and fresh vibe, though softer colors are also used.

Many guests play hard at the SAX, where entertainment comes in many forms. There is a 10-pin bowling alley for a little retro fun and a sixth-floor lounge powered by Microsoft, but the Crimson Lounge is the jewel in the crown. It is the happening haunt where bright young things gather for VIP bottle service and DJ or live music. Don't worry if you're not a night owl, since not all of the fun happens when the sun goes down. Bin 36 is an inviting spot to sample wine and small plates all day.

Chicago ▶ River North

337

Trump International Hotel & Tower

401 N. Wabash Ave. (bet. Hubbard St. & the Chicago River)

Phone: 312-588-8000 or 877-458-7867
Web: www.trumpchicagohotel.com
Prices: $$$$

Grand (Red)

229 Rooms

110 Suites

William Huber

Go big or go home seems to be Donald Trump's mantra, and the Trump International Hotel & Tower shows off these principles in all of its glorious, shimmering style. The hotel, part of a 92-story mixed use tower, stands out among the Loop's skyline for its curvaceous, elegant design of sleek stainless steel and tinted glass. It grabs your attention, but there's nothing flashy about the well-heeled sophistication peddled here.

Bright with large windows, the Italian limestone-clad lobby has a surprisingly intimate character. The highly professional staff handles everything in a seamless manner. Trump Attachés or personal concierges offer the highest level of personalized attention.

The Donald's own gold-loving style is never evident; the guestrooms and suites are the very definition of cool and contemporary with grey, black, and soft brown color schemes. Whether it is Bose clock stereos and iPod chargers on the bedside tables or Miele cooktops and Bernardaud china in the kitchenettes, the accommodations showcase the world's leading brands.

From the guestrooms and the 14th-floor health club to Sixteen's dining room and Terrace, the real VIP here is the show-stopping view.

Westin River North

320 N. Dearborn St. (bet. Kinzie St. & the Chicago River)

Phone: 312-744-1900 or 877-866-9216
Web: www.westinchicago.com
Prices: $$$

 Chicago (Red)

407 Rooms

17 Suites

The Westin Chicago River North

It may be located across from the legendary House of Blues, but guests at the Westin aren't singing the blues. Instead, they're whistling a happy tune, thanks to a good night's sleep in one of the many spacious and comfortable rooms and suites. This mod respite enjoys an ideal location. Sitting at the edge of the river, the hotel is a convenient base; it is a business traveler's favored perch—they flock here as much for the conferences held in the more than 28,000-square-feet of meeting space as they do for the restaurants and accommodations.

The guestrooms and suites are appointed with a subtle sophistication. Clean, simple furnishings crafted of polished woods and soft, muted colors are used to create a restful and relieving atmosphere. Westin's signature Heavenly beds make you want to jump right in, while the Heavenly Bath with therapeutic spa showers will help wake you up or wind down.

Some of the better features of the Westin are its three distinctive entertainment venues. Ember Grille sates all carnivores with fire-roasted entrées and prime steak; Kamehachi Sushi Bar serves basic Japanese; and Hana Lounge is just right for catching up over cocktails.

Chicago ▶ River North

339

Affinia

A1

166 E. Superior St. (at St. Clair St.)

Phone: 312-787-6000 or 866-246-2203
Web: www.affinia.com
Prices: $$

Chicago (Red)

215
Rooms

Affinia Chicago

The Affinia Chicago, bookended by the ever-popular Gino's East restaurant and a new condo tower, is terrifically located, near a prime stretch of Michigan Avenue. The bright lobby, with large windows, white terrazzo floors, and stainless steel accents is the first sign that this hotel subscribes to the clean and uncluttered look.

The rooms echo the lobby's look with ivory color schemes and simple furnishings, while the bathrooms get a little crazy with metallic orange-toned wallpaper and black granite-topped vanities. Affinia also offers a host of comforts. Pick one of six styles from the pillow menu or enjoy an "experience kit" (walking tours with loaded iPods and stayfit kits with equipment and DVDs).

This hotel is in the thick of it (you'll hear street noise even 18 floors up), but that's why you want to be here. Another reason is the food. C-House, overseen by celebrity chef, Marcus Samuelsson, is all-out fantastic. The menu is seafood and chops with tasty sides that are a gourmet riff on classics. With a bellini in hand, head up to the C-View rooftop bar and lounge. Not only does this heavenly haven offer a great scene, but it also boasts a magnificent bird's eye view.

Chicago ▶ Streeterville

Allerton

701 N. Michigan Ave. (at Huron St.)

Phone: 312-440-1500 or 877-701-8111
Web: www.theallertonhotel.com
Prices: $$

Chicago (Red)

359
Rooms

84
Suites

Nathan Kirkman Photography

Relive a part of Chicago history while staying at The Allerton. This Gold Coast landmark was built in 1924 and was one of the first high-rises on North Michigan Avenue. With a beautiful Italian Renaissance design, intricate stone details, decorative brickwork, and iconic neon signs, this vestige is an architecture and history buff's dream.

Regarded as a gorgeous getaway, The Allerton represents a welcome departure from the modern towers that line the Magnificent Mile. But there's nothing stuffy or antique here: checkerboard terrazzo flooring sets a stylish tone in the lobby, though it is in the rooms and suites where the design really gleams. From the white tufted leather headboard to the Lucite cube bedside lamps, it is art deco all the way.

Each evening, this inviting home-away-from-home hosts a complimentary wine hour for guests to mingle and munch. Other trappings include a 24-hour health club and the sleek M Avenue Restaurant and Lounge with its upscale dining and comfortably chic setting. The lobby-located flightboard displaying airport departure times and accompanying printer kiosk is certainly one of the most convenient gestures.

Chicago ▶ Streeterville

Inn of Chicago

162 E. Ohio St. (at St. Clair St.)

Phone: 312-787-3100 or 866-858-4430
Web: www.innofchicago.com
Prices: $$

 Grand (Red)

339 Rooms

20 Suites

Scott Thompson

If you have caviar taste but a burger budget, the Inn of Chicago is just the place for you. It may be a half-block away from the Magnificent Mile, but you don't need a lot of moolah to stay at this value-oriented hotel that offers the same coveted neighborhood without the sticker shock.

The Inn of Chicago has enjoyed a long history–first opening in 1928 as the Hotel St. Clair–but this space is rooted firmly in the present with its modern design and high-tech amenities. It may not be pricey, but this hotel does not skimp on the extras—large screen plasma televisions, dazzling views, and large walk-in showers are among the standard offerings. All guests are welcomed with open arms, but business travelers are especially well cared for here, with conference rooms, a business facility, and a fitness center.

Though the hotel does not have its own restaurant, the Lavazza coffee shop hits the spot with pastries and sandwiches; and the InnBar is the in-place for a post-work or post- sightseeing signature cocktail. Of course, the hotel's real pièce de résistance is the 22nd floor Skyline Terrace, which opens during warmer months and showcases stunning city views.

Chicago ▶ Streeterville

InterContinental

505 N. Michigan Ave. (bet. Grand Ave. & Illinois St.)

Phone: 312-944-4100 or 800-628-2112
Web: www.icchicagohotel.com
Prices: $$

 Grand (Red)

717 Rooms

75 Suites

InterContinental Chicago

Like an aging starlet with a story to tell, the historic InterContinental has lived many lives. Like old photographs or letters, there are several signs of the hotel's former incarnations—there is even a blue Majolica-tiled pool complete with terra-cotta fountain of Neptune that was the training site of Olympic athlete Johnny Weissmuller.

Don't be put off—just because it revels in its history doesn't mean it ignores modern needs. 24-hour room service is timely, the business and fitness centers are convenient, and the dining choices are enjoyable. The exquisite lobby is the showpiece of the InterContinental. They just don't make grand entrances like this anymore and this magnificent four-floor rotunda with handcrafted mosaic tiles of onyx and marble is worthy of attention. Though not as grand, the accommodations are decorated in the same old-world vein.

InterContinental spices up the old with the new at its dining establishments. ENO is a unique concept managed by the master sommelier and offers flights of wine, chocolate, and cheese from around the world. Their take-home gifts make wonderful souvenirs. The hotel's main restaurant, The Continental, has a modern American flavor and feel.

Chicago ▶ Streeterville

Orrington

1710 Orrington Ave. (bet. Church & Clark Sts.), Evanston

Phone: 847-866-8700 or 888-677-4648
Web: www.hotelorrington.com
Prices: $$

256 Rooms

13 Suites

Hilton Orrington

The Orrington now is proof positive that everything old can be new (and renewed) again. This hotel first opened its doors in 1925 and has achieved landmark status, but a multi-million dollar renovation has brought this elegant hotel seriously up to snuff. The location, not far from downtown Evanston's shopping, dining, and entertainment, is ideal for those journeying on business, pleasure, or visiting nearby Northwestern University. The convenience factor is par none.

Black wood furnishings set against dramatic red and yellow walls, striped fabrics, and clean lines set a modern tone in the range of rooms and suites. The accommodations are well-suited for corporate travelers with ample work spaces and comfortable chairs. The Orrington is dog-friendly. Look out for the bowls of biscuits and water at the entrance. Whether you need to check in to the office (24-hour business center) or check out at the fitness center (24-hour gym), The Orrington has all your needs covered.

Two dining options include the Globe Café & Bar for all-day dining with a focus on lighter fare (salads, sandwiches, et al), and Indigo Lounge for martinis and mixed drinks.

North & Northwestern Suburbs

Oak Brook Hills Marriott Resort

A3

3500 Midwest Rd. (at 35th St.), Oak Brook

Phone: 630-850-5555 or 800-228-9290
Web: www.oakbrookhillsmarriottresort.com
Prices: $$

348
Rooms

38
Suites

Oak Brook Hills Marriott

The Oak Brook Hills Marriott Resort is a business traveler's dream. Visit this suburban Chicago resort with the confidence that you won't feel "stuck" at a conference or the like. It's not just about the event and meeting space, though there certainly is a lot of it. This Marriott branch entices guests with an 18-hole golf course, indoor and outdoor pools, fitness center, tennis courts, and easy access to area shopping.

All the rooms and suites are sunny, spacious, and extremely comfortable. From plush duvet covers to ergonomically designed desk chairs, the accommodations treat guests to a wonderful plethora of amenities.

Of course, all of the action takes place outside the rooms. The Audubon certified Willow Crest Golf Course is a definite morale booster. Lessons, equipment rentals, and putting green are all part of this first class facility. Need to calm your colleagues? Take them to one of three area spas or hit up the Oak Brook Center or Yorktown Mall. Brought the whole family along for the company conference? Take them to nearby Brookfield Zoo. Back at the Marriott, there are four restaurants all showcasing American cuisine, and many of them boast scenic views of the golf course.

● Where to **Eat**

● Where to **Stay**

Indexes

Alphabetical List of Restaurants

Restaurants by Cuisine

Indexes ▶ Restaurants by Cuisine

Peruvian

Rios D'Sudamerica	✖✖	66
Taste of Peru	😊 ✖	276

Pizza

Burt's Place	✖	264
Coalfire Pizza	✖	51
Connie's Pizza	✖✖	80
Crust	✖	52
Edwardo's Natural Pizza	✖	96
Gino's East	✖	207
Giordano's	✖	207
Great Lake	✖	23
Lou Malnati's	✖	268
Pequod's Pizza	✖	165
Pizano's	✖	103
Pizza Rustica	✖	144
Pizzeria Uno	✖	217
Roots Handmade Pizza	✖	66
Sono Wood Fired	✖✖	168
Spacca Napoli	😊 ✖	36

Polish

Andrzej Grill	✖	44
Smak-Tak	😊 ✖✖	274

Scandinavian

Ann Sather	😊 ✖	133
Tre Kronor	✖	277

Seafood

Fish Bar	✖	138
Fulton's on the River	✖✖	205
GT Fish & Oyster	😊 ✖✖	209
L20	🌣 ✖✖✖✖	163
Mariscos El Veneno	✖	62
Oceanique	✖✖	270
Reel Club	✖✖	296
Riva	✖✖	232
Shaw's Crab House	✖✖	221

Southern

Big Jones	✖✖	20
Dixie Kitchen & Bait Shop	✖	266
Table Fifty-Two	✖✖✖	108

Spanish

Azucar	🍱	113
Café Marbella	🍱	264
Mercat a la Planxa	✖✖	84

Steakhouse

Benny's Chop House	✖✖✖	197
Chama Gaucha	✖✖✖	289
Chicago Cut	✖✖✖	199
David Burke's Primehouse	✖✖	201
Fleming's	✖✖	204
Gene & Georgetti	✖✖	206
Gibson's	✖✖	97
Harry Caray's	✖✖	209
Keefer's	✖✖✖	212
Mastro's	✖✖✖	213
N9NE Steakhouse	✖✖	248
Rosebud Prime	✖✖✖	179
Rosewood	✖✖✖	273
Smith & Wollensky	✖✖	222
Wildfire	✖✖	300

Thai

Always Thai	✖	132
Amarind's	✖✖	262
Arun's	✖✖	113
Elephant (The)	✖	267
Jin Thai	😊 ✖	26
Opart Thai House	😊 ✖	31
P.S. Bangkok	✖✖	144
Rosded	✖	34
Royal Thai	✖	145
Siam Noodle & Rice	✖	35
Spoon Thai	🍱	36
Sticky Rice	✖	146
TAC Quick	✖	147
Thai Classic	✖✖	147
Thai Grill & Noodle Bar (The)	✖	38

Cuisines by Neighborhood

CHICAGO

Andersonville, Edgewater & Uptown

American
M. Henry	🙂	✗	30
Over Easy Café		✗	31

Asian
Fin	✗	23
Jibek Jolu	✗	25

Chinese
Mei Shung	✗	30

Contemporary
Acre	✗	18

Ethiopian
Demera	✗	22
Ras Dashen	✗	34

Filipino
Isla	✗	25

French
Bistro Campagne	✗✗	20
LM	✗✗	28

Gastropub
Hopleaf	🙂	✗	24

Indian
Marigold	✗✗	29
Paprika	✗	32

Italian
Anteprima	✗	18
Antica Pizzeria	✗	19
Due Lire	📧	22
Pizza D.O.C.	✗	33

Japanese
Blue Ocean	✗✗	21
Katsu	✗✗	27
Sunshine Cafe	✗	37
Tank Sushi	✗	37

Korean
Hae Woon Dae	📧	24
Jin Ju	✗	26
San Soo Gab San	✗	35

Latin American
La Fonda Latino Grill	✗	28

Mediterranean
Ceres' Table	🙂	✗✗	21

Mexican
La Ciudad		✗	27
Los Nopales	🙂	✗	29

Pizza
Great Lake		✗	23
Spacca Napoli	🙂	✗	36

Southern
Big Jones	✗✗	20

Thai
Jin Thai	🙂	✗	26
Opart Thai House	🙂	✗	31
Rosded		✗	34
Siam Noodle & Rice		✗	35
Spoon Thai		📧	36
Thai Grill & Noodle Bar (The)		✗	38
Thai Pastry & Restaurant		✗	38

Vietnamese
Ba Le	✗	19
Pho 777	✗	32
Pho Xe Tang - Tank Noodle	✗	33
Tien Giang	✗	39

Bucktown & Wicker Park

American
Bedford (The)	✗✗	46
bin wine cafe	✗	47
Birchwood Kitchen	✗	48

Indexes ▶ Cuisines by Neighborhood

Starred Restaurants

Within the selection we offer you, some restaurants deserve to be highlighted for their particularly good cuisine. When giving one, two, or three Michelin stars, there are a number of elements that we consider including the quality of the ingredients, the technical skill and flair that goes into their preparation, the blend and clarity of flavours, and the balance of the menu. Just as important is the ability to produce excellent cooking time and again. We make as many visits as we need, so that our readers may be assured of quality and consistency.

A two or three-star restaurant has to offer something very special in its cuisine; a real element of creativity, originality, or "personality" that sets it apart from the rest. Three stars – our highest award – are given to the choicest restaurants, where the whole dining experience is superb.

Cuisine in any style, modern or traditional, may be eligible for a star. Due to the fact we apply the same independent standards everywhere, the awards have become benchmarks of reliability and excellence in over 20 countries in Europe and Asia, particularly in France, where we have awarded stars for 100 years, and where the phrase "Now that's real three-star quality!" has entered into the language.

The awarding of a star is based solely on the quality of the cuisine.

Exceptional cuisine, worth a special journey
One always eats here extremely well, sometimes superbly. Distinctive dishes are precisely executed, using superlative ingredients.

Alinea	XXxxX	155

Excellent cuisine, worth a detour
Skillfully and carefully crafted dishes of outstanding quality.

Charlie Trotter's	XxX	158
Ria	XxxX	104

€3

A very good restaurant in its category
A place offering cuisine prepared to a consistently high standard.

Blackbird	XX	240
Boka	XX	156
Bonsoirée	XX	114
Courtright's	XxX	290
Everest	XxxX	176
graham elliot	XX	208
Longman & Eagle	X	120
L20	XxxX	163
Moto	XxX	249
NAHA	XxX	215
Schwa	X	68
Seasons	XxxX	106
Sepia	XX	254
Spiaggia	XxxX	107
Takashi	XX	71
Topolobampo	XX	223
Tru	XxxX	233
Vie	XxX	299

Bib Gourmand

This symbol indicates our inspector's favorites for good value. For $40 or less, you can enjoy two courses and a glass of wine or a dessert (not including tax or gratuity).

Under $25

Brunch

Late Dining

CHICAGO
CHICAGO
CHICAGO PUBLIC RADIO & DIREC TV
PRESENTS THIS AMERICAN LIFE
CHICAGO PUBLIC R
& DIRECTV PRES
THIS AMERICAN

Alphabetical List of Hotels

Notes

YOU ALREADY KNOW THE MICHELIN GUIDE,
NOW FIND OUT ABOUT THE MICHELIN GROUP

MICHELIN
A better way forward

The Michelin Adventure

It all started with rubber balls! This was the product made by a small company based in Clermont-Ferrand that André and Edouard Michelin inherited, back in 1880. The brothers quickly saw the potential for a new means of transport and their first success was the invention of detachable pneumatic tires for bicycles. However, the automobile was to provide the greatest scope for their creative talents. Throughout the 20th century, Michelin never ceased developing and creating ever more reliable and high-performance tires, not only for vehicles ranging from trucks to F1 but also for underground transit systems and airplanes.

From early on, Michelin provided its customers with tools and services to facilitate mobility and make travelling a more pleasurable and more frequent experience. As early as 1900, the Michelin Guide supplied motorists with a host of useful information related to vehicle maintenance, accommodation and restaurants, and was to become a benchmark for good food. At the same time, the Travel Information Bureau offered travellers personalised tips and itineraries.

The publication of the first collection of roadmaps, in 1910, was an instant hit! In 1926, the first regional guide to France was published, devoted to the principal sites of Brittany, and before long each region of France had its own Green Guide. The collection was later extended to more far-flung destinations, including New York in 1968 and Taiwan in 2011.

In the 21st century, with the growth of digital technology, the challenge for Michelin maps and guides is to continue to develop alongside the company's tire activities. Now, as before, Michelin is committed to improving the mobility of travellers.

MICHELIN TODAY

WORLD NUMBER ONE TIRE MANUFACTURER
- 70 production sites in 18 countries
- 111,000 employees from all cultures and on every continent
- 6,000 people employed in research and development

Moving
for a world

Moving forward means developing tires with better road grip and shorter braking distances, whatever the state of the road.

CORRECT TIRE PRESSURE

RIGHT PRESSURE

- Safety
- Longevity
- Optimum fuel consumption

-0,5 bar

- Durability reduced by 20% (- 8,000 km)

-1 bar

- Risk of blowouts
- Increased fuel consumption
- Longer braking distances on wet surfaces

forward together
where mobility is safer

It also involves helping motorists take care of their safety and their tires. To do so, Michelin organises "Fill Up With Air" campaigns all over the world to remind us that correct tire pressure is vital.

WEAR

DETECTING TIRE WEAR

The legal minimum depth of tire tread is 1.6mm.

Tire manufacturers equip their tire with tread wear indicators, which are small blocks of rubber moulded into the base of the main grooves at a depth of 1.6mm.

Tires are the only point of contact between vehicle and road.

The photo below shows the actual contact zone.

NEW TIRE

WORN TIRE
(1,6 mm tread)

If the tread depth is less than 1.6mm, tires are considered to be worn and dangerous on wet surfaces.

Moving forward
means sustainable mobility

INNOVATION AND THE ENVIRONMENT

By 2050, Michelin aims to cut the quantity of raw materials used in its tire manufacturing process by half and to have developed renewable energy in its facilities. The design of MICHELIN tires has already saved billions of liters of fuel and, by extension, billions of tons of CO_2.

Similarly, Michelin prints its maps and guides on paper produced from sustainably managed forests and is diversifying its publishing media by offering digital solutions to make travelling easier, more fuel efficient and more enjoyable!

The group's whole-hearted commitment to eco-design on a daily basis is demonstrated by ISO 14001 certification.

Like you, Michelin is committed to preserving our planet.

Chat with Bibendum

Go to
www.michelin.com/corporate/fr
Find out more about Michelin's
history and the latest news.

QUIZ

Michelin develops tires for all types of vehicles. See if you can match the right tire with the right vehicle…

Solution : A-6 / B-4 / C-2 / D-1 / E-3 / F-7 / G-5

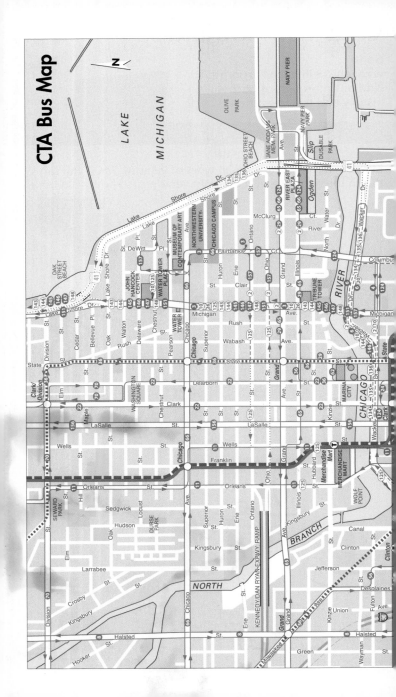